"As humans, our 'ascension' potential is our birthright, and in *The Return of the Rebel Angels* Wyllie proclaims that we're all 'doomed to become perfect.' Way to go!"

NEXUS MAGAZINE

"Timothy Wyllie's multivolume narrative, of which *Rebel Angels in Exile* is part, is a masterpiece of writing. It is essential reading for any who would explore the cosmic dimension of mercy suggested in the parable of the prodigal son and the role of those often known as Starseeds in its manifestation upon this and many other worlds."

ROBERT DAVIS, DIRECTOR OF THE DAYNAL INSTITUTE

"*Revolt of the Rebel Angels* and its series is recommended to everyone who is interested in where we have been and where we are going as a planet and as individuals. It will explain a little of what is out there. Once again I can hardly wait for the next volume."

JENNIFER HOSKINS, NEW DAWN MAGAZINE

"In *Wisdom of the Watchers* Timothy Wyllie and his guide, Georgia, continue the deep revelations of the hidden histories and lost legacy originally detailed in *The Urantia Book*. *Wisdom of the Watchers* is the nexus of a history and destiny that is both personal and universal."

RANDY MAUGANS, OFFPLANET RADIO HOST

"*Awakening of the Watchers* is the latest masterpiece by the always inspiring Timothy Wyllie. This book expands you and compels the reader to go deeper into the mystery that is all around and within us. A captivating read that is hard to put down."

PAUL SAMUEL DOLMAN, AUTHOR OF
HITCHHIKING WITH LARRY DAVID

"Timothy Wyllie's *Awakening of the Watchers* is a memoir of the dimensional ecology of the Lucifer Rebellion and the Process Church that creates a living dialogue between the New Earth density and we the reader—the individual soul—a bottom line in any Universe."

ALFRED LAMBREMONT WEBRE, AUTHOR OF THE OMNIVERSE:
TRANSDIMENSIONAL INTELLIGENCE, TIME TRAVEL, THE AFTERLIFE, AND
THE SECRET COLONY ON MARS

Secret History
OF THE
Watchers

Atlantis and the
Deep Memory
of the Rebel Angels

TIMOTHY WYLLIE

Bear & Company
Rochester, Vermont

Bear & Company
One Park Street
Rochester, Vermont 05767
www.BearandCompanyBooks.com

Bear & Company is a division of Inner Traditions International

Library of Congress Cataloging-in-Publication Data
Names: Wyllie, Timothy, 1940– author.
Title: Secret history of the watchers : Atlantis and the deep memory of the
    rebel angels / Timothy Wyllie.
Description: Rochester, Vermont : Bear & Company, 2018. | Includes
    bibliographical references and index.
Identifiers: LCCN 2017052480 (print) | LCCN 2018016106 (ebook) |
    ISBN 9781591433194 (pbk.) | ISBN 9781591433200 (ebook)
Subjects: LCSH: Cosmology, Ancient—Miscellanea. | Atlantis (Legendary
    Place)—Religion. | Occultism. | Spiritual life. | Angels—Miscellanea.
Classification: LCC BF1999 .W975 2018 (print) | LCC BF1999 (ebook) |
    DDC 133.9/3—dc23
LC record available at https://lccn.loc.gov/2017052480

Printed and bound in the United States by Lake Book Manufacturing, Inc.
The text stock is SFI certified. The Sustainable Forestry Initiative® program
promotes sustainable forest management.

10   9   8   7   6   5   4   3   2   1

Text design and layout by Virginia Scott Bowman
This book was typeset in Garamond Premier Pro with New Baskerville used as the
display typeface

Some books are crooks
they steal your time
but worse than that
some melt your mind
of all the books I've ever read
I prefer the ones that raise the dead.

TIMOTHY WYLLIE

Contents

Timothy's Spiritual Legacy

An Update for the Reader

"I live on!"

That's what Timothy would be saying had he not physically passed on October 4, 2017.

Timothy admired my cheekiness—and even dubbed me "The Cheeky One"—so I know he'd appreciate the humor. If anyone would laugh at death, it would be Timothy, so I hope you will too.

My name is Daniel. Timothy was my "surrogate father"—and I proudly his "surrogate son"—and he has entrusted me to carry the torch that had been given to him by powers higher than us and honed by him over the course of more than seven decades.

We spent countless hours going over his vision, and my directed mission was clear: "Reach as many people as possible. If my writing, my art, and my music inspires them, I want it to be in their homes."

To that end, I fully intend to publish his remaining books. He and Georgia had completed the final *two* books in this series already. They are on my computer, and I will be working with his "team" to have those published over the next couple of years.

His website is also in the process of being totally revamped. Timothy and I had created his first ever website back in 2002, but we turned it over to his hired help in 2003 and—let's just be nice and say it wasn't in the decade where he wanted it to be. The new website will have *all* his books, writings, and artwork, so please do check it out. The web address will still be www.timothywyllie.com.

I have been asked by many people about purchasing prints of Timothy's drawings, and they will be available as well. In an effort to get Timothy's art into the homes of people who are drawn to them as Timothy had desired, there will be cards, prints, limited edition prints, and possibly even some originals (which are in the studious care of Timothy's "artner," the wonderful June Atkin).

Timothy was so much more than a surrogate father to me, and he was so much more to so many other people as well (maybe even you, dear reader).

When I received the news that he was rushed to the hospital and that "it doesn't look good," I instantly dropped what I was doing and flew to Albuquerque to be by his side. He recovered enough to bring light to the hospital floor—the nurses and doctors absolutely loved him—but he also recovered enough to look his doctor in his eyes and *console the doctor* when he said, "Look, I know you want to save me, but I am seventy-seven years old. I have lived a wonderful life, and it is time for me to move on. I've died before, and I am not afraid of dying again."

So Timothy Wyllie checked himself out of the hospital and into in-home hospice care—in my home with my family 1,667 miles away in Pittsburgh. If you have read Timothy's books in the past—and therefore know of his amazing exploits—then you will not be surprised to read that in typical Timothy fashion, we drove. It was the most miserable trip either of us had ever taken—despite definitely having assistance of the angelic sort along the way—but what an adventure!

The misery we felt proved worthwhile as soon as I got Timothy into his bed that my wife and seven-year-old daughter dutifully prepared. Timothy cozied up, smiled like a cherub, and said, "I am so glad I made this trip."

He passed on two weeks later, but it was a splendid two weeks, and it served as a primer for what was to come after he passed. Timothy and I had been preparing for his "falling off his perch" (his words) for a while, and it was such a lovely affirmation that—after he passed—I picked up everything exactly as we had planned.

There was also such a powerful energy unleashed—accompanied by a ratcheting of enthusiasm—after he moved on, and that energy was experienced by others with whom I have spoken. It has been nearly half a year, and I *still* get communications from his friends and loved ones stating that they feel even closer with him today.

So let us say this for him—and mean it—because Timothy *does* indeed live on (as you, the reader, will see).

Enjoy!

DANIEL MATOR

Note to the Reader
Regarding a Glossary of Terms
and the Angelic Cosmology

In this work the author has coined or provided specialized definitions of certain words, some of which are derived from *The Urantia Book,* a key source text. A complete list of these terms and their meanings has been provided in the glossary at the back of this book for your ready reference. The reader will find a brief overview of the Angelic Cosmology, also drawn from *The Urantia Book,* in the appendix.

An Intuitive Truth

Calling All Rebel Angels, Homo angelicus, and the Approaching Planetary Transformation

I would imagine anyone reading these words has already come across Georgia's previous books. For those of you who haven't, I will elaborate on who Georgia is and how we've come to collaborate together on six volumes of the *Confessions* series, of which this book is the sixth.

I had never been one to believe in angels, nor had I spent much time thinking about the issue of whether they existed. My first contact with Georgia was a fleeting one that occurred when I was in my twenties. It wouldn't be until many years later that I fully accepted who she was, and, when I did, she became a welcome constant in my life.

I now believe I couldn't fully initially understand her because I didn't have the emotional or spiritual maturity to fully grasp that such a being as she could even exist in the first place! It would be the profound near-death experience (NDE) that I underwent when I was thirty-three years old that finally and irrevocably opened my eyes to the reality of other realms of existence, in general, and which prepared the ground for me to truly accept the reality of Georgia, in particular.

As I describe later in this book, during my near-death experience I was ushered into the presence of a celestial choir of angels. I then met my own companion angels before undergoing a medical procedure that fully restored my ailing body. Once that was done, my spirit was returned *to* my body and I "awoke" from my experience, completely confounded by it but not able to remember many of its more salient details.

Be this as it may, and as a direct consequence of my transformative NDE, I now know that a personal knowledge of the angels is the birthright of every human being on Earth—a birthright robbed from us by a unique and uniquely distressing event that transpired in heaven more than two hundred thousand years ago.

This event, which affected thirty-seven inhabited planets and which included Earth, was a battle among the celestial angels who'd been tasked with tending the spiritual evolution of the mortals in their purview. In the historical record this event is variously referred to as the Lucifer Rebellion or the War in Heaven. Indigenous cultures and myth likewise depict it as a celestial uprising that occurred in antiquity. Semantics aside, this event destabilized the celestial status quo and influenced human life on Earth in a profoundly deleterious way.

For those of you who would like to learn more about this seminal conflict and its consequences, I recommend (in addition to Georgia's books in this series of *Confessions*) *The Urantia Book*. First published in 1955 in Chicago, this definitive, esoteric cosmological narrative details complex information about the celestial realms and other lifeforms. Its breadth spans four sections, which cover the following topic areas: the Nature of God and the Central and Superuniverses, the Local Universe, the History of Urantia (their name for Earth), and the Life and Teachings of Jesus Christ. In short, *The Urantia Book* outlines a history of God, the Universe, and Everything.

The Urantia Book also seeks to set the record straight as to the truth about Lucifer, Satan, and the rebel angels, all of whom have gotten a bad rap down through time. This assignment of blame is due primarily to the human tendency to invent a "bogeyman" or scapegoat responsible for all of humanity's perceived troubles. It's ironic that Christianity, allegedly a religion whose cornerstones are love and forgiveness, has been largely unable or unwilling to apply these fundamental tenets to its falsely created enemies: Lucifer and Satan and the rebel angels.

Georgia joins with the mandate of *The Urantia Book* to present the complicated truth about this maligned trifecta as she, from her unique standpoint, understands it to be. In this, she separates the facts of the celestial rebellion from the politically motivated untruths associated with it and takes the demonizing brush from the hands of those who have tarred Lucifer, Satan, and the rebel angels with it throughout time.

Her essential findings deduce the real reason for the rebellion: a desire, on the part of both angels and mortals, for greater independence and autonomy—to get out from under the wings of the hierarchical and oppressive order of the Multiverse Administration. (For further reading on the particulars of the Angelic Cosmology, please refer to this book's appendix.) In articulating and explaining this true motivation of Lucifer vis-à-vis his rebellion, she effectively removes the stigma of "devil"—not only from him but from Satan and the rebel angels as well.

Georgia then goes on to make further distinctions between "devils" (or "demons") and "angels" so that we're clear from the outset that real demons do not exist, whereas real angels *do*.

Allow me to explain. An angel is a being of a very high frequency who inhabits the higher celestial dimensions. What we sometimes interpret as a "demon," on the other hand, is nothing but a thoughtform—a human construct, not a divine one. A thoughtform is the matrix of a core emotion that has accreted over time; quite literally a figment of the collective human imagination.

While thoughtforms reside primarily in the astral realms, they're capable of residing within the inner life of an individual as well. As such, thoughtforms may be generated by one's emotions—anger for example, or sadness, envy, and so on. Intense and emotionally laden thoughts, directed at another, are thoughtforms. If one should be troubled by being the recipient of a thoughtform that has found a home in one's subtle energy body, it's best to dissipate it by sending a beam of love to it from the heart chakra.

From my own experience I can tell you that thoughtforms are in no way spiritual beings—a view that Georgia wholeheartedly corroborates.

In any event, thoughtforms, angels, demons, Lucifer, Satan, and the rebel angels have been grossly misrepresented in the course of human history. I hope I've now made clear the differences between them, as it will enhance your understanding of this book you're about to read.

My collaboration with Georgia on this series of books has, in many regards, been a grand experiment. That said, one of its designed purposes is to awaken others of my kind. By "my kind," I mean those of us who are rebel angels and who have chosen to incarnate into a human body for this lifetime—which presents both an opportunity and a challenge. I am comfortable acknowledging the true nature of my identity, because I know I am one of *many* rebel angels currently living a human life on Earth.

That there are multitudes of us is evinced by the letters I receive from a growing number of people who recognize themselves as rebel angels too. These are smart, sensitive, highly intuitive individuals who have, throughout their lives, felt profoundly different from their peers. They are unable and unwilling to accept the status quo and, instead, question various forms of authority as well as everyday norms. Typically these are the folks who become spiritual seekers and travel down myriad spiritual roads in attempts to arrive more fully at themselves.

Georgia describes us as Homo angelicus and goes on to tell me that in the past we have been unaware of who we really are. However, with planetary transformation on the horizon, which is getting closer by the moment, transparency is the new order of the day. In this, rebel angels everywhere are becoming aware of the nature of their true essence. As this awakening transpires on the collective level, deep psychic and emotional tensions that have been extant for thousands of years across the Multiverse are dissipating and withering away, lauding the advent of a new golden era on Earth.

After this cycle is complete, the Multiverse will be forever changed for the better. What we have experienced for the past 203,000 years might, in the future, be thought of as a drama of titanic proportions, or a hybridization project between the dimensions, or an experiment in individual liberty—or all of the above. But whatever it's called doesn't matter. It's part of our great cosmic homecoming for, in the end, as

Georgia likes to remind us, we're all doomed to become perfect.

As Georgia has explained, she has been preparing me to produce this collaborative work for a very long time. Of course, over the years there have been moments of doubt and testing on both sides, but mainly on my part. By the time we started on these books together I'd learned to master my doubts and self-censorship, so that by this sixth volume we've been able to establish between us a discernible difference in voice and personality. (This is further noted by our respective asides in the text.)

Our relatively untroubled working relationship has allowed the narrative to flow more fluidly than ever, as well as encouraging Georgia, I've noticed, to become bolder in her revelations as well as more detailed in her descriptions and analyses.

I'm writing this introduction having completed the primary draft of this book, so I have the advantage of knowing the end before the beginning. And "the end" is full of some revelatory insights that truly astonish me. Not simply because the insights were ones I'd never thought of before—those occur on almost every page—but because the insights covered issues I don't think I ever would have thought of independently of my angelic friend.

It's such a delicate and tender balance, this collaboration with Georgia, and it brings me the most consistent joy I have yet experienced in my life. Georgia has made no pretense that if she is writing for anyone but the two of us, it is for all those incarnated rebel angels out there who will find that what we have to share is of considerable personal interest and value to them.

I would like to believe that when this volume is published there will be a far greater awareness among those rebel angels among you, about who you are, and why you have chosen to incarnate at this key point in human history.

Much of what you read here will be intuitively familiar to you, for truth is like that: you feel you know it already. You will find other material that will illuminate issues you may have been puzzling over. Some of it might pass over your head. No matter. Not all of us are interested in the same things.

If by any chance you have picked up this book and, having read this far, you already find that what has been written is unappealing, then you may want to slip the book back where you found it. Georgia's words are probably not intended for you.

And for those of you who have been anxiously waiting for the next book in this series to become available, I don't think Georgia is going to disappoint you.

She certainly hasn't disappointed me!

As it has been, and apparently ever has been,
gods superseded, become the devils
in the system which supplants their reign,
and stay on to make trouble for their successors,
available, as they are,
to a few for whom magic has not despaired
and been superseded by religion.
                    WILLIAM GADDIS, *THE RECOGNITIONS*

A visual culture cannot distinguish
between fallen and unfallen angels,
since we cannot see either
and are forgetting how to read ourselves,
which means that we can see images of others,
but cannot really see either
others or ourselves.
                    HAROLD BLOOM, *FALLEN ANGELS*

Jesus said, "If you bring forth what is within you,
what you bring forth will save you.
If you do not bring forth what is within you,
what you do not bring forth will destroy you."
                    THE GOSPEL OF THOMAS

1

Into the Heart of Darkness

Lucifer's Cosmic Alchemy, Conditioned
Responses, the Manhattan Microcosm,
Hypnosis, and a Watcher's Amnesia

Once again, I feel I acted out of cowardice.

These are so curious, these human emotions. I truly believed that
I had faced my timidity, that I'd mastered my fears when I chose to
stay on this world during the painful global catastrophes that struck
throughout the thirteenth and twelfth millennia.

Yet here I am, doing it again.

I previously left off my narrative as this world, suffering under
the yoke of Prince Caligastia's increasingly capricious and high-
handed dominion, was about to enter the eighth millennium BCE.
It was no particular convenience that caused me to stop at that point,
but I realize now, as I pick up where I left off, that I must have a
real fear and reluctance to report on what I had observed over the
ensuing millennia. Usually I write quite fluidly from millennia to
millennia, from era to era, and this has been reflected in the ease and
rapidity with which I've been able to move from volume to volume
of my *Confessions*. My enthusiasm has been such that I've started the

subsequent volumes on the very same day that I'd completed the previous one.

Not so this time.

It's been a month and a half of avoidance, of convincing my collaborator of his need to read through the previous volume—something he hasn't done before—before embarking on this one. I've been encouraging him to respond fully and with generous attention to the intelligent letters he receives from the readers of his books; in fact, anything I could conjure up to distract him from plunging back into our work together, and doing this without him becoming aware that I was exerting any undue influence over him.

The reason I'm including this confession of my avoidance and the manner that I accomplished it for almost two months is both to fulfill my pledge to write openly about my nature as a watcher and also to alert my collaborator to the subtle influences he has taken on by agreeing to work so closely with me. After we completed the previous volume I was aware that he wanted to take a break of a few days, or even as much as a week, but after a month had gone by I knew he was starting to feel that *he* was doing the procrastinating. Although this obviously puzzled him—given that he clearly enjoys our writing together—it didn't lead to any serious self-recrimination on his part. I think he'd agree that he was able to put the time to valuable use—(he does. T.W.)

Since the 2011 publication of his book *The Return of the Rebel Angels,* he has been getting letters from readers who resonate with the proposition he presents in the book—that the rebel angels have been, and are currently, incarnating in mortal vehicles. These are readers who don't appear to be lightweights. They're clearly not stupid or deluded. Instead, they are serious men and women who have struggled all their lives with their sense of being different from those around them. As I've contributed in small part to some of his replies, I am speaking with some authority when I say how impressed I've been with the lucidity and emotional maturity of almost all those who have written to him.

My collaborator tends to be more reserved than I am in making his assertions, preferring, as he says, to launch his propositions into the collective "as a dolphin might sonar the seabed for reflected information." He believes that he has no need to persuade anyone of the existential truth of what he has discovered. He reasons that—if it is indeed true that the rebel angels are incarnating into the human line—it will be self-evident. He feels that the appropriate people will recognize their angelic heritage as an inner resonance, while the others will most likely dismiss the whole concept as a harmless delusion.

As you can see, I'm still finding reasons to try to put off starting this volume. It's only in writing these words and being pushed by my collaborator to confront my resistance that I now recognize it has been my fear and distaste for what I need to narrate over the course of the ensuing eight millennia that has caused me to procrastinate.

On the redemptive side of the issue, my procrastination has made me aware that I need to be constantly vigilant as to the state of my emotional body, lest my fears unduly affect the clarity of my intention.

However, writing now with the knowledge of retrospect, I confess that it does pain me to report that the next eight thousand years will be the most difficult and spiritually challenging period that humans have encountered in the half a million years that I've been observing this world—at least up until the years following World War II. Those eight millennia were certainly the most dangerous era ever endured by a rapidly expanding planetary population. This had been a time, too, when there was more than one occasion upon which we could have seen the extinction of the human species.

Yet for all the dangers and the horrors of those terrible times and, as I'm starting to grasp, *because* of the challenges they presented, so also did some magnificently strong and brilliant souls emerge out of the spiritual darkness that has shrouded the planet since Lucifer's revolution.

Was it in this way that Lucifer can justify his experiment in cosmic alchemy? Are these brave, emergent souls the spiritual gold extracted from the base matter and corruption of planetary life? Is the desperate confusion and chaos of those eight millennia better understood as a preparation for an event so extraordinary that it will transform absolutely everything on this world from that point on?

These are just some of the questions I hope to address as I continue my narrative. But first let me turn to Mein Host's biography, which he has agreed to let me relate. He tells me that he's discovering from my unique point of view much of what he was unaware of at the time.

* * *

It was when Mein Host was driving down Park Avenue late one rainy spring afternoon in 1972, soon after he'd arrived in Manhattan, that he received what I've heard him call "a perfect gestalt of New York City life."

He had just relocated to the city with the express aim of negotiating a distribution contract for the album that he and the Version, the Process rock band, had cut up in Toronto at Thundersound Studios. So far, it had not proved to be a successful mission.

My ward was now living with four other Processeans in a large, once opulent apartment, on the 91st Street block of Park Avenue, just past where Spanish Harlem nudged its way into the genteel apartment blocks that line the avenue. Nannies with their prams and double-walkers seldom ventured this far north on Park, and even dog walkers, being jerked along clutching the leads of as many as a dozen dogs of every breed—even they turned back well before 91st Street. However, the fifth-floor apartment was large, relatively inexpensive for Manhattan, and it allowed them the conceit—impressive, they hoped, to anyone not a New Yorker—of living on posh Park Avenue.

On the particular afternoon that my ward had his gestalt experience he was driving one of the large Winnebago RVs the community was using for its outreach programs. This one was down from the Boston Chapter with six or eight young Processeans in the RV's spacious interior. Mein Host was dropping them off on propitious midtown street corners, two by two, to sell their bundles of PROCESS magazines on streets paved with gold.

This involved my ward negotiating a large and ungainly vehicle through a maze of taxis and trucks unloading on the narrow cross streets. On top of this it was pouring cats and dogs. Pedestrians kept dashing into the traffic, risking crushed legs as they squeezed between the cars jammed nose-to-tail that inched forward in unpredictable jerks.

As he moved slowly down Lexington Avenue, letting off a couple more Processeans before turning back toward Park Avenue, it looked like a particularly vicious gust of wind had simultaneously blown a number of flimsier umbrellas inside out. This presented the sadly comical scene of furious, cursing people trying to return the loose, flapping silk and the bent and broken spokes to their original form; turning their busted brollies this way and that, hoping fruitlessly to catch another gust that might reverse the damage.

"Sometimes it works," my ward was saying laconically, leaning forward to wipe condensation off the windshield with the loose end of his long black robe. "You can jerk 'em back . . . but those are the cheap ones you get on the street—they're made to break!"

He was interrupted, stomping on the brakes to avoid hitting a smartly dressed young couple dashing in front of the RV, each with a soggy copy of the *New York Times* held overhead in a forlorn attempt to keep the downpour at bay.

There was a crashing sound behind Mein Host as a couple of Processeans fell against one of the built-in wardrobes. "Sorry about that . . ." he called out over his shoulder. "New York rush hour . . . better hold on tight!"

He turned the awkward vehicle back up Madison Avenue. The sidewalks were besieged by office workers streaming from their buildings, momentarily pausing, bewildered by the fury of the rainstorm. They blocked already crowded entrances before they dove into the crush of black umbrellas. Bicycle messengers were threading their way through the rush-hour traffic, the sharp pitch of their whistles cutting through the rumble of trucks and the deafening roar of the buses heaving their way up Madison, black smoke belching in oily clouds from the behemoths' exhausts.

Aiming to drop off the last two Processeans close to Waldorf Astoria Hotel, he turned the Winnebago back toward Park Avenue, threading his laborious way through taxis and double-parked Town Cars. It took so long that by the time he turned south on Park the rain had stopped. The wet streets were now gleaming in the sheen of shimmering brake lights and—because Park was free of trucks and buses—from the elevated height of the RV's driving seat my ward looked out over the tops of an endless sea of yellow cabs.

The event I'm leading up to relating occurred on the southwest corner of Park and one of the streets in the mid-40s. It might have gone unnoticed were it not for two factors special to Park Avenue: no noisy trucks and buses, and its linked traffic lights. This could produce two quite different effects, which on this particular afternoon happened at the same time. The lack of heavy vehicles made Park Avenue the quietest of Manhattan's north/south avenues, which under a certain configuration of traffic lights could produce an almost unearthly quietness. And because the traffic lights up and down the avenue changed at the same time, dependent on the crosstown traffic, this can sometimes leave a complete city block on Park entirely free of cars and taxis.

So it was that as Mein Host pulled the heavy Winnebago around the corner and accelerated south on Park, he was to find an empty block ahead, and one of those strange moments of quietness. He might not have noticed the sudden silence, he told the others afterward—or the empty road ahead—were it not for a sudden crackle of gunfire.

"That was startling enough," he said. "I knew it was gunfire immediately; I used to shoot. But that wasn't it. I hit the brakes. It was happening right in front of me, like it was a theatrical set. The lighting, the sound . . . everything was perfect. What it was, my gestalt moment, was how the people in the street reacted. There was this crack, crack, crack sound, maybe seven, eight times. It was loud and close-by—too close, though I couldn't see anyone running or who had fired the shots."

And it *was* close, I can confirm that; it was an armed robbery just around the corner that he was approaching when he slammed on his brakes.

"I could see everything spread out before me—except what actually went down. But here's what happened to the people on the pavement . . . there were, what? About twenty on both sides of the street and maybe half a dozen crossing the avenue in front of me. There was a brief pause after the last of the shots, a theatrical beat, I thought. And then, as if they were one person, every single man and woman on the street in front of me threw themselves flat on the ground! Bang! People didn't look at each other . . . there was no domino effect. No ripple. They all went down at once! It was like they were trained for it . . . really! It was like a vast movie set; the actors knew exactly what to do. And here I was sitting high up in the P-Car, kind of insulated from the action, watching this surreal event unfolding in front of me like it was a scene created just for us."

That was Mein Host's gestalt image of New York life—a city that was both entirely artificial, and yet at the same time, utterly real. A permanent film set, and every man and woman on it an actor, with each person as unaware that they were acting out their unique drama of life, much as we angels were ignorant of the cosmic drama being played out through us at the time of Lucifer's revolution.

Manhattan, the Big Apple, had raised her voluminous skirt for a moment, permitting my ward a glimpse of a naked thigh beneath. The reality that all was not as it seemed became an insight that would serve him well during his twenty years of living in the city. It would be Manhattan's very artificiality that would impel his spirit to leave the city in 1990 for a more natural life in the high desert of the American Southwest.

Perched uneasily on a long thin island, there is very little that is truly natural to Manhattan save the occasional glacial boulders, remnants of the receding ice twelve thousand years ago, and the dramatic outcroppings of Manhattan schist found in some of its parks. Central Park, like other of the smaller parks on the island, is a wholly man-made place, designed with ingenuity and planted to heighten the aesthetic pleasure of human beings. The parks are simulations of nature; they were as self-consciously fabricated in their time as were the more recent skyscrapers and high-rise apartment blocks sitting on their patches of landfill—the reclaimed land at the southern tip of the island.

Unlike most European cities—which have grown gradually over the centuries, expanding their city boundaries naturally to accommodate a growing population—Manhattan's restricted location surrounded by water has forced every square foot of space to become utilized in some form of service to humans.

I don't say this in any critical sense. I'm aware, even if it's not currently a popular viewpoint, that human beings are every bit as much a part of Nature as trees and eagles and crocodiles, and Manhattan is a perfectly natural product of the human imagination. I have no quarrel with that. My point digs a little deeper. Although I'm sure that I am not the first to suggest that Manhattan is cut off from natural cycles, it is the subtle effects of living under these thoroughly unnatural conditions that interests me.

What changes do humans go through when living so separated from natural cycles? Freed from the constraints and burdens imposed by the rhythms of nature, do humans then live the artificial life imposed on them by the rhythms of the artificial simulation? Or are the psychic pressures of living in a wholly artificial setting, paradoxically enough, unusually conducive to original acts of the creative imagination?

Conversely, does living and working in such artificial surroundings as a city like Manhattan support the development and use of lifestyles and technologies antithetical to natural conditions? Does such environmental artificiality breed a subconscious contempt for nature? Or does it liberate the mind to open and soar into new and unknown territories?

If Lucifer's intention was alchemical, as he had once told me, then what could represent the Nigredo stage of the process better than New York City? More than any other city in the world, Manhattan is a microcosm of the world. I've heard my ward speculate that the city must contain a person from every single town and village on the planet— both the best and the worst—living in relative peace.

The years Mein Host would spend living, as he liked to say, "deep in the heart of darkness," would prove to be rich in life lessons for him. It would also be a turning point for me. It would be the first time since the Lucifer Rebellion more than two hundred thousand years ago that I would feel there is some real hope for us all.

* * *

Ten thousand years ago, as the world was entering its eighth millennium before the birth of Christ, human beings had been around as recognizable human beings for about a million years. The different races of color, as with the various distinctions science draws between Neanderthal and Cro-Magnon, for example, are subsets, mere twigs on the branch that carried humans from the primate bough on the evolutionary tree of life.

Half a million years ago saw the first of the interventions from the Multiverse Administraion (MA). At this time, a small group of what my collaborator calls "intraterrestrials" were posted on the planet with the directive to support and help humanity's climb up from its animal roots. I too was part of this original mission, which I have previously written about more fully as regards the arrival of the Prince and his staff of one hundred intraterrestrials. Thus I don't necessarily need to go into all that here.

The Lucifer Rebellion broke out on Jerusem, the capital planet of this System, 297,000 years later, thus affecting this and thirty-six other inhabited worlds within this System. It was this revolution with which I and many other watchers aligned. As it turns out, it started what I have to admit has been the long dark age that, as I turn to the eighth millennium, is only going to get darker.

I'd had great hopes for the revolution. I respected and loved Lucifer as System Sovereign and as my superior, and from what I'd observed of life on Jerusem and on this world, a profound shakeup of MA's stagnant bureaucracy was sorely needed. Even I could see that!

I've never believed many of the accusations the MA's agents hurled at Lucifer and those of us who aligned with the revolutionary cause. I don't believe we were blasphemers, just as I don't believe that Lucifer can be dismissed as having been driven insane by self-inflation. He was too fine a spirit to ever descend into madness. I can do no better than to reprint the brief piece my ward was privileged to receive from Lucifer in 1981, which he originally included in his first book, *The Deta Factor: Dolphins, Extraterrestrials & Angels.*

I know the transmission came through in one fluid and unbroken piece of automatic writing in 1981, and although I wasn't present at the time my ward received it I have no reason to believe it to be anything but an authentic statement from Lucifer (expressed through my collaborator's sometimes confused vocabulary).

This is what Lucifer had to say:

The Multiverse Administration (MA) talks of our rejection of the Invisible Father. But I made no such rejection. I knew the Father. I had seen the Father and I felt the presence of the Father stirring inside me.

It was this that none could understand. They accused me of blasphemy; of usurping the role of the Unseen One. How could I have seen and felt and heard what so many magnificent beings knew nothing of? They proceeded in faith and trust, obeying traditions laid down at the dawn of time. They made no allowance for the vastly changing nature of the evolving universe of universes. They saw not that we carried that very change, as you do now. We were the missing link, the changelings, propelled into new and strange territories.

They called us traitors and betrayers, but we betrayed no one. Free choice was given freely to all to follow, or not, according to how the voice inside so dictated. We coerced no one. I myself progressed with immense caution—overlooking, ignoring, vacillating, and damming up my feelings within a castle of privacy for almost a hundred thousand years. I thought and felt and dug deeply inside my being, reaching for the quiet internal guidance that emanated from my Father's presence.

Michael knew. Michael understood. He has never doubted me, nor I him. We have known each other long and well. Yet something had to bend; I could no longer tolerate the ambivalence. And mercifully, one day, I could feel Him no longer, and my true Father, implicit inside my heart,*

---

*Michael refers to Jesus Christ, the "Michaelson" of our Local Universe who incarnated as Jesus Christ.

faded from my troubled mind. At last I could act. The contact needed to be cut, but with the sweet promise of the long return home that I always carried in the depths of my soul; that was never forgotten.

In this transmission Lucifer has presented a rather different story from the one touted by the MA's agents. Naturally, there are two sides to any issue, and an event as polarizing as a revolution among the angels is likely to create serious differences of opinion and some extremely harsh attitudes—especially among those administrators most negatively affected by the revolution.

At the core of Lucifer's declaration was his assertion that his revolutionary thinking was well-known to his superiors and possibly even quietly condoned by them. Lucifer's statement that Michael never doubted him, and that Michael knew and understood what he was going through, points to the crux of this complex situation: *Lucifer's revolution was never against Michael.* It was aimed at shaking up what could be called the MA's middle management, the level of the celestial bureaucracy most intimately connected with mortal life on their third-density worlds. This therefore would not likely have been reported by the MA's agents.

He speaks in this transmission of his revolution as being an inevitable personal response to the rapidly evolving conditions occurring in the Multiverse, changes of which many of his colleagues and his immediate superiors appeared to be unaware. It was for this divergence of vision, so he states, that he was cast as betrayer and blasphemer.

He seems to say that this is what administrations do when they are challenged by original ideas and unconventional approaches. Little or no consideration is given to the new concepts, and instead, those who propose them will be demonized. There are few administrations that ever favor personal liberty or full self-determination for those they administer, and the Local System's angelic administration proved to be no different.

As a watcher, I find the most touching part of Lucifer's statement is his indelible memory of the "sweet promise of the long return home."

It gives me courage and supports my faith to know that Lucifer always possessed the knowledge that there was a deeper purpose to his revolution, and that however demonized and despised he would likely be labeled by the very authorities he was opposing, he always knew he was loved and trusted by our Michaelson.

However, as I was observing the unrelenting bloodshed on this planet at the dawn of the eighth millennium, the result of the vastly increasing number of humans pouring in to Europe from the south and east, I was not feeling nearly so confident about the revolution and how it was working out in practical terms.

I had continued to hold Lucifer in the highest regard. He was generous enough to grant me an interview that I had recorded. Though I emerged from it greatly encouraged by what I'd heard, afterward I had no memory of what was discussed. Regardless of this temporary amnesia—which I've only recently learned was drawn down on me by Lucifer at the end of the interview—I found myself hopeful and trusting that there was a deeper purpose and meaning to our revolution than a mere political struggle between minor celestial functionaries (or worse, the monstrous betrayal it has been portrayed as by agents of the Administration).

No indeed, I hadn't lost my confidence in Lucifer, even though paradoxically I had no knowledge of what he told me. I have since thought that this says much about the persuasive charisma of a System Sovereign, deposed or not, that he can so deeply reassure another being of the rightness of his cause. Apart from that one meeting, I have barely ever caught a glimpse of Lucifer, given that he has been taking care of his many responsibilities on the other rebel-held worlds.

After the revolution had taken hold and the thirty-seven Planetary Princes had cast their lot with the rebel faction—and as I've previously mentioned—Lucifer and his main aide, Satan, divided the supervision of the thirty-seven planets under their control. Lucifer took authority over nineteen worlds, and his aide the remaining eighteen. The Earth, it should come as no surprise, was one of the eighteen worlds falling under Satan's charge.

The alert reader will have noticed that Satan has scarcely been mentioned so far in this narrative. If Earth falls so directly under Satan's egis, it might be thought of as a serious oversight not to have paid him more attention. But there is a reason for this. I had seen nothing of Satan after the few visits he made here to argue the rebel cause at the time of the uprising. It is possible that Satan may have come and gone while I was away on Zandana or on one of the other worlds I visited, but I'd heard nothing of it. Astar, one of my sister watchers who knew me only too well, had once, when we were discussing Satan's possible whereabouts, likened him to "an absentee landlord."

I'd been confessing to her my relief that I hadn't yet had a confrontation with Satan, that I hadn't even seen him around since the early times of the revolution.

"And now you want to meet with him?" Astar said sharply.

That took me aback! Astar has a way of cutting through my equivocation. She knew I hadn't taken to Satan the one time I'd had a chance to observe him in action—and that's probably the best way of expressing my mild aversion. I hadn't taken to him at all, and certainly not in the same way that I have always felt a powerful natural affection and admiration for Lucifer.

Astar spoke again. "You need to understand there is nothing unnatural about how you feel. Some have found their natural affinity for Satan, you for Lucifer. You are polarized toward the light of revelation and the exposure of Lucifer the Light Bringer; others are drawn toward the darkness of the mystery yet to be revealed that is Satan, the Noble Adversary."

I felt grateful to Astar for putting it in these detached terms. I'd been concerned that my reaction to Satan was going to land me in trouble at some point. And from the little I'd seen of him haranguing the staff and midwayers back in the days when Dalamatia was a thriving city, I feared his scornful anger and had no desire to be subjected to his hurt pride.

"And yet, now you desire to meet him?" Astar's voice in my mind was completely without attitude. It pulled me back in, reminding me that she thankfully gave no credence to my timidity.

I had not been aware of any such desire; in fact, rather the opposite. Astar's neat explanation of my polarization toward Lucifer had certainly clarified my reaction to Satan. I had no reason to find any further cause for my aversion, if such a polarization was merely characteristic of my nature.

It was then that Astar hit me with something that I had never given any consideration. Had I thought it through more thoroughly, I might have realized that there was indeed something improbable about my never having seen Satan, not even once, since those early days of the revolution. Earth was one of the eighteen worlds under his authority, after all.

"If I am reading you correctly," Astar murmured with a sly grin (for she'd never yet read me incorrectly) . . . "if I'm correct numerically, you have observed Satan, and even been in his presence . . . nineteen . . . no, twenty times, since the revolution."

No, that couldn't be! I'd *seen* him *twenty* times?! I guess it's possible that once or twice I might not have *noticed* him—although that was hard to believe. Satan was hard to miss. No, surely, Astar must be having some fun at my expense, setting me up with that absentee landlord quip.

"Twenty times!" Astar was laughing aloud now at my incredulity. "A couple of times you were well within his field and looking right at him! Right at him!" There was more laughter from Astar, throwing her head back, her silver hair swinging behind her with the beguiling, slow-motion elegance, as my collaborator suggests, of a model on a Revlon TV commercial.

It always charmed me when she did that. Astar has a long, slim, adorable neck, and her laughter, which issues from an open throat at a far deeper pitch than might be expected from such a delicate form, always has this deliciously arousing effect on me . . . clouds seemed to clear in my mind, revealing a sandy windblown beach . . . waves beat against a massive rock formation at the far end of the bay . . . a narrow path threaded its way up to a castle standing on top of the . . .

It was then that it came to me that I must have been drifting off into a time-shifted memory of a future era in fifteenth-century Japan, a time when Astar and I had become more closely bonded because our wards had met as mortals and suffered deeply as a result of their love for one another.

"Georgia, you really *don't* know, do you?!" Astar's tone cut through the soft haze of memory.

"I don't know . . . *what?*" I really didn't know what she meant. I remember thinking at the time *I'm a watcher, aren't I?* I pride myself on observing everything in my ken. Of course I couldn't have missed any being as noisily flamboyant as Prince Satan. *Could I?*

"It's not that you didn't *observe* him, silly! Each of those twenty times you *did* see him. Does that surprise you? Each time you *saw* him, and you forgot it immediately afterward."

I was thrown into confusion by this. If I had forgotten seeing Satan, what else had I forgotten? Astar might have been laughing at me, but this was no joke. I could sense she was only telling me this because she didn't want me to appear to be a complete fool if and when I encountered Satan again.

Astar's tone softened in my mind. "Remember you told me about your interview with Lucifer? How elated you were afterward? You were glowing with inspiration and going on about how much you loved him, whatever he'd done . . . Then, when I asked what Lucifer had actually told you, you went completely absent for a moment . . . You must remember *that!*"

Went *absent?* Whatever could she mean? And then, of course, it struck me. I recalled some whispers among my sisters back on Jerusem about a facility said to be possessed by all System Sovereigns. They'd called it "drawing down"—a sort of telepathically induced posthypnotic amnesia . . .

Astar cut into my thought. "You never heard it officially discussed, did you? Always just a rumor, right? The Multiverse Administration didn't want us to know that our memories could be so selectively manipulated or erased. I'll warrant you even forgot about it until now!" We both laughed again at that. It was true, I *had* forgotten that I'd forgotten that I'd forgotten . . .

"An infinite regression of forgetfulness," Astar said, her tone turning thoughtful. "Yes, that must be it!" She beamed over at me as if I'd thought up something rather clever.

Now she was thinking out loud: "Infinite regression . . . so that's how it's done . . . set up whatever original posthypnotic suggestion fits the need . . . let's say complete amnesia . . . such and such an event never occurred . . . you'll remember nothing of it, and never will . . . and that could be accomplished by using an infinite regression of forgetfulness . . ."

"So the memory falls into a black hole . . . ," I said, hoping I was still being clever.

"Well, something like a black hole, Georgia!" I felt Astar was humoring me—there was an edge of impatience in her tone. "In a black hole, once you've passed the event horizon, there's no getting out. This is much more sophisticated. It's incremental, don't you see? Lucifer drew you down on the contents of your meeting, but not on the beneficial effects it had on you. I would think that at some point in the future there will come a time when what you were told by Lucifer will come forth. Incremental, see? The memory hasn't disappeared *forever* in a black hole . . ."

"Although it *could*," I said, determined. "It could if it just kept on infinitely regressing . . . At some point the memory just disappears into the hole, doesn't it? Forever."

I thought Astar was going to mock me again, but no, to my relief her tone had turned kindly again. "It wasn't exactly the point I was making about the incremental nature of infinite regression, but yes . . . in fact, that's exactly how Satan drew you down. Even now, when I tell you you've encountered him twenty times here on this planet since the uprising, you still have absolutely no memory of those events, do you?"

It was true. If it wasn't Astar telling me this—whom I basically trusted, even if she had her little ways—I don't think I would have believed it. I was horrified when the truth of my amnesia struck me. It wasn't simply what I might have missed as an observer, as a *watcher,* for goodness sake! But more seriously, it caused me to doubt what I *had* observed. If my memory could be so easily manipulated such as to make me forget that I'd already encountered Satan as many as twenty times, what else could have been induced posthypnotically? To what extent have System Sovereigns been shaping my thoughts? If they can telepathically wipe out my memories, what might they have telepathically posthypnotically *implanted* in my mind?

Yet as I mulled this over, I realized that the answer to my question was essentially unknowable, at least at that point in time. If I was being telepathically manipulated by a System Sovereign and had no awareness of it, the reality of it was that there was little I could have done about it. Perhaps at some point in the future it would become clear to me, but right then, with Astar favoring me with her wisdom, another question seemed more pressing. I felt that all those erased encounters must have left their psychic shadow on me. Was it this shadow that Astar had read in me and was reflecting back to me when she proposed that I was wishing to meet with Satan?

I could only wonder what was going to happen when I *did* next encounter Satan. I wanted to ask Astar for her insights and any advice she might have to offer. Besides, I wasn't sure I had really grasped her explanation of the incremental nature of infinite regression. But when I turned back to her, Astar had already disappeared, leaving only the slightest tremor in the ether.

Regardless of what might happen in my next encounter with Satan, it remained my hope that I would be able to meet with Lucifer again. Yet by the eighth millennium my request for an audience still hadn't been granted. Neither, I might add, had I yet "seen" anything of Satan. This, at least, gave me one insight. Simply *knowing* that I would be vulnerable to Satan's ability to telepathically draw me down evidently wasn't enough to negate his induction—if indeed he had been visiting and casting his shadow over me.

In Lucifer's case, I was aware how busy he must have been, and I had no wish to make a nuisance of myself. I would see him whenever he had an opening—I was sure of that. I had no doubt that Lucifer knew I loved him—that he had my deepest respect.

Allow me to return to my original grievance, but now with the uneasy feeling that by entirely missing Satan's presence I'd been focusing my criticism on the wrong being.

Here's the issue: As I've previously related, I'd been increasingly distrustful of the policies of Caligastia, the Planetary Prince of this world. It didn't appear to me that he was truly honoring the principles of Lucifer's revolution, not if the freedoms we have won have resulted merely in a planetary free-for-all.

After the initial rush of exalted liberation that we felt in the early years of the revolution had died down, and the reality of the situation we had got ourselves into on a planetary level dawned on us, the prospects became a lot darker. I've written previously about the terrible loneliness that descended on us during those dark days when we first realized that the MA had quarantined Earth. And then to discover later that this whole System of one thousand planets had been isolated as a result of our revolution had demoralized us even further.

The sixty members of the Prince's staff and the many midwayers who had aligned themselves with the revolution were soon taking advantage of their new freedoms. Over the millennia since the uprising this has led to conditions becoming progressively harder and more dangerous for human life. Almost all the developments and social advances made by humanity before the revolution had disappeared, and in the chaos many tribes had little choice but to return to a simple nomadic existence.

A new mood had sprung up among the Prince's staff and the rebel midwayers. No longer was the spiritual and social advancement of mortal life the central rationale of the Prince's mission, for there had been a profound shift of mission intention.

It had already been the openly expressed opinion of a number of the staff that human beings were rather more trouble than they were worth. Even though all one hundred members of the staff had once been mortals on planets of their origination, and not so very long before volunteering for this mission, the sixty who had aligned with Lucifer and Caligastia seemed to have forgotten their own humble mortal roots.

The MA would have calculated that—because the staff had been so recently living mortal lives on their own worlds—this should have created sufficient identification with human beings to ensure that they wouldn't abuse their power over humanity. After all, the staff had been carefully handpicked for the Prince's mission back on Jerusem, and it was thought of as a great privilege to have been selected. There were always many more volunteers than those chosen, because this first mission to an inhabited world was typically regarded as crucially important.

However, no one anticipated that a revolution would break out on Jerusem and change everything. After a while it had upended so many of the hallowed traditions of the Multiverse Administration that all that remained was raw power. And as far as raw power was concerned, human beings were always bound to become the victims in a far larger game than they were aware they were playing.

It was now going to be about the rebel staff and midwayers. This kicked off what had become by the eighth millennia an endless struggle between them for power and influence. Human beings had become pawns in the cruel games the midwayers have been playing in their guise of the gods and goddesses of the paleolithic pantheons. And behind this midwayer power mongering and manipulation was Prince Caligastia. Aided by his deputy Prince Daligastia, he has seemed to me to have become increasingly obsessed over the centuries with gathering the reins of power to himself, using any methods to accomplish this, however brutal and genocidal, and with absolutely no care for human beings.

I've been thought too tenderhearted by some of my sister watchers when I've admitted to turning away in horror at Caligastia's ruthless exercise of power over and through the many rebel midwayers under his direct control.

The rebel midwayers, in their manifestation as gods and goddesses and in what I thought was a slavish emulation of their Prince, had become increasingly autocratic and demanding of human beings. These self-proclaimed divinities had discovered that they were able to draw off energy from the worshipful devotion of their human followers, and this in turn was feeding their pride and self-delusion. The competition between these false divinities had grown so increasingly bitter by the eighth millennium that wars were continually breaking out between the followers of different gods.

Unbeknownst to those midwayers—yet painfully evident to me at the time—was that the more they became addicted to feeding off human energy, the more they needed to stir up the latent fear and aggression in their human devotees to satisfy their habit. This wasn't the glorious liberation I'd risked everything for when I'd chosen to follow Lucifer into the great revolution. This seemed to be every being for itself and was every bit as tooth-and-claw as the animal world they liked to believe was so far beneath them.

Perhaps the most dismaying of Prince Caligastia's many excesses had been his proclamation that he was "God of the World," as well as his demand to be known and addressed as such. Even *I* saw the fallacy in such a ridiculous claim. Yet as a watcher there was nothing I could do but observe.

I believe it was then that I first started having fears for the outcome of our revolution.

2

Harbingers of the End

A Deteriorating Metropolis, Relishing the
Apocalypse, Unique Spiritual Paths, and
Revealed Dynamics of Alien Abductions

As the winter of 1972 edged its way uneasily into the spring of 1973, America was becoming increasingly riveted on the events unfolding in Washington, D.C. Yet while the Watergate scandal may have been mildly titillating for a stolid Midwesterner, for the average New Yorker it became a daily obsession.

It was only in mid-June of the previous summer that the abortive break-in had occurred at the headquarters of the Democratic National Committee in the Watergate complex in Washington. Now that it was leaking out, the New York–based media cabal was feasting on the corrupt corpse of the Nixon presidency. There had always been a palpable tension between New York City and Washington, and being able to report on the unraveling of President Nixon's crooked and venal machinations had become a regular scribbler's pot of gold.

My ward had commented on how the quality of life in New York City seemed to have been steadily deteriorating throughout the late 1960s, so that arriving back there in 1972 after a four-year absence the city felt to him as though it had become shrouded in depression. Two terms of Mayor John Lindsay—a period characterized by devastating strikes, major corporate headquarters fleeing the city, as well as continual intractable labor struggles—all this and more was bringing the city to its lowest ebb.

Mayor Lindsay, I heard it generally agreed, had only made the difficult situation that the city faced far worse when he took over in 1966. On his very first day in office, New York bus and subway workers had gone on strike. This lasted for twelve days while Lindsay dithered and delayed, infuriating the entire city when he walked the four miles to City Hall proclaiming what a "fun city" it was. His lack of empathy with both the striking workers and the average New Yorker made him the focus of a bitter sarcasm from which he never really recovered when he attempted to become the U.S. president.

Mayor Lindsay had promised to be a liberal's dream; he was charming, bright, and good-looking in the American way, and he'd proved himself to be a courageous maverick during his time as a Republican in Congress. However, as mayor, he turned out to be a weak and divisive negotiator. His presumably well-meaning but feeble attempts to break union power, for example, created a legacy that would leave the city in tatters for years to come. It seemed that for a few years everyone was striking. Teachers, transport workers, construction workers—there was even a three-day strike by the theaters on the Great White Way. But worst of all for New Yorkers was the rotting garbage that accumulated on city streets as a result of the strike, which occasionally even caught on fire. So reviled had Mayor Lindsay become by 1968 that police snipers had to be brought in to cover one of the mayor's public appearances. Although there never was a serious attempt on Lindsay's life, he should have been thankful that his maladroit insensitivity had not provoked his demise at the hands of a furious citizenry.

His inept handling of a freak snowstorm in 1969 that killed and injured people throughout the city's five boroughs found the mayor throwing the city's resources into cleaning up Manhattan, while leaving the other boroughs to cope with fifteen inches of snow on unplowed roads.

Strikes continued into the early 1970s, and there was rioting in the streets as the reality of the Kent State shootings struck home. Protests were gaining strength against the American invasion of Cambodia and the endless war in Vietnam. Obviously Mayor Lindsay can't be held responsible for the tragedies of Kent State or Cambodia, but his bungled handling of both police and protesters earned him the ire of just about everybody and prompted even more strikes.

Lindsay had been defeated by a Republican contender in the mayoral primary. Thus he switched parties to that of the N.Y. Liberal Party and squeezed in a second term, much to the horror of most people. The slippery way that he'd accomplished his ambition and the prospect of four more years of his ineffectual leadership did little to further endear him to New Yorkers. It was all this and more that caused a reputable political historian to call John Lindsay the worst New York City mayor of the twentieth century.

However, I will give the poor man credit for one trait not shared by many politicians: He was rightly ashamed of his poor performance. Indeed, when Abe Beame took over the office of mayor in December of 1973, the departing John Lindsay was reported to have broken down and rued that he had bungled opportunities to enhance the welfare of his constituents.

The reason I've sketched out Mayor Lindsay's miserable record in office is to get across something of the social unrest that was roiling in Manhattan when Mein Host arrived in the city in 1972.

America itself was in turmoil, with passionate antiwar protests increasing in size in every major American city. Richard Nixon had just been elected president—a man who appeared so patently mean-spirited and conniving that I heard my ward comment at the time that "you don't have to be psychic to see the guy's a crook." This was well before the guy himself found it necessary to publicly protest that he wasn't one.

It must have seemed to Mein Host and the others in the community that their dire predictions of the imminent ending of civilization were being fulfilled around them. Racial tensions were rising all over the country. The Vietnam War was continuing to gorge relentlessly on America's young men. Daniel Ellsberg had leaked the Pentagon Papers to the *New York Times,* which they'd published on the front page in mid-June of the previous year. The horrifying reality of the lies and deception of both Congress and the Johnson administration was open-ing the eyes of many of those stalwart citizens who had never previously doubted the integrity of their government.

The criminal behavior of President Nixon and his coterie of advis-ers was being revealed daily as more of the lies and cover-ups rolled out of a slathering media. This served to merely confirm for those in the Process that the End of the World was indeed nigh.

"And getting nigher by the week," adds Mein Host.

Although we haven't made a general practice of breaking into the narrative, I'm inviting him to continue.

Mein Host writes, "We in the Process were completely convinced that it was coming to a head, and, tell the truth, we were delighted at the thought. I know that I'd had a brief encounter with an extraterrestrial back in '63, when he told me they could pick the rockets out of the sky, but I must have salted that event away. I'm sure I was as certain as all the others that the world was going to end soon."

"Then why," I ask him, "did everyone in the Process bother to work so hard to build up your organization if you thought the world was going to end so soon? Why not simply retire to the country and dig in and try to survive?"

"That wasn't the point, Georgia. We told ourselves that we *relished* the End. We were looking forward to it. We didn't think of surviv-ing it. We *wanted* to go out with a bang, not a whimper. That was one of Mary Ann's favorite maxims. It was her scorched-earth policy. Perhaps some of the junior members may have believed that our join-ing the Elect of God—that's what we called ourselves—would have meant we'd be the ones to be saved . . . but I don't recall any plans for what we'd do then."

I ask, "Do you think this belief came from Mary Ann?"

"Well, it certainly was absolutely central to her belief system. In fact, I'd go further; I think her entire belief system was structured around the world ending. In her mind we were the harbingers of the End. We were the elect who were picking up our people before the End—although it was never clear what we'd do with them.

"But I think your question goes deeper than that. I know, Georgia, that you've already written earlier in this narrative of my generally pessimistic viewpoint throughout the late 1950s, '60s, and '70s, from your perspective. But your seeing this quality in me, and my feeling of the weight of it are two quite different experiences. In fact, it only dawned on me fairly recently just how blinkered we had become when I realized how so many of my generation had made no plans for the future. In those key years between, say, the ages of fifteen and twenty-five, when kids are normally planning their futures, many of us were partying with no *care* for the future; it was the era of the beats and the hippies."

I ask, "Were you aware that you weren't planning for the future at the time?"

"Perhaps some of us were, but most of us hadn't really put it together. I think the prospect of nuclear annihilation was so existentially terrifying, it was like background radiation. We knew it was there and it was going kill us and there was nothing we could do about it. Not only that, the life-or-death decision to hurl all those bombs was in the hands of politicians in whom we had absolutely no confidence; or it would be one of those rogue generals featured in Kubrick's film *Dr. Strangelove*.

"I think most of us just shoved the horror of it down deep inside and distracted ourselves in different ways. It was good for the music scene—that was really the social context which incited and nurtured rock and roll. It was our generation's channel for rebellion; our way of feeling that at least we were telling it like it was, telling our truth to power."

"So the time wasn't entirely lacking in value?" I query.

"Well, Georgia, we probably had a great deal more fun than any succeeding generation—and probably a few previous ones too!"

I didn't disagree. Life had certainly become a great deal more serious for subsequent generations since the 1970s. But I wanted to grasp the moment to explore another, more personal theme.

I said, "Let me give you another viewpoint and, if I may, use you as an example. You write of the group's bravado in the face of nuclear annihilation, but underneath your macho posturing was a more psychological impulse. Your reaction to the terror that you likened to background radiation was to try to find your security in a community of like-minded souls—some safety in numbers. When Mary Ann revealed herself as a goddess to you, you gave over your autonomy and your power in exchange for the certainty—delusory though it may have been—of an autocratic goddess."

"It's rather humbling to hear you lay it out so baldly, Georgia. Of course I knew I'd given away my power, but I'd never seen my joining the Process as a grasping for security."

I say, "I know you are now aware that your fifteen years with the community was a vastly accelerated learning curve; a training, if you like, for what you've encountered in your past thirty years working with the angels. This is what I want you to understand: It was precisely your complete negation of a possible future that allowed you to follow your intuition so freely and has given you the chance to explore the Multiverse in a manner few others have had the time or opportunity of doing. Having qualified as an architect, had you then settled down to a long career in the profession, and were you then to marry and raise a family—as might have been expected of you—you would never have been able to devote your life to working so closely with the angels . . ."

"And I'd never be collaborating with you, Georgia! Which makes me wonder if I *had* chosen that path of settling down and raising a family, would you be collaborating with someone else?"

"A meaningless question. Though you may have believed at the time that you had a choice whether to make a career out of architecture, you really didn't. You had already plotted out the key turning points of your life with your companion angels before you entered incarnation. It was always your destiny to do what you're doing. This was written long before your current lifetime."

"Georgia, let me stop you there. I know you've touched on this concept of predestination before, but you must be aware that it's a difficult concept for the human mind to wrap itself around. Admittedly some aspects of life do seem mandated—our sexual preferences, for example— but the concept of free choice is so central to what it means to be a human being that the idea that we are simply acting out a predestined role in some vast theatrical melodrama of someone else's devising defies so much of what we believe to be true; why, it's very hard to grasp."

I reply, "Much of the confusion arises from humanity's profound ignorance of the true nature of a mortal being. I say this not to flatter: human beings are far more significant and powerful in ways you've yet to discover. And this applies every bit as much to incarnate rebel angels, but in a slightly different way.

"All mortals do, of course, possess free choice. Here is how it works. Each mortal has her or his own unique spiritual path. It's an arrangement, if you like, made in the deep mind between the human personality, the person's companion angels, and the Indwelling Atman, and it will be shaped by a person's genetic endowment and their environment. You can detect the output of this arrangement from the general level of enthusiasm an individual brings to their tasks in life.

"However, of more interest to you, and perhaps your readers too, is the case of mortal reincarnates. And this will also hold true for those other reincarnates with different spiritual heritages than the rebel angels who have their own reasons for being present on the planet. Your unique spiritual path will have been a journey through any number of previous lifetimes. Many of the choices that you had freely exercised in a past life will have consequences that affect your current lifetime in ways that might make you think you had no choice in them."

"An example would be helpful, Georgia."

"Here's one from your own life, and another of a more general application. You will recall that when you were at your English public school, Charterhouse, at the age of thirteen or fourteen you had to fight off the constant bullying homosexual demands of a much senior boy. You could well have thought of that as a situation in which you had no choice—as something that was happening to you against your will.

"Yet you have since discovered the nature of the sexual torture you endured in a previous lifetime and how you created a deep need to reclaim your honor in this lifetime by successfully repulsing that senior boy's brutal advances. Thus what appeared to be a situation in which you had no choice—by which I mean you had no choice *but* to react to the bully—was brought about as a result of a decision you made before you came into this incarnation.

"Now take the reports of alien abduction. In almost every case you'll read of abductees protesting that they were taken against their will, that resistance was useless, that they had no choice but to submit to their abductors and endure their examinations. Yet you can be sure that each one of those abductees had chosen prior to incarnation to volunteer for their mission, whether or not they consciously recall it—and a few do. Or they are told the truth of who they really are in the course of their abduction."

"So Georgia, abductees are really contactees; they just don't know it? Are they actually members of the abductor's race? Is that it?"

"It's important to understand the context for these so-called abductions—they are, in fact, very small threads in a much larger cloth. As with much else that is happening behind the scenes, what occurs during an abduction is simply one small part of the preparation for the coming shift of consciousness.

"To answer your question, most of those abducted have agreed, as members of another planetary species, to take part in a hybridization project. This is a technically advanced race from an older third-density world, one of the other thirty-seven planets won over by Lucifer's uprising, which has become genetically weakened by its overreliance on technology. They evidently know of the coming transformation, and I imagine they fear for their race's physical survival."

"How does this hybridization project work, Georgia? Is it legal? Is it allowed?"

"If Lucifer gave his permission, it's permitted. Since this project is occurring within his sphere of influence, his retooling of the subtle energy grid governing the normal mortal ascension process permits the reincarnation of souls within the Local System.

"So in this case, a soul on her planet of origination will have volunteered, after dying, to then incarnate in a human vehicle for the continuation of its species. As a human being, she—and the soul will almost always choose a female body for potential breeding purposes—will have no memory of her previous existence. She will most likely grow up thinking herself to be the most normal of women. She'll have no memory of the many times she'll have been picked up and examined over the course of her childhood and adolescence. She will most likely marry young and have genetically normal children with her husband. But more immediately significant for the visitors—here I'm calling them simply the 'visitors' as it doesn't fall to me to reveal their identity—the woman becomes available to them as a host-womb.

"During her fertile life she will be frequently abducted and go through the amnesia process afterward. She'll be impregnated with sperm from the finest specimens of the visitors' race, and after the hybrid embryo has gestated for a few months, she'll be lifted off again, the embryo will be removed and will continue its development in shipboard birthing vats."

"And the woman will know nothing of this?"

"She may have the occasional feeling something strange was happening. Perhaps she'll have some unusual dreams. Her menses will unexpectedly cease for a few months. Maybe she'll have some unexpected pains; she might even think she's pregnant. Then, just as unaccountably, she won't be. The embryo will have disappeared. After this occurs a few times—and it will, if she proves to be a good genetic host for the visitors—she learns to ignore it. Don't forget, she's almost certain to be a conventional housewife. Even if she did voice her suspicions, she would be thought mentally unbalanced by those around her. It is far easier for her to simply blot out the idea—which, of course, efficiently reinforces the posthypnotic amnesia placed there by the visitors.

"This is not a particularly widespread phenomenon. I'm told no more than five or six million women are involved. However, almost all of them live in the advanced Western countries, with a small number in the more advanced and stable Eastern cultures. As a result, the few

women who have become self-aware—some of whom have written publicly about their encounters—have been generally dismissed as hoaxers
or hysterics by a culture blinkered by millennia of planetary isolation."

"No surprises there, Georgia, but why are these so-called abductions
so concentrated in the advanced nations? Aren't they all the more certain of being dismissed by a disbelieving scientific community and a
cynical press than if the women were spread more evenly around the
world?"

"Astar tells me the primary reason that the hybridization project is
occurring in the developed nations is continuing social stability. The visitors' intention has always been to set up familial lines of mother, daughter, granddaughter, and so on and so forth, as it best serves their interests.
Most favored are socially stable areas like the American Midwest, where
in some cases there are matrilineal lines of four or five generations of
abductees. It is hoped that living in these areas will ensure that these
host-womb women live in optimally secure conditions so that both their
eggs and the implanted embryos will not be subject to undue stress.

"Besides, by conducting their program among people who will have
their reasons not to come forward, or be publicly scorned if they did
speak openly about their experiences, works to everybody's advantage.
So in a way, that too suits the visitors; their project has been a secret
that conveniently keeps itself."

"It seems a great deal of trouble to go through, Georgia—all that
toing and froing, keeping the posthypnotic amnesia in place, placing
the woman in an impossible situation . . . why don't they simply fertilize
the woman's eggs in test tubes, like doctors do in fertilization clinics? I
mean, if the embryos are going to be incubated in those vats, what's the
difference?"

I reply, "Even when humans with their compatible DNA contribute
eggs and sperm for test-tube fertilization, it's not always successful. The
nature of the visitors' genetic coding, while sufficiently similar to that
of human DNA to permit cross-fertilization, had long been in a deteriorating condition. They had started the project with in vitro fertilization but had so little success with it that they'd had to resort, somewhat

to their distaste, to using living wombs for those first few months of gestation."

"Somewhat to their *distaste,* Georgia?"

"I'm just passing on what I heard from Astar, and she was pointedly courteous in her descriptions. However, the impression of the visitors that I got from her was one of guilty embarrassment. They felt shame at being reduced to combining genes with another species, whom, even though physically vigorous, they considered vastly inferior to themselves. In their focus on technological advancement they'd become so detached from the natural cycles of life that discovering they would need to work with living wombs had initially disgusted them.

"And yet they'd had to get over their qualms—it was too serious a situation for them to allow for such sentimentality. The birthrate on their home planet had been dropping rapidly for generations and the visitors believed that their species would be extinct within a few hundred years. This is the only reason the visitors undertook the hybridizing project to begin with—they were becoming desperate. They were a proud race, and the thought of mixing their genes in such a crude way with a species from another planet, however repugnant, had to be overcome. But, as Astar observed with a toss of that beautiful head, she could always tell from the rigid and controlled way the visitors carried themselves around humans that they never entirely lost their disdain.

"Here's what did work out to their benefit. They were able to take advantage of Lucifer's modification of the energy grid, refitting it to allow for local reincarnation. Under normal conditions in Nebadon this would never have been possible.

"I heard most of the details on this project from Astar, who possesses a more widely developed scientific knowledge than I do. It was she who told me that the visitors had begun with their disappointing in vitro experiments and the reluctance they felt when they'd had to turn to using a host-womb for those first few months of gestation. It was far more laborious and complicated, but ultimately it was successful in producing hybrid embryos. After all, in the visitors' minds the future of their species was at stake, so however onerous and time-consuming the process, their survival made it worth their while."

"I've only come across one of these women in my travels, Georgia, so I got the impression it was pretty rare. Has their program been going on a long time?"

"The one woman you met with the hybrid children on the craft was indeed rare—she was one of the very few hosts who has retained a conscious memory of her abductions. You've met a few others, but because they were unaware of who they were, or the purpose they were serving, there was no need for you to know.

"As for timing, Astar tells me there were a number of false starts over the centuries, but the project started in earnest with a few hundred familial lines in the latter part of the nineteenth century. The project gained momentum throughout the twentieth century as many of the female human offspring of the contactees, in turn, also became host-wombs for the hybrid children. You will find the visitors frequently favor specific maternal genetic lines, so that a contactee might well discover that her mother, grandmother, great-grandmother . . . back as many as half a dozen generations in some cases, all have been host-wombs."

"Will we ever get to meet these hybrid children, Georgia, or will we come across them as adults?"

"Very few hybrids have walked the Earth as adult males. There'd been a few early attempts, which had produced some unfortunate results. Breeding males was never the visitors' primary interest, for it was the females who would ensure the survival of their species. Astar estimated that they were using a ratio of one male child to every seventy females. Most males, as they grew to adulthood, chose to live out their lives on the visitors' more advanced planet, but a few have insisted on a life on Earth.

"Some of these hybrids were driven to schizophrenia by the demands of living in two realities simultaneously. A few were shunned, or even killed, by their communities. Even when one of them managed to maintain his mental and emotional equilibrium, it was precarious at best. They were frequently brilliant thinkers and ahead of their time, which seldom worked out well for them.

"I am permitted to give you Nikola Tesla as an example of one of the more well-known of the male hybrids who chose a life on this planet. He paid a heavy mental and emotional price for his genius and his curiously idiosyncratic ways, as well as for some of his advanced discoveries that, were they to fall into a dictator's hands, would have threatened the fabric of the energy grid. After the potential Nikola Tesla fiasco the visitors became far more cautious about whom they permitted a life on Earth."

"Enough!" I said. "I'm aware this is interesting to you but I have allowed the intensity of your interest to divert me from the issue of free choice. So to return to the original paradox as to how free choice can exist alongside predetermination, the simple answer is that one's free choice is exerted to the extent that one chooses to follow a predestined path—whether one chooses to fight it or ignore it."

"So what you're saying, Georgia, is the only real choice we exert is that which opposes our natural spiritual path?"

"An oversimplification, given that some of the choices you make are taken to return to your path, but apart from that, yes, correct. As I explained earlier in this narrative, it is only the key watershed moments in your spiritual path that you determine beforehand—how you arrive at these key points is up to you and the choices you make. If you arrive at one of those predetermined turning points, it's quite possible to take the wrong turn and miss the opportunity. Do that, however, and you'll find that the events in your life and your responses to them will conspire over time to prompt you back toward your destined path.

"It is in paying close attention to these corrective events in life that occur when you inevitably fall off your path that you come to appreciate the Multiverse as a magnificent device for learning and personal transformation."

* * *

It wasn't long before the Process set up its first New York Chapter intended to be open to the public. This was on East 38th Street. During their previous time in the city, four years earlier, the chapter on

Cornelia Street was far too small for public activities, and, besides, the group itself was on its way back to Europe. Their move to New York in 1972 would come to be the start of a new phase for the community and, as it will turn out, would be their last opportunity to become successful as a religious organization.

A gradual change had been taking place at the core of the Process over the previous couple of years. It was a subtle shift of focus. Although it was evident to me, I saw no evidence that Mein Host was yet aware of this unacknowledged redirection of the group's energies. The members of the community who'd originally come together in England in the early 1960s had done so in part because they had grown disenchanted by the society within which they'd grown up. When the community moved wholesale to Xtul on the Yucatán Peninsula in 1966, my ward and most of the others in the group were quite sure they were turning their backs on the conventional society they had come to revile once and for all.

Now here they were, six years later, incorporated as a church that they would have considered absurd only ten years earlier, with success coming to mean a full house at their religious services, packed coffee-houses, and, of course, with that, the money was rolling in.

The Process chapters in Boston, Toronto, Chicago, New Orleans—and to a lesser extent the chapter in Miami that had never really taken off—were now being regarded primarily as moneymaking machines by the Omega (otherwise known as Mary Ann and Robert, heads of the Process Church). A chapter's success was judged solely on how much money it made. The weekly financial reports coming into the Omega from the chapters were skillfully used by Mary Ann to galvanize the competition between the Processeans. As well, they gave her a reason to pour scorn on the masters in charge of the failing chapters.

Mein Host would have no choice but to recognize this when the word came down in a few months to discontinue the PROCESS magazine in favor of what my ward has called their "tediously self-glorifying" newsletter. Considerable financial outlay was needed for a print run of two hundred thousand copies of a classy and controversial four-color magazine. Much more money could be made on the street selling an inoffensive, single-color newsletter.

Mein Host has pointed out that there was no real need to drop the magazine, because money was already pouring in. Previously, the emphasis for the magazine had always been on achieving the highest possible production values, along with a unique approach to graphic design and provocative images. The magazines were powerfully exuberant visual representations of the unconventional beliefs of the Process Church. They were colorful, confident, and startlingly original, and have become far more highly valued now, more than forty years later, than they ever were when they were being sold on the streets of American cities. In contrast, the newsletter—predictably enough named *THE PROCESSEANS*—was merely a dozen or so pages of self-serving propaganda and the most mundane black-and-white photos of happy-faced Processeans going about their daily tasks. As PROCESS magazine had once been a vibrant outpouring of original thought, eccentric design, and the spiritual insights and revelations of a contemporary Gnostic community, *THE PROCESSEANS* was created exclusively to pander to people on the street and persuade them to part with their money.

This shift in emphasis I mentioned earlier can probably be most clearly seen in the way in which their publications that once proudly proclaimed—and in some cases, shouted—the community's controversial beliefs were now becoming a few pages of inoffensive piffle and photos cynically chosen to tug at the buyer's heart. Who could resist a cover shot of a pretty young Processean cradling a cuddly kitten, a dreamy Madonna smile on her fresh, open face, her pupils dilated with adoration as she gazed sweetly into the camera? Who could turn away from *that*?!

While the decision to phase out the magazine might have made hard-nosed sense for a profit-driven business, I believe that for a church—a so-called nonprofit religious organization—it was a sure sign that greed was starting to settle in.

Mary Ann and Robert had been living for the past couple of years in relatively modest style, for them, in the house they'd rented for themselves on the outskirts of Toronto. However, with the establishment of the New York Chapter, they would have taken it as a sign to relocate to New York. Mary Ann, in particular, had always held up the Big Apple as the ultimate goal of the Process Church: "Be a success in New York City," she liked to announce, "and we will succeed everywhere."

Mein Host had seen nothing of Mary Ann and Robert since he moved to America, so I made it my business to keep the Omega intermittently under observation when they were still in Toronto. It was there that I was able to identify the source of this new shift of direction.

The subtle balance of power that existed between Mary Ann and Robert, which had worked so well for them for the first three or four years of the Process, was now starting to tilt progressively more toward Mary Ann. Although they went on putting on a good face in front of the senior members of the Toronto Chapter during their meetings, behind the scenes the tension between the pair more frequently erupted, as Mary Ann's fury grew ever more volcanic in the face of Robert's apparent inability to fulfill her impossible demands.

Robert had always been the least materialistic of men, quite content to talk and argue endlessly into the night whether he was living in a one-room shack or a mansion. He seemed entirely lacking in personal ambition, and his rather detached and passive nature—characteristics that had originally made him of such value to Mary Ann—were now regularly infuriating her. This fury, in turn, exposed one of the deep contradictions in her own personality.

Her megalomaniacal ambitions, for example, seemed to be more often than not thwarted by the poor choices she made in trying to achieve them. Her conviction in her own divinity would have demanded a partner of matching spiritual significance and, as I've heard my ward comment, "Poor Robert, he's a sweet man, but he's no messiah for all her badgering!"

I've already related some of Mary Ann's efforts to turn Robert into a messianic figure by virtue of her Nietzschean formula of attempting to destroy him to make him stronger. But it hadn't worked. Even though a retouched, glamorized portrait of Robert still decorated a prominent

wall of each chapter, the man himself had no public charisma whatsoever, however elegant the styling of his hair and the clothes Mary Ann
selected for him.

It's my observation that it was in Toronto that Mary Ann reluc-
tantly began to realize she might be unable to mold Robert into her
own malleable messiah. Equally, it was clear from her viciously scornful
treatment of him in their rows that she was certain it was Robert who
was to blame for being chronically incapable of rising to her expectations. This is a tension that must surely exist in many relationships in
which one partner is more ambitious than the other, but they're unlikely
to be freighted with such grandiose demands, nor will such unreasonable demands be met with such intransigent passivity.

It certainly wasn't as if Robert hadn't tried his best over the years
to fulfill Mary Ann's improbable ambitions for him. He had tolerated
more abuse and humiliation at his wife's hands than any man rightly
deserved. His two public lectures, at the Oxford Union and the London
School of Economics, given eight years prior back in the early days of
the Process, had exposed his inability to communicate with an audience. From that point on Mary Ann hadn't permitted Robert to make
any more public appearances, believing, I imagine, that she would be
able to lick him into shape with her indomitable will prior to presenting
him to the world as the long-awaited messiah.

I am unable to enter a mortal's mind without being consciously
invited, thus I was unable to read Mary Ann's true motives in her dealings with Robert. She may well have always intended to use him as
a launching pad for her own ascendancy. Then again she could have
started off with the dream of being one of a divine pair—the magical
dream of a fatherless child, born illegitimate into the most degraded of
circumstances—only to find no man was capable of fulfilling the role.

Not surprisingly, given her background, Mary Ann had a generally
poor opinion of men in general. Her years of working as a call girl—"a
high-class call girl, *if* you please," I've heard her emphasize more than
once—had taught her what she needed to know about men. I doubt
she ever stopped to think that she might have been generalizing her

low opinion from a somewhat limited and self-evidently compromised sample.

As can occur with other women of power, she would have thought of men as helpless children, fearful and needy and ridiculously easy to manipulate. No doubt her time as an expensive call girl had given her a taste for money, but more importantly, it had opened her eyes to that aspect of the human male that can fixate on a strong, controlling woman—in the same way, as a baby, he once might have been imprinted upon by his mother. Mary Ann would also have invariably noticed that it seemed to be a secret desire of many wealthy, powerful men to be dominated by a more powerful woman. While this will be no secret to a career dominatrix—and probably not to most women—Mary Ann's particular talent lay in applying the same principles within a religious setting, along with the associated insight that with skill and a callous disregard for another's self-determination, men could be made willing slaves to her every desire. What's more, the men wouldn't even know they were slaves.

This skill would manifest in constructing a sufficiently interesting and complex cosmology to compel the attention of her followers' mental intelligences while she held the cords with which she could manipulate their emotional bodies. It would have been for the task of creating this complicated theological structure that she must have initially needed Robert, a man who could spin a cosmology out of a hat before it dropped.

How consciously aware she was of concocting this situation for herself wasn't easy to discern. She was not a bad woman. I never observed, for example, her taking any sadistic delight in the harsh treatment she doled out to those who fell from her favor. If she had started with such cynical thoughts in the early days of the Process, I suspect she must have slowly come to buy into her own propaganda.

Had she always believed herself to be the Goddess? Or did she merely allow others to believe it of her? Had she become convinced of her divinity from the devotion she engendered from those in her inner circle? Was she playing the old "who-say-ye-that-I-am" game of official deniability?

Could she perhaps have assumed the cloak of divinity only to discover, over time, that what she was manifesting was the dark side of the Goddess? Or was it the dark and troubled aspects of Mary Ann's own character that, by nature of correspondences, had drawn in the dark side of the Goddess?

In posing these questions about Mary Ann, I trust I'm communicating something of the extent to which she still remained an enigma to me in the spring of 1973. I found it too simplistic to treat her as deluded—believing that she was merely fooling everyone with her pretension of divinity. Mein Host has claimed that just too many inexplicable and synchronous events had occurred at her instigation for her to be dismissed so casually. He also reminds me that there are a number of Eastern religious cultures in which incarnate goddesses are readily accepted and revered in much the same way as he, and the others who were close to her, felt a devotion to Mary Ann.

I am bringing these brief observations of Mary Ann's personality into the narrative at this point to illustrate the gap between what I thought of Mary Ann and what my ward was going through while he remained firmly convinced of her divinity. To me this seemed somewhat strange, but as both of his companion angels were continuing to support his choice to be part of the Process, I could only step back and wonder.

What I couldn't have known was that in a few months my ward's life would profoundly change in a way he could never have imagined.

3

Unnatural Selection

Genetic Predispositions, the Somme Valley,
the Invasion of Europe, Elect of God,
a Satirically Unnatural Death, and
the Mary Ann Mini-Me

There are a number of purely practical explanations as to why similar events can occur in the same location even though those events are separated by thousands of years. Owing to reasons of geographical necessity, invasions have tended to follow this pattern over time. Mountain ranges, wide rivers, and large bodies of water most frequently define the boundaries of tribal and, later, national identity. These barriers can generally be overcome only in certain places: a pass over high mountains, the place where a river can be most readily forded, or a sheltered bay.

However, there are locations where, for no obvious reason, terrible times of bloodshed have occurred again and again in the same place down through history. The Somme Valley in northern France is one of these places. It is best known for the more recent Battle of the Somme in the fall of 1916 when—in four and a half months of fighting—there were more than a million casualties. On the very first day of the Somme offensive the British Army suffered an unheard-of sixty thousand casualties with almost twenty thousand dead. The flower of the empire's manhood—20 percent of the British fighting forces—were killed in one day. The few months of trench warfare from July to November 1916 won the British and French a mere few miles of territory for all those losses.

Lesser known was another battle in the Somme Valley, this one occurring in the late seventh millennium. It was every bit as terrible, yet with a far more significant result than the more recent war. The battle that occurred in the seventh millennium—if I can really call it a battle—lasted for more than five hundred years and transformed the racial composition of Europe forever.

While clan and tribal loyalties have always been the primary form of self-identification, racial identity became increasingly significant as the various races increased in numbers and moved around. By the eighth millennium, Europe, more than any other continent—some of which were sparsely populated—had become a racial melting pot that was spoiling for an explosive collision.

Here I should insert a brief note for those unfamiliar with my previously related references to the different races of the human family. It may be a truism, but race has always been important. For many people, their race is still their basic point of personal identification. Even though the overall racial situation has become vastly more simplified over the past ten millennia—and despite America being rightly claimed as the most advanced nation of the early twenty-first century—there are still white Americans and black Americans, Hispanic Americans, Japanese Americans, and Chinese Americans.

I have observed that a lot of talk of the different races, as well as their slightly different genetic endowments—whether physical, intellectual, or spiritual—have been badly distorted in modern times by the weight of historical guilt. Whether it has been the brutality of colonization, the dark reverberations of the slave trade, the problematic issue of eugenics, or centuries of anti-Semitism, discussions of racial differences can easily slip into minefields of misunderstanding.

Almost ten thousand years have passed since the decisive five-hundred-year war along the Somme Valley, and, even though the different races are far more assimilated now than then, an individual's race, even more than their religion, is still the primary form of self-identification for most people around the world. If race remains such a central issue in the lives of so many people, and is such an awkward subject for others to broach in serious discussion, it shouldn't be hard to picture just how paramount racial differences might have been in a more belligerently uninhibited era.

So if I write more openly about race than might normally be expected, it's without bias or judgment. Racial differences have been baked deliberately into the evolutionary process. They are unavoidable. The various mortal races of color are standard fare on third-density inhabited worlds. Differences between the races are calculated to provoke a certain amount of creative tension between them, with the ultimate intention of producing a human race through the process of natural selection that carries the finest aspects of every race.

Some races will happily interbreed and assimilate. Others are able to coexist, however uneasily, while others are aggressively intolerant of a different race. For example, about one hundred thousand years ago the orange people were as good as entirely wiped out as a result of a genocidal hundred-year war with those of the green race. Most of the fighting took place in the Nile Valley, and after the dust had settled it was the green race who subsequently spread throughout southern Egypt.

One of the features of the green people was their giant build; some of their great leaders were well over nine feet tall. Unfortunately for the green race they weren't as generously gifted with intelligence as they were with their noble physical attributes. Soon they too went into a lingering decline, making few significant advances while consuming themselves with internecine fighting. Within a few thousand years the remnants of the green race were, in turn, absorbed by the indigo people when they arrived sometime later in North Africa. The genetic predisposition among the green race for giantism, although now somewhat muted in the mix, can still be observed in the singularly tall build of the people of some African tribes. One of them—the seminomadic Masai people who are known for their unusual height—still have an oral tradition of having originated in the lower Nile Valley.

Although human beings have become substantially more socially compliant over the many intervening millennia, and the different races have become far more assimilated and integrated, racial identity obviously continues to drive some of the most intractable and bitter conflicts of the modern world.

Enough about the racial tangle. And believe me, I have simplified the situation. Trusting I've gotten across something of the complex mix of races roiling around the Middle East and Europe in the eighth and seventh millennium, I'll pick up the trail of the invasion again—one that so profoundly altered the racial balance of Europe.

It was as I was accompanying a caravan of migrants through the mountains of Eastern Europe that I started to overhear talk of the war that had been going on endlessly in northern France. It was this that seemed to be preoccupying the men traveling north as they sat around their fires at night, shivering in the colder climate.

As so many of their people had done before them, they had followed the trail from Mesopotamia up through Turkestan and southern Russia to arrive hopefully at one of their rapidly growing settlements in Denmark. They were an intelligent and ingenious people. They carried a generous endowment of the violet blood inherited from their distant ancestors: the two off-world visitors and their descendants who had settled some thirty thousand years earlier in the Land of the Two Rivers.

As the millennia passed, the endowment of violet blood had become more widely distributed as clans sprang up by interbreeding with other native tribes. But in doing this, the people had become more assertive and aggressive, so by the time they had reached northern Europe they'd developed more of a taste for invasion. This is what the five-hundred-year war centered on the Somme Valley really was: a brutal invasion that set the stage for the race now identified as the white European type.

So for simplicity's sake, and because by the eighth and seventh millennia this race was now mixed with others, I'll call these invaders the white race. These were the people who had been massing in Denmark and casting their hungry eyes toward the land in the south and east.

The people who faced these white invaders and who had been the dominating racial mix in central and southern Europe for thousands of years were the blue people. We met them earlier in my narrative as a small group of hunters who had, over the centuries, interbred with the Cro-Magnon people, who were mainly to be found around the foothills and mountains of southern France. This Cro-Magnon and blue people mix proved to be a physically hardy one, but it wasn't of great benefit in raising the intelligence of the blue race. The Cro-Magnon genome dominated in the mix, which, over the generations, led to a reduction in the general level of intelligence in the Cro-Magnon/blue race. While they had become expert workers of flint tools and weapons, they never progressed much further than that.

Whereas the blue people, they were bright. I've heard it said it was they who first invented the spear. Yet being a peaceful river people, they had used the spears almost exclusively for spearing fish!

However, from what I had observed, whether pureblood blue or Cro-Magnon mix, prior to the invasion they were an essentially peaceful and industrious people who had set their genetic, artistic, and cultural stamp on the land during the thousands of years they had spread throughout the continent. And while the blue people may have been relatively bright and industrious by nature, they proved no match for the far more ingenious and aggressive white race.

Moving out from their settlements in Denmark, the white invaders cut a swathe through central Europe. The blue people had little chance of resisting the marauding bands of mounted cavalry. In most cases, when a settlement was overrun, the locals had never seen a horse before and were so frightened they were easy to cut down. In fact, for at least half a century the blue people were convinced that both horse and rider were a single creature, a tribe of centaurs who became their merciless angels of death.

I'd seen so much of death and destruction on this world by this time that I found I was able to observe the massacres happening all over the land with a new detachment. Having rid myself of what I had come to believe was sentimental self-indulgence, I was able to see with clearer eyes the level of planned intention the invaders brought to their purpose. They weren't simply raiding parties that attacked the indigenous encampments and settlements, looting and carrying off their women and then riding off not to be seen again for a few years. These invaders knew what they wanted and went about it with an implacable ferocity. They had migrated on a long, hard journey up through the barren mountains in the East to find a new homeland, and the endless pastures, the fertile soil, and virgin forests of central and western Europe would have seemed to them a promised land.

While many races over the course of history have used this justification for their invasions—whether racial or religious—they invariably discover that they have to deal with those people who are already living in their promised land.

The racial transformation of Europe that took place over the next few thousand years was not so different from the expansion of the European white race throughout the North American continent from the seventeenth century until the present. Here was the same impulse to usurp another's land. Here also was the corresponding need to dehumanize the enemy as an acceptable reason for trying to eradicate any vestige of their existence.

I happened upon an example of this after a particularly ferocious clash between the invaders and a force of the Cro-Magnon blue people who had fought bravely, but fruitlessly, to defend their village on the western bank of the Somme River. Bodies lay strewn around, both in the village and in the bordering forest, some in small heaps and others in pairs, still locked in their death struggle. Despite my newfound sense of detachment, it was when I looked at those heaps of bodies more carefully that I lost my emotional equilibrium. They were children. Boys of all ages, their contorted limbs were improbably twisted, some with their throats slit, others with their little heads smashed open. There were babies too. Tiny little creatures, mercifully dead, I thought.

Yet as I stayed to observe, this revealed an element which set it apart from what I'd seen of the wholesale massacre of Native Americans. While there were a number of older women lying dead, I saw nothing of dead or dying younger women or adolescent girls. I hoped, naively perhaps, that they'd been secreted away in the forest by the villagers before the attack. I should have known better.

I had already taken note that when the white and blue people had the opportunity to mingle relatively freely with each other they'd discovered there was a natural affinity between the two races. I knew the women of the blue people seemed to find the men of the white invaders better breeding material than the males of their own race. What I hadn't understood until then was that the white males, in turn, were not only enjoying the sexual advantage of this natural attraction, but they also appeared to be purposefully impregnating as many women of the blue race as possible.

At first I thought this was simple lust. Though there was much of that too, as I moved around the fringe of the forest where most of the coupling was taking place, I realized the purpose behind it. Above and beyond the men's sexual release—or their instinct to dominate and humiliate the women—lay a more considered intention. It seemed to me that they were deliberately setting out to genetically overwhelm the indigenous blue race. But surely this wasn't a conscious calculation, was it? Were they operating under instruction? I wondered. Was Prince Caligastia's hand in this?

I knew the blue race had been particularly shaken up by the rebellion. They'd been one of the races who'd responded best to the teachings of the Prince's staff before the uprising. Over the following millennia, with the final death of the staff and Caligastia's leadership becoming increasingly bizarre, the blue people had been thrown into turmoil, never again quite sure who or what to believe. Even though that had occurred many hundreds of generations in the past, the blue race lost much of its confidence and went into a long decline. They had only regained some of their old racial vigor after they'd more fully populated

Europe. Yet despite this regeneration they were invariably outwitted by the invaders.

Although they would become gradually assimilated into the white race—who themselves were already a genetic cocktail of violet, red, and yellow races—it would be essentially a mix of these two races, blue and white, which would lead most directly to the ancestors of the contemporary European type.

I realized then that Prince Caligastia would never have ignored a chance to take his revenge on a people he felt had betrayed him. He had a long memory. He had originally been unnaturally proud of the blue people; "God's special children," he used to call them. After the uprising and the confusion had set in, in the Prince's mind it was *his* special children who had betrayed *him*! He would never have forgiven that!

I'd imagine it must have been beyond him to have seen and accepted his own part in the betrayal. He never had been strong on personal responsibility. When the time came that the blue people finally turned away from their "God," I've no doubt the Prince could have started plotting his revenge. After all, he must have felt he had all the time in the world.

It was this that allowed me to more deeply understand the dynamics of resentment. As well, it opened my eyes to the real power behind the white invaders as they overran central Europe.

Was there a purpose to Prince Caligastia's support of the invaders, I wondered, or was it merely an expression of his revenge against the hated blue people?

* * *

It was within no more than a few months of opening the New York Chapter on East 38th Street that the group found it needed to expand to a building across the street.

The city was going through its desperate times in the early 1970s, and this general sense of malaise was proving to be fertile turf for the community. Disillusionment was at its height among young people. The revolutionary zeal of the sixties had turned sour with Nixon's vicious drug war, Kissinger's realpolitik, the endless war in Vietnam, Watergate—everything that was occurring in the world seemed to be proving the Process right. Everything was falling apart.

The number of disciples was growing. These were people who wanted to become part of the community and who had embarked on the long testing period—between six months and two years—to establish their commitment. Disciples continued with their jobs and normal lives but were expected to devote more and more time to the Process. They were required to tithe money, attend courses and classes, attend the Sabbath Assembly and the weekly Midnight Meditations, work around the chapter, and go out on the street enthusiastically selling magazines whenever they had any free time.

Later, when the number of disciples had swollen to more than twenty, they were encouraged to share apartments as a way of readying themselves for the intensely communal life of the Internal Processeans, or IPs. IPs were those who were living within the community versus the disciples, who were Outside Processeans, or OPs. The OPs—those identifying with Process ideals—if serious about their intention to join the community, were required to refrain from alcohol and drugs (nicotine was not included); commit progressively more of their time, energy, and money; agree to maintain sexual abstinence; and finally, to sell or give over all of their personal possessions and finances to the Process.

So challenging were the demands made on those wanting to join the community full-time that it could be said the Process Church had really condemned itself to remain a small and insignificant cult, with little or no impact on the culture from which it sprang.

I have heard my ward insist that the long harsh testing period was intentional as it efficiently screened out the fainthearted, the poseurs, the wannabes, and the layabouts. The period soon revealed who possessed the self-discipline that would be required of them once they were IPs. However successful, wealthy, or powerful a person considered themselves to be in the outside world, when they joined the community they found themselves at the very bottom of the hierarchy. This was quite enough to dissuade those with an exaggerated sense of self-regard.

Also, the people who viewed the community as an easy escape from the world or a safe refuge from real life could be discouraged early on, before too much time had been wasted on caring for them.

After all, the IPs thought of themselves as the Elect of God! It *had* to be a small and select club. Besides, they would tell you there wasn't one of them who had not taken on and surmounted the obstacles and met the same demands they required of those who wished to join them. A central maxim of the group was never to expect or require another person to do what one hadn't done oneself, or what one was unprepared to do.

They would have agreed it was the prime purpose of the hierarchy. People had the same opportunity to work themselves up from the bottom, doing the most mundane of tasks and yet being given every chance to reveal unexplored talents. In this way the hierarchy also functioned as a meritocracy. Someone like Sister Jessica, for example, with a gift for illustration, might recuse themselves from street selling to work full-time in the art department. Another person with a talent for public speaking might be scooped up to host their radio shows. Mein Host's cousin Andrew, who had joined the group well after they'd returned from Xtul, had been shooting up the hierarchy due to his organizational skills.

Within the community, they were enthusiastically greeting the deteriorating conditions in the outside world as well as the depressing state of the city as being sure signs that the End of the World they had long been predicting was drawing closer by the day. I had the chance to observe the incongruous pleasure they seemed to take in the news of every catastrophe. These were collected daily from newspapers and read out at the evening meeting; interpreting, for example, a riot in Indonesia, an earthquake in Japan, or a bridge collapse in Chile through the lens of their apocalyptic belief system.

I must admit that I found the psychology of their enthusiastic response to such an ominous global collapse somewhat hard to fathom. They weren't callous people. They took no sadistic pleasure from human suffering. Should the news report include an item about a bus of pilgrims crashing off a precipice in India—an astonishingly frequent event—it wasn't cruelty that caused them to applaud the crash and the body count. It was merely another sign of the End.

Was it merely bravado? Was it the community's way of managing their own fear of death as individuals? Were they perhaps just following the party line as dictated by Mary Ann and Robert? Did they think that they were in training to cope emotionally with the very disasters they were predicting? Or were they simply sensing the community's impending demise and projecting it out onto world events?

I have since understood that this demonstrated one of the most puzzling features of human psychology. It would appear that the more tentative people are in their beliefs—even on a subconscious level—the more vociferously they need to proclaim those beliefs. And its inverse: the more closely a person's beliefs are aligned with their higher truth, the less need they will have to bray their beliefs from the rooftops.

Any impartial analysis, of course, would have revealed the conviction that the world was soon to end was obviously an uncertain and unrealistic belief, absurd enough in the popular mind to be relegated to unkempt old geezers with sandwich boards. Worse still, as my collaborator points out, these sorts of apocalyptic predictions are such a familiar trope in the dynamics of cult psychology that, taken together with the prediction's perennial lack of success, are always sure to invite incredulity. Having to overcome this not unreasonable initial skepticism shown by any thoughtful person required a level of passionate certainty bordering on the fanatic. Much of the energy behind their displays of excessive enthusiasm at any sign of the imminent apocalypse resulted from having to support such a preposterous premise.

However, from what I was able to overhear and deduce at the time, these were not questions or issues to which anyone in the Process was giving much attention. Yet it was just these sorts of uncertainties that I found were disturbing their emotional bodies whenever I cared to look.

My ward agrees with me that this accurately reflected the general feeling within the community at the time.

However, had they delved somewhat more deeply, they may well have found themselves confounded by the evident paradox of their situation. On the one hand, those in the community spent almost all their time promoting or evangelizing for the Process Church in one way or another. They believed in the rightness of their cause—of course they did!—and they felt proud and fulfilled in their mission, as anyone would, and particularly when other people recognized this and joined them.

On the other hand, believing themselves to be the Elect of God was in itself a conceit of outrageous elitism. It could only be supported and validated by making it almost impossible to achieve. Any elite, by definition, has to be small and select; the Elect of God would have to be the smallest and most highly select. Logically, either all human beings are the Elect of God or it would have to be confined to the very few. Within this paradox resided both the success of the Process and its inevitable failure.

The problems presented by this paradox hadn't yet occurred to my ward or any of the others, for they had thrown themselves into expanding into the apartment on the north side of East 38th Street. However, this arrangement soon became impossible too. They were living so closely together that they were tripping over one another. People were being sent to New York from other chapters because so much more money could be made on the streets of Manhattan. This only made living more constricted than ever, with sleeping conditions that were ridiculously cramped. The truth of it was straightforward, or so I heard my ward joking to a couple of the others in the tiny, jerry-rigged art department: it was simply that their accommodations were a great deal smaller than other places they'd inhabited.

I find in writing that sentence my collaborator has turned suddenly thoughtful. He'd forgotten he said that somewhat revealing remark. It seems to suggest he was more aware of yet another of those subtle shifts of direction and purpose that was leading the Process into its inevitable decline.

It was indeed true that as the community became more financially successful, the chapter houses had become increasingly spacious and comfortable. Even the apartment that Mein Host shared with the other three priests in Toronto was large and elegant and at the top of a modern high-rise apartment block—so high they overlooked the city all the way to the lake. It was much the same for the Processeans who had been sent to New York from other cities.

Until recently, their individual comfort would have been the least important aspect of their lives. They had prided themselves on a hardy indifference to their creature comforts. Their years of hitchhiking around Europe with no money—trusting only in their intuitions and the kindness of strangers—had taught them the spiritual value of simplicity.

The chapter in London at Balfour Place may well have been a Mayfair mansion, but they slept on the floor, six to a room. The Rome Chapter was in a sumptuous palazzo, yet the community shivered in the frozen cellars of the palace. The New Orleans Chapter was now in a magnificent old building on Rue des Ursulines in the French Quarter. Impressive though it might have been from the outside, the building's dilapidated state permitted the cold, damp, Gulf winds to whine through corridors, freezing the sleeping Processeans.

In short, these were young men and women who had tested themselves to destruction, who had turned their back on material comforts, and who had given up money and personal ambition in service of the gods they professed to represent.

It was going to be another challenge as more and more money poured in to the Process coffers. It is no difficult task to be frugal when living with so little money. How would the community respond as they began to think of themselves as wealthy and moved in to buildings they hoped would reflect this change of status in the eyes of the world?

Yet even as I pose that question, I find I need once again to discern the degree to which the desires and the dreams of the individual members were aligned with or merely reflected Mary Ann's ambitions for the group. While it is certain the Process would never have existed if it hadn't been for Mary Ann's drive, psychism, and charisma, the various chapters were now being run by senior Processeans, with an increasing degree of autonomy.

What happened over the next few months would find Mary Ann making a series of increasingly unrealistic decisions, which would be driven ever more brazenly by her personal ambition than by any real thought for the good of the community. Robert had never really been a match for Mary Ann in the power stakes, although he'd put in a good showing over the years. At best, Robert might have been able to rein in the more unreasonable and excessive of his wife's demands in the early days, but, as stated earlier, the years hadn't been kind to him. Mary Ann had been waging a war of attrition—first to break him down and then to rebuild him to become her messiah. Following this, she'd set out to destroy him for not fulfilling her grandiose expectations.

The necessity of Robert's being able to rein in his wife's ambitions would be most sorely needed the following year, but the reins were fast slipping out of his hands. Besides, there were a couple of other matters waiting in the wings that would have a far more serious effect on Robert and, ultimately, on the fate of the entire group.

* * *

As I observed the after-battle gathering on the banks of the Somme on that overcast winter afternoon, I was surprised to see the sophistication with which the victors applied the principle of what Mr. Charles Darwin would much later refer to as the evolutionary process of natural selection. How *natural* their technique was, I will leave to the reader to decide.

The white Europeans who invaded and settled in North America generally showed little interest in interbreeding with Native Americans. It was by the Somme River, with the huts burning in the background and the air thick with smoke and the stink of death, that I observed a rather different ritual taking place.

There was a double line of perhaps fifty or sixty men of the blue race standing with their backs to the river, and, from their dejected and in some cases bloodied appearance, they must have been the surviving prisoners of the attack on their village. The women of the clan were nowhere to be seen. I assumed from what I heard of the squeals coming from the woods bordering the burning village that they were being enthusiastically ravaged by the victors.

An early snow had gathered in small drifts to the north side of each tree, each a white streak etched against the dark earth. I can only liken this to looking at a massive negative photograph. The pitch black of the nearby tree trunks, each with its white shadow stretched out behind it, contrasted with the churned black and bloody mud. The spiky leafless limbs of the trees in the forest on the far bank of the river; the birds circling noisily overhead, eager to feast on the bodies of the dead; the moans of the wounded warriors punctuated by a sudden shrill scream of a dying horse; the hiss of icy rain as clouds heavy with water finally split open—this formed an appropriate mise-en-scène to this disturbing ritual.

At first I could just make out an old woman walking uncertainly out of the smoke, accompanied by four heavily armed warriors of the white tribes. Behind them and starting to gather in a semicircle were about a dozen men, whom I took for priests from their more elaborate attire and their stern bearings.

I was surprised to see that the old woman, now that I looked at her more distinctly, was a Cro-Magnon/blue mix. Whatever was she doing here, being escorted in such style? Were they going to execute her? And the priests; why were they here and looking so solemn?

The old woman was being led unsteadily toward where the prisoners stood. Drawing closer I could see, from her build and the shape of her head as she stumbled along, supported between two of the white-skinned warriors, that there was quite an evident bias toward the Cro-Magnon in her facial features.

Now that was odd! Her Cro-Magnon blue race were particularly staunch defenders of their land and invariably received the harshest treatment when captured. And yet here she was, seemingly healthy and being treated with unusual care by her escort. I couldn't make any sense of how she might fit in to what I was watching play itself out.

It wasn't long before I understood.

Beginning at the end of the first line of prisoners and working her way slowly, one by one, along the terrified men, as each in turn was pushed roughly to their knees, the old crone bent over and sniffed at their bodies. For some prisoners, one sniff was enough. With others she started at the head and then would straighten up and stand back for a moment as though considering her judgment before bending down again to more attentively smell the body. Sniff . . . sniff . . . sniff. Down the line she slowly shuffled, sniffing and shuffling . . . sniffing and shuffling . . . sniffing and shuffling . . .

She stopped her shuffling and sniffing about every tenth prisoner, painfully pulling herself as erect as the curvature in her spine allowed. One of her attendant warriors handed her a clay bowl, which, as I looked closer, appeared to be spherical with a small circular hole at the top. It also had a little thin spout extending from one side.

I imagined it must contain water. Yet rather than drinking from the vessel, the old woman solemnly jammed the spout up one of her nostrils. She tilted her head back and snorted noisily, clearing her nasal passages, before blowing a stream of water onto the ground beside her. She repeated this with her other nostril and then handed the bowl back to her attendant, ready to move on to the next man.

I couldn't help noticing the care she took to prevent the water from touching any of the prisoners when she was spewing it out of her nose. Even her warrior attendants made sure their feet didn't touch the water as it puddled on the muddy ground beside her.

Her nose clear again, she moved on to the next man, and the sniffing and shuffling started all over again and continued for the next ten men when the same little ceremony was repeated.

What struck me as so uncanny was the pall of silence that enveloped the entire process. It had floated down almost imperceptibly over the gathered men like a noise-canceling blanket. The moans of the wounded had died away; the screams and squeals of fear and pleasure from the forest had quieted down; the prisoners, unsure of what was happening to them, were standing passively silent; even the birds circling high above this puzzling drama seemed to sense the significance of what was occurring below them and had ceased their raucous cries.

Not a word was spoken; not a whimper heard. The old woman

doddered down the line stopping and starting, sniffing more carefully at some than others in a manner I found quite arbitrary. I couldn't see the difference between most of the men. There must have been some sign passing between the woman and the warriors that I wasn't able to perceive. The priests too seemed to be responding to hidden cues.

As the old woman moved slowly down the line, sniffing and shuffling, in some cases one of the warriors, in others a pair of priests, would step forward and lead a prisoner away—the warriors going in one direction, the priests with their prisoner in the other.

Over and over this happened, with a clockwork precision. There was no protest from the prisoners, and whether they knew what was about to befall them I couldn't tell. They seemed to be moving like automata, in whichever direction they were being led.

The number of prisoners in the two lines steadily diminished as the woman shuffled her way toward the end. Two priests then took the last of the men off to join the others gathered in a meadow bordering the river some five hundred steps south of the village. I hadn't seen where the warriors were taking their prisoners.

Obviously physically exhausted, the old woman was teetering on her feet by the end of the last line. Yet as I attended more closely to her emotional body, I could feel her pain was mixed with a wash of guilty exhilaration.

And with good reason, I thought. I had a better idea of what was going on by that time!

At first I hadn't been able to make out the difference between those prisoners being led off by the warriors and those taken by the priests. The captives had appeared to be in much the same state to me— hopeless, broken, dejected men; all no doubt facing an unpleasant fate. I got my first clue when I noticed that a few of the prisoners accompanying the priests had the robust build of a Cro-Magnon, as well as heads with the broad flat forehead that made them so recognizable. And as I've said, most of the prisoners who were being led off by the priests looked much the same to me as those who were taken by the warriors. What *was* I looking at here?

Then it struck me.

I realized I'd been paying too much attention to the state of the captives' emotional bodies—which, of course, tended to be similarly miserable. No wonder they looked the same. I'd entirely missed the obvious. Now I could see that the invaders were deliberately and knowingly separating out those men of the blue race who carried even the smallest trace of a dominant Cro-Magnon gene. The old woman had been sniffing them out!

I'd observed much of this kind of activity back in the days when the Prince's staff were frantically mating with humans and attempting to nurture their bloodlines, yet this only really occurred among the Nodite ruling aristocracy. In the many battles and massacres I have observed in my time here, I had never witnessed this level of racial sculpting being carried out with such ruthless and mechanical efficiency.

It was later in the night that I discovered the full picture.

I followed the direction the warriors had taken their prisoners and soon found them. They were clustered in a tight group of some thirty or thirty-five tired, cold, and bewildered men. Huddled on the muddy patch behind the village, they lay and sat where earlier they'd so laboriously cut and cleared the trees back to the edge of the forest.

This was also the place where most of the slaughter had taken place, and the dead still lay where they'd fallen. Many of the prisoners were sleeping. A few were sitting on felled logs or squatting on the ground, quietly talking among themselves, seemingly indifferent to the corpses around them—mostly of their own race. I have no doubt that the dead were fathers, brothers, and cousins—members of their extended family; men with whom they had so recently been out hunting or feasting together, or sharing the danger and excitement of spearing fish in their sacred river.

I looked across this sad tableau of jumbled bodies and for a moment, as the thick clouds split open to reveal the moon, there seemed little difference to me between the living and the dead.

There had been no change in the prisoners' dejected passivity. I imagined that the idea of escape must have been the last thing on their minds. The small number of warriors guarding this disconsolate group was clearly a sign of how confident they were of their dominance. A handful of them were standing close together warming themselves around the single roaring fire and casting only the most cursory of glances over at their captives.

My mood suddenly shifted. By including the warriors in the tableau, it now seemed to me that there was a particularly shocking contrast between the living and the dead. Here were these five large men, after all, who were carelessly laughing and drinking together, intensely alive and still pumped up by the fighting—and yet seemingly oblivious to being surrounded by a field of corpses.

Slipping closer to the warriors, I was able to overhear them boasting to each other about their day of fighting. They were comparing the number each had killed and relishing the skill with which they'd gone about it. When I heard them joking among themselves about which of the captives slumped around them would make the best slaves and taking wagers on which would die first, and which ones would last longest, it confirmed what I'd started to suspect. The sorry lot of them were going to be slaves. And, as I overheard one of the warriors comment with what might have been a rueful laugh, the lucky ones were those who had been killed in the fighting.

I didn't know what that meant until later when I saw one of these skirmishes in action. It seemed to be a tactic the invaders employed when it wasn't practical to send in their cavalry. It must have been an accepted ploy at that time, and it won't be unfamiliar to those callous enough to use it to this day. Acting as human shields, the prisoners were prodded ahead of the warriors in their sneak attacks on the more inaccessible settlements and cliff dwellings.

I found this more cynical than callous. It was a trick. It relied on the ignorance and sentimentality of the defenders. When they saw people of their own race approaching them they could be relied upon to let down their guard and rush out to greet their fellows, thus allowing the invaders to pounce. It was true—in the subsequent scuffles it was inevitable that some of the slaves in the human shield would be among the first to die.

After seeing this tactic repeated a few times, I later came to appreciate the rueful subtext to the warrior's remark about the dead ones being the lucky ones. It was often the slaves whom the defenders would kill first in their confusion at being deceived by their countrymen. At least that's what I believed at the time.

It was only after I'd watched this ruse playing itself out four or five times with much the same results that I saw the irony of the gambit—although I doubt if the invaders would have appreciated it.

As for others of his race, in the conceptual framework of the warrior who made the remark, the very worst that could happen to them was death in battle at the hands of one of their own people. For them it meant cowardice and was said to ensure a direct passage to the "Land of Shadows." Such a death for white invaders was believed to be the ultimate humiliation.

Ironically, the blue people believed just the opposite, and just as firmly. *Their* conceptual framework, inherited from a long and merciful tradition of ending the lives of their infirm and elderly, held that there was no greater privilege than to be killed by one of their own race. They believed such a noble death would assure them of their place in the "Shining Land beyond the Sky."

It was only many years later, when the two races had become largely assimilated and the invasion was merely a tale from the distant past, that I heard this irony had become legendary and was now being used by wandering storytellers as a basis of satire.

If any should doubt that such intangible concepts as irony and satire would be found in Stone Age men and women, think of how much more closely entwined and interconnected were their lives than yours. They would have spent their entire lives existing intimately close together, day and night, with little chance of being able to get away from one another. Most of them would never have left the confines of their settlements and villages. And these were men and women not so unlike yourselves who, while not possessing quite the mental intelligence of a modern human, were every bit a match in the realm of emotional wisdom.

The ability to laugh at themselves was a gift that would become a survival skill for early humans who had no choice but to live under those pressure-cooker circumstances.

Humor, I thought, was all very well in such intimate social situations. However, I felt I owed it to my more complete understanding of what I'd been watching throughout the afternoon and night to visit the priests and observe what they were doing with their prisoners.

This was not an event I was looking forward to—I'd seen quite enough of human brutality and cruelty. I managed to procrastinate by putting off the visit until early the next morning, when what I discovered only further surprised me about the nature of the mortal creature.

* * *

In contrast to the generally depressing atmosphere in Manhattan, my ward was about to enjoy a remarkable run of good fortune and personal success.

I could see it hadn't been easy for him to recover from his disappointment at Mary Ann's reaction to the album that he and the Process band, Version, had recorded in Toronto. Once again it was his friend Mother Juliette who helped him turn the corner.

Juliette was one of the few of his fellow Processeans to whom he felt safe to open his heart without fear it would reach the ears of the Omega. It had been to Juliette he'd confided his ET encounters, his lucid dreams, and his revelation of Mary Ann's divinity. He liked the woman and clearly felt comfortable and trusted her in a way he withheld from most of the others. As well, he obviously enjoyed her wry humor and intelligence. They'd had a brief fling some ten years ago, well before the Process had proclaimed itself celibate, in which they found they valued their friendship a great deal more than their rather uninspired sexual congress.

When Mary Ann had been conducting her orgies with those of her inner circle in London and Toronto, I heard my ward and Juliette agreeing with some amusement after one of the gatherings that they were relieved at not having to replay their earlier lackluster sexual encounter. Which is to say they were close enough in heart and spirit to be able to laugh at themselves in an arena that many would find awkward and embarrassing.

I have written more fully about Juliette's pre-apartheid, white South African background in a previous volume and how her move to London as a qualified architect had resulted in her meeting the Process and throwing in her lot with the community. She'd joined before they'd left England for Mexico and was with the community in Nassau and at Xtul, in the Yucatán. She was also one of the handful of Processeans who had stayed at Xtul for an extra year to build it up when the others returned to London.

Juliette was a tall, naturally elegant woman in her midthirties; no great beauty, but with a long slim neck and an oval tanned face already slightly wrinkled by the African sun. Mein Host had evidently always found her physically attractive. I had noticed by this time that he had an obvious, narcissistic preference for tall, slim, long-legged women, with their characters written largely on their faces. Juliette's features resolved into a pleasantly placid somnolence, betrayed only by her remarkably light blue eyes that were full of intelligence that sparkled from under uncharacteristically epicanthic lids. Her eyes weren't the cornflower blue of my ward's but seemed to glow with unnerving translucency of the lightest blue-green aquamarine.

As an original member of the group, Juliette had risen in the hierarchy alongside the others, but her retiring nature invariably kept her in the background. If you were to look through the many photographs of Processeans in their magazines and newsletters, you would be hard put to find more than a couple shots of Juliette.

Although she would have considered herself one of the Omega's inner circle—and this was particularly important for the senior Processeans as they jostled with one another for their time in the sun— Juliette had never become one of Mary Ann's favorites; rather the opposite. She frequently found herself a convenient scapegoat for all that Mary Ann believed was wrong and defective about her followers. Many times I'd heard the Oracle mercilessly berate Juliette for her passivity and her lack of self-confidence—the kind of control and aggression that Mary Ann liked to see in her matriarchs.

The Oracle preferred to work through her matriarchs, or so she frequently claimed, yet Juliette was seldom included among them as she appeared almost entirely lacking in personal ambition. Among the six or eight senior matriarchs, Juliette was the only one who did not qualify for inclusion among those I heard my ward once caustically refer to as "that bossy little group of Mary Ann Mini-Mes."

Mother Juliette might not have been the most highly respected of the senior Processeans, but she was surely one of the most beloved by the junior members. Unfortunately for Juliette in Process terms, much of what contributed to her being a genuinely nice person was a gentle innocence that bordered on naïveté. I don't believe, for instance, that she had any idea, at the time, of quite the degree to which she was being consistently excluded from positions of responsibility.

While her placid nature and apparent lack of ambition stood in the way of Juliette's rising to glory within the Process, it was just those same qualities that allowed her to be kind, trustworthy, and nonjudgmental.

I am sure Mein Host would have recovered his equilibrium over time, for he has a natural tendency to bounce back. However, it was Mother Juliette's empathic sensitivity and employment of humor that allowed him to release the resentment he was feeling toward the woman he believed was the Goddess.

4

New Residences

A Watcher's Dilemma, the Value of Intuition,
Ceremonial Deaths, the Basques, the Gods
Are Smiling, and a Lakeside Walk

My ward had the chance to speak to Juliette soon after she was sent to the New York Chapter. It was the first time he had been able to openly express his anger and frustration at Mary Ann's careless killing of the Version's album. This had killed off the band too. Soon after the recording was completed the band members split up, and some of them, like my ward, were sent to different chapters.

"Look, I *know* that album was good," he was insisting to Juliette after they had stolen away to a local coffeehouse on Lexington Avenue. "We couldn't have made it any better than we did. Of course, we might have mixed it differently, but that wouldn't have made it any better. We were in top form after all those rehearsals. Seriously, Juliette, we were playing at the very peak of our abilities. Hell, we *knew* it was good!"

His voice had been steadily rising in pitch. Several of the other customers sitting at the long counter jerked around, looking over at them nervously as New Yorkers are wont to do, never quite sure what will happen next. Mother Juliette smiled serenely at them, and they turned back to their newspapers and their coffee refills.

My ward's voice dropped to an angry hiss. "See, it simply doesn't make any sense. Shitting on us like that! Shitting on us from a high place!"

There! He'd said it. He seemed surprised at his own audacity and paused for a moment to look at Juliette to see whether he'd gone too far. Her face, however, was its usual impassive self, but for those translucent blue eyes that glittered with interest.

Encouraged, my ward continued with what sounded to me like a shtick he'd rehearsed a few times in his mind. His angry tone had shifted to one of incredulity.

"That producer who worked with us, Chris whatever . . . he loved it! He was never one to fluff us up—he could be mean, that man! Mean but fair . . . Don't get me wrong, Juliette, he was just what we needed to lick us into shape. All I'm saying is he'd have been the first person to tell us it was bad."

He broke off talking while they ordered coffee and took a look at the menu from the waitress who'd appeared at their booth a few moments earlier so unnoticed by them that she'd had to flip the pages of her notebook particularly noisily to get my ward's attention. She was a beautiful woman, somewhere in her midthirties, who wore her uniform with an unusual elegance, and to my surprise, was wearing high heels. She was not happy, and not being noticed sooner was clearly making her unhappier by the moment. As an actress who'd come to the city from a small town in Ohio with her high hopes for stardom . . .

(And here I have to catch myself before I slip into what I call "the Watcher's Dilemma." You see, we observe so much. In her case, the waitress's testimony to her failed career as an actress hung in her aura. How could I not have become curious? But, for the purposes of this narrative, our waitress plays no greater role than narrated herein.)

Coffee ordered, the waitress had click-clacked her way back to the counter, her swaying rear end evidently intended to provoke my ward's interest. She had little obvious success, for my ward was still stewing over the injustice of it all.

"The recording studio," he hissed, "they liked it so much they even gave us hours and hours of extra time for free, and the engineers who mixed it, they *really* got into it . . . everyone who heard it dug it . . ."

Juliette interrupted, "Didn't you say that music lawyer you took it to—didn't he really like it?"

"Yeah, everybody . . . everyone *except* Mary Ann!" Mein Host said, ignoring her question. I imagined he was feeling out Juliette's reaction to his more implicit criticism of the Oracle.

Happily she was unfazed at what most of the others would have considered all but blasphemous. Juliette simply replied that if Mary Ann wasn't behind it, then the album wasn't going anywhere, however good it was.

"Right there, Juliette! But here's what's really pissing me off. We'd sent her earlier tapes. She'd heard the music. She knew we were creating the songs for a popular audience; for God's sake, we were writing *pop* songs. The kind of music you'd hear on the radio. And then to discover she'd sneered at our music and dismissed the songs because she thought they were just like the stuff you'd hear on the radio! That was the last straw!"

He continued ranting along much the same lines for several minutes before he ran out of steam and Juliette had a chance to speak.

"Perhaps it was never about the album," she suggested tentatively, reaching across the tabletop to stroke his hand. "Maybe it was more about your reaction to the failure."

I could see that stopped my ward in his tracks.

His body tipped backward with a thud against the back of the booth before he leaned forward again to grab his packet of Camels. His hands were shaking as he scrambled to remove a cigarette, and he'd lit one up before he realized he still had one half burned in the ashtray.

"What do you really care about what happens to the result?" Juliette continued, overlooking his emotional reaction and capitalizing on her insight. "Think of it as being about *you,* Micah—you and the rest of the band. It was the band that had the actual *experience* of making an album from scratch. It wasn't just a pipe dream. You and the band made it happen, and you did it as well as you could. That's what's important, isn't it? That's what you take with you. That's what counts! It's the experience itself that's of real lasting value."

Our normally placid Mother Juliette was by now leaning forward over the table, emphasizing her points by stabbing the air with her cigarette—I'd never seen her so animated!

"You must see that, Micah! What did the Oracle get out of it? Nothing, right? Each of you in the band actually lived through it; you know how much you learned." Juliette's voice subtly changed with her enthusiasm. It was one of the few times I'd heard the hint of a clipped South African accent breaking through in Juliette's normally soft voice.

The waitress arrived with two cups of coffee and slid them over the table as my ward pushed the ashtray aside. She gave him the brief smile of an automaton, checked to make sure there was sufficient sugar—there was—straightened up, and giving him another smile, this time a tad warmer, asked in a tired voice if there was anything else they wanted.

Before the waitress had the chance to get too far into her endless list of pies and cheesecakes, my ward cut her off with an understanding and kindly gesture. At this she seemed simultaneously relieved at not having to deliver her spiel—it was the end of her shift—and mildly irritated. I imagined that she was anticipating the disappointingly small tip—it had been a slow day—and she turned back toward the counter, walking languidly while slapping the menus against her thigh.

Juliette cocked an eyebrow at this little drama, trying to get a grin out of my ward, but his mind was still elsewhere.

"That's fine for you to say, Juliette." My ward wasn't going to surrender quite so easily. "But all that work! Those months and months of rehearsals, wasted. Thrown away. And, we pushed ourselves way beyond the limit, practically killing ourselves! All those shows we did now mean shit? Is that it? And that miraculous twenty-four hour recording session, how it came together . . . the whole operation was like it was meant to be."

"C'mon Micah, now you're just feeling sorry for yourself. 'Course you've got a reason to be angry. You put your heart and soul into making the album. That's true. But it isn't really the point, is it? It's the *process* of creating it that's important—promoting and selling the thing afterward is kind of beside the point."

Juliette allowed a couple of beats before delivering her coup de grâce. "You silly! We do call ourselves *the Process* for good reason, don't we?!"

Well, that seemed to break the dam.

The futility of his holding on to his resentment and the obviousness of her resolution must have struck home. A slow heave of laughter was rising up from deep inside him, and within moments first he and then Juliette were roaring their heads off. It really was so silly. He believed he was the one who'd actually named the community the Process in the first place and for just that reason. Yet here he was, falling into the same old trap again!

Somewhere within this noisy jubilance and amid his spluttering, I thought I heard him saying something along the lines that the answer to his problem was hiding in plain sight. While they were both laughing uproariously I took the opportunity to observe Mein Host's emotional body more closely.

At the time, this wouldn't have occurred to my ward, but on an emotional level this situation was very similar to an earlier wounding rejection. When he was a twenty-year-old back in London and three years before he'd joined the community, his girlfriend Vicky, with whom he'd been living for more than three years, had upped and left him for his best friend, without a word of warning from either of them.

In the same way that he now thought the album was good, he also believed his relationship with Vicky to be a good and happy one. In both cases the shock of hearing otherwise was compounded by the fact that the news was so completely unexpected.

I've written in a previous volume about how firmly Mein Host had repressed his pain and anger at this earlier double betrayal. Now, of course, I was curious when I was observing his emotional response as to whether he would repress his feelings again this time.

I'm happy to say he didn't. Perhaps it was their humor that dissolved the anger and frustration, because it seemed to me they just could not stop as the waves of laughter almost overwhelmed them.

It turned out to be a lesson well learned and one that has served my ward in his later life as an artist and writer. It has allowed him to follow his own inner creative leanings without having any real concern for how what he produced would be received by others. His consuming interest in nonhuman intelligences—in dolphins, ETs, and angels—which ultimately led to our collaboration, is a relatively new area of study. Continuing his research for more than thirty years outside of academia as he has—as well as writing up his investigations in a series of books— very much benefitted from his focus *on process*.

Much of contemporary writing is directed purely at the effect it will have on the reader. It's much the same in the visual arts. A shark in a tank of formaldehyde, a pile of bricks, or an unmade bed are created solely to shock, surprise, or disgust the viewer. Nothing is learned. There's no inspiration, no higher aspirations. Forget beauty or truth. Little skill or craft is involved in the making, and what is made is probably done by an assistant or subcontracted out to a professional craftsperson . . . don't get me started on what is called "art" these days!

However, there is a contrast I am trying to make here. If popular success is measured by a work's general acceptance, and a successful artist or writer is the one who becomes wealthy, the drive to tailor one's creations to appeal specifically to the public has become almost irresistible. This essentially commercial view has become so deeply ingrained in contemporary cultural life that to suggest that popular acclaim is irrelevant will sound idiosyncratic at best.

Yet it has been precisely this devotion to the *process of exploration*— particularly in an arena as ephemeral and subjective as extraterrestrials and angels—that has allowed the two of us such a close collaboration, given that ours is a relatively rare but not unprecedented working relationship. Thus I should express my appreciation for my collaborator's dogged persistence in pursuing this narrative with no concern as to how it will be received, while simultaneously having no illusion about how readily the work is likely to be ridiculed in a materialist culture.

Having finished with my views about the contemporary art scene I'll continue the narrative by following Mein Host as he was walking the streets of midtown Manhattan in the spring of 1973. It appeared he was back in Mary Ann's good graces, for she had put my ward in charge of finding a new residence for the priests.

He would have taken this instruction as a renewal of trust in him. She knew he would use his intuition to find the correct property for them, and she liked that.

This was an intriguing contradiction in her personality. Although she was extremely autocratic by nature and always appeared implacably confident in her own rightness, she also liked to encourage people to follow their intuition when it served her purposes for them to do so.

As it happened, this was turning out to be invaluable training for my ward and one that would have been hard to find in any other walk of life. In all the places he'd located for the community over the years he had never needed to consult real estate agents or resort to combing through the back pages of newspapers. He had always simply allowed his inner prompting to guide him.

Over the course of this *process* (there's that word again!) of listening to the inner whispers, of watching for the signs, and of feeling his way through the elegant side streets of Manhattan's East Side, subtle clues were starting to manifest. Within a few days he had closed in on an unassuming-looking building in a terrace of five-story houses on East 49th Street. He soon discovered it was owned by the celebrated theatrical couple Ruth Gordon and Garson Kanin, who, by chance, were hoping to rent it out furnished while they were working and living in Hollywood.

As unassuming as the house was from the outside, the inside of 242 East 49th Street was rather the opposite. Oh, nothing too ostentatious, mind you, but it had a faded opulence designed to impress the visitor with the owners' commitment to the arts, and to demonstrate their indifference to the riches it brought them.

Clearly the rooms had been furnished and decorated by a successful and wealthy, but somewhat sentimental, elderly show-biz couple. The armchairs and sofas were old-fashioned and overstuffed, the side tables were ridiculously delicate and, like the shelves, were covered in a proud display of hundreds of tchotchkes. These were pricey little trinkets that had been accumulated over the years from admirers, with the decorative taste of another era.

A lesser painting by Grandma Moses hung over the mantelpiece. It was a farming snow scene, a mostly white landscape with some barns, a few cows, horses, trees, and a handful of people scattered across the canvas, scratched out in her childish hand. It had the unfinished look of a piece rushed through to pay the rent. And yet, the painting's crude simplicity felt like a welcome contrast to the ornate puffery of the furnishings and finicky trinkets.

French doors at the far end of the living room opened onto a small balcony, and a wrought iron staircase led down to a well-groomed garden. This was one of a row of gardens behind the terraced townhouses on both East 48th and East 59th Streets.

Magnificent full-grown trees were starting to bud, and the flowering bushes, some already blooming and radiant, peeked charmingly over the garden walls. The gardens shared a strip of pastoral greenery stretching the entire block between the two avenues and enclosed at each end to create a sense of a secret garden in the heart of all that Manhattan madness.

Standing on the balcony overlooking this lushly verdant scene, my ward's nose was wrinkling happily under a barrage of the intoxicating floral scents of a warm spring afternoon. With the constant roar of city traffic, now thankfully baffled by the buildings and reduced to a faint rumble of distant thunder, the whole place had the quality of an urban oasis, enjoyed only by the rich and famous.

Well, weren't they going to be surprised!

* * *

A dull gray dawn was breaking over the eastern hills when I thought to follow the trail through the forest in the direction the priests had been leading their prisoners. By this time I had a better idea of what was going on, and I wasn't looking forward to what I would find.

In a large clearing in the forest about a dozen of the captive blue people knelt in the mud at the riverside with their heads bowed. A ceremony was taking place. There was a low drone in the air that, as I moved closer, I could hear coming from the priests whom I had seen earlier. The priests were now lined up in two rows, at right angles to the river, one row on each side of where the captives knelt.

The mumbled drone abruptly ceased. After a heartbeat, two priests separated themselves from the others, moved to either side of one of the prisoners, and raised him gently to his feet.

Yes, gently! That surprised me.

The man was making no attempt to struggle; he didn't try to run for it. He was every bit as passive as he had been earlier when standing with his fellows waiting to be selected. Had he already known his fate—even back then?

The captive allowed himself to be led to the water. The priests on either side of him barely needed to guide him. They moved slowly and deliberately, almost as one person. There was no sign of fear in the prisoner's emotional body. Was I missing something? This wasn't mere passivity I was seeing. I had the feeling that once again I was somehow overlooking an essential truth—some fundamental difference between our two species that, as an angel, I didn't feel equipped to understand.

The three of them stood side by side facing the river for a few moments before the captive was led into it. Once it was up to mid-thigh, the two priests pushed the prisoner's face firmly down into the water. Once again I was struck by the captive's seeming lack of a struggle as this was happening. It was as if he was greeting the river, kissing it even, embracing her wild wetness in his death throes. Within moments of the man's head being underwater his spirit ascended, leaving his body to shudder, his legs kicking feebly until there was no further movement of them.

The priests straightened up when the droning sound started again. As it did, they released the dead body of the prisoner to the swift current, captive no longer, to be taken back into the welcoming arms of the goddess of the river.

This solemn ceremony continued until no prisoners remained and the priests had completed their ritual by disrobing and washing themselves ritually in the river. The thunderclouds of the night had fled, and the sun had broken through, drying their naked bodies as they lay in the stubbly dead grass beside the swiftly running water.

No one was speaking.

The birds were no longer circling overhead, having eaten their fill of the blue people killed in battle on the previous day. A pall of silence seemed to fall over the meadow when a cloud blocked out the sun. I felt a wave of terror rising from where the men were now huddling together for warmth. A freezing wind had picked up, ripping through the bare trees and sending the shivering priests running back to where their garments lay carefully folded on a patch of dry ground behind them.

They then tucked themselves back into their outer robes, which was a rather time-consuming business given that the donning of each layer—and there were many layers—had to be accompanied by a silent ritual. They must have done this together many times before, because it had the look of a synchronized performance piece.

After they were dressed they lined up in a single file, and, still not speaking, they trudged back along the path that wound through the forest to the settlement of the blue people. Smoke was rising from the smoldering heaps, which was all that was left of the village's crude mud huts. The bodies of the dead villagers had been pushed to one side of the clearing and lay in a pile of torn and bloated flesh. There were perhaps fifteen large birds hopping awkwardly from body to body, wings flapping, beaks tearing at the soft tissue—eyeballs were always the first to go—and lunging aggressively at any other bird who tried to poach. The only sound was their angry squawking and the deafening buzz of insects gathering in a thick cloud around the heap of bodies, which together with the growls and snarls of the settlement's dogs feeding on the flesh of the dead masters, created a symphony of death.

I was surprised to find that there was no one around. I imagined that the priests must have retired to wherever they slept. There was no sign of the invaders; they seemed to have moved on as silently as they had arrived. The captured slaves too were no longer to be seen. The settlement was now simply a deserted disaster zone.

One of the larger huts had been left standing so I took the opportunity to look more closely at how it was built. It was some ten feet high at the highest point, circular with a diameter of about twenty feet and surrounded by a shallow ditch that collected the rainwater from the roof and kept the inside dry. The interior had either been cleared out by the invaders, or it was normally kept that way by the original occupant. All that remained was the bare earthen floor and a central pole, rich with carvings, which seemed to be supporting the structure's domed roof.

I adjusted my vision so as to permit me to peer deeper into the structure of third-density material. I soon saw the ingenuity that had been used in making the building. This wasn't quite the crude mud hut I'd taken it for from the outside. Long pliant willow stems had been bent to curve up to the top of the central column where the ends were gathered and bound together to create a solid plate resting lightly on top of the column. I could see how this would allow the dome to move slightly to be able to absorb the impact of strong winds without prejudicing the hut's structural integrity.

Clever as this was, I have to admit that the incessant creaking of the plate as it rubbed against the top of the pole had soon started to irritate me, distracting me while I was trying to examine the hut's interior.

I found that thin strips of willow ran horizontally around the dome, each piece tied carefully to the verticals at each joint with narrow pieces of leather. On top of this skeleton the builders had then strewn layers of dried reeds thrown down every which way to create a relatively solid membrane.

I asked myself the obvious question as to how they had been able to do this without the reeds slipping down while they were building the dome, and once again I found myself admiring their ingenuity. The reeds hadn't been thrown down quite so casually as I'd originally believed. The first layer was indeed a random crisscrossing of reeds, but I could see a more specific pattern in the way the additional layers had been packed to form the membrane. It was the randomness of that first layer of reeds that was somehow allowing it to adhere to the frame. Curious about this, I thought at first that some sort of glue made from boiling down bones had been used on the reeds, but drawing closer, I caught the pungent scent of pine resin.

Now, that *was* interesting. They could have used rabbit-bone glue. It was far easier to make in quantity than pine resin. Yet they had evidently chosen to expend their energy in patiently collecting enough drips of dried sap sufficient for their purposes. I can't imagine how much time it took to scrape up enough resin to melt down for just this one roof. (I hadn't known at the time that this was the head priest's hut.)

It was only later that I learned this was done as an act of appeasement to the divinity they believed lived in the forests surrounding them. They felt, or so I heard, that the constant scent of pine resin would remind their priests of the bargain struck with their gods to keep themselves safe from the fires that ripped so unexpectedly through the forest.

Before I continue further, I apologize to those reading my words who might be less interested in the structural details of the hut than my collaborator—a "lapsed architect," as he likes to call himself. Please feel free to skip to the next section—if you haven't already!

Over this thin blanket of reeds the builders had placed horizontal rows of bundles of the same dried reeds that grew so plentifully along the banks of their river. They would have needed to start at the base where the willow stems had been dug into the soft ground. They then must have worked their way up the dome, fixing the bundles in place with river clay as they made their way to the top. It would have been this thick layer of tightly packed reeds that provided the insulation. A final coating of river mud, mixed with straw to give the mud some tensile strength, had been smeared over the entire structure, which had then been left to harden in the sun.

When it was finished I have no doubt that the hut was a thing of beauty. But from the state of it now, with large patches of mud torn away and clumps of dried grass sprouting from the gaps—some of which had caught fire and were still smoldering—there was little left of its original distinction. The dome's remarkable structural integrity ensured it would continue standing for years, but these were a superstitious people, and they would never use that hut again. Soon enough, for all its elegance, the dome would return back to a tumble of muddy sticks.

It was later that day when, after following the river a long way upstream, I came across a large clearing in the forest on the east side of the river in which the victors had set up camp for the night, or so I initially thought.

Open fires around the clearing were flaring in the deepening twilight. Loud laughter drifted up from the men who were eating and drinking while gathered around the fires. The smell of burned meat hung thick in the air. Someone was singing, with others joining in the choruses under a lean-to down to my right on the edge of the clearing. I could see that they had posted guards at regular intervals in the surrounding forest. At the far side of the clearing their horses were tethered loosely to trees and were grazing on piles of dried grass.

It was those stacks of hay that had clearly been there for some time that allowed me an insight into how the invaders were operating. This wasn't simply a place where they had stopped off to make camp for the night. This was evidently their main base, from which they sent out raiding parties like the one I'd just observed. Theirs wasn't quite the massive invasion force I had anticipated before traveling north, with armies of many thousands facing off against one another in battles across the breadth of Europe—it would turn out to be nothing like that.

Compared to the burgeoning population of the Middle East, Europe was still relatively sparsely inhabited, and the blue people's settlements were too isolated for them to ever raise a coordinated army. That the blue people were able to put up a fight for as long as they did—it took around five hundred years for the races to become broadly assimilated—was a consequence of their familiarity with the continent's river systems. Once they understood what was occurring—that people of another race were coming like white ghosts to burn their settlements and steal their women—they were able to use the network of rivers to sometimes escape. If they were lucky, they could alert others of their kind or—at other times—to raise what opposition they could from the assorted clans and tribes.

I was mulling this over when I heard a loud bleat on a ram's horn. Soon people were emerging from their tents and lean-tos, and many more from the forest, and were streaming toward where they'd started to gather on the eastern side of the clearing.

It was getting darker now, and torches were being lit. In the center of this widening circle of people stood half a dozen biers, and as I moved closer I could see that on top of each lay one of their warriors who had been killed in the previous day's fighting.

When the last straggler had joined the throng—and there were only about ninety raiders total—there were another three blasts on the ram's horn. Here was another ceremony, I thought, as six of their warriors stepped forward with torches held high. Another long honking bleep on the horn and the torches were lowered and the biers lit as the warriors slowly circled the gathering flames. The crowd remained silent as the fires consumed the six bodies. Individuals then drifted back to their tents to talk quietly among themselves before retiring for the night.

But that wasn't what had gotten my attention.

It was that they were *burning* their own dead!

I must have been in Europe for too long. Perhaps I had become too accustomed to the burial practices of the Cro-Magnon and the blue people, because I'd not seen cremation used since I was last in the Land of the Two Rivers.

Much later I would realize the relevance of this observation when I overheard some modern anthropologists puzzling over the unusual dearth of human remains subsequent to the times of the Cro-Magnon. This has led contemporary science to some confused thinking regarding the unlikely evolutionary leap from Cro-Magnon to modern human. Further testing of mitochondrial DNA will doubtless settle this issue over time, but for the moment, a direct genetic connection from Cro-Magnon to the modern European type has remained hard to establish.

By the final centuries of the seventh millennium the invasion forces had spread over the entire continent, including Britain. These forces enslaved their prisoners, killed those who opposed them, and purged as much Cro-Magnon blood from the genetic pool as they could. In some of the inaccessible mountainous regions of northern Spain and southwest France, for example, small numbers of the Cro-Magnon race managed to live on and became gradually absorbed into the general population.

Over time, these people who spoke their own language and with their own distinct ethnic and cultural identity would come to be known as the Basque. They would spread up through the west coast of France to settle in Ireland and Wales and freely interbreed with the tribes already inhabiting those countries. Yet they would always maintain their indigenous claim on the Basque country centered around the western end of the Pyrenees mountains that stretched from northern Spain to encompass much of southwestern France.

Having been horribly repressed by the Spanish fascist dictator General Franco—from his victory in the Spanish Civil War in 1939 until he died in 1975—the Basque people had been trying to reassert their separate ethnic identity in a long-lasting campaign for self-determination. I suspect that in the vigor and persistence of this campaign—which continued throughout the latter quarter of the twentieth century and is now mainly remembered by outsiders for the bombings of the Basque extremists—there is an apt demonstration of the toughness and staying power that can be found in a racial type that contains a healthy dollop of the Cro-Magnon genome.

As the fair-skinned invaders continued to permeate the continent, they interbred with the blue race for well over fifty generations. By the mid-sixth millennium both racial types had become assimilated into a single race. This race would eventually yield the ancestors of the modern white European—those women and men who have been termed officially and erroneously *Caucasian*.

And yet the conditions on Earth were peculiar. It had been the scene of continual racial conflict, torn apart by natural disasters, and been the stamping ground of a progressively unbalanced Planetary Prince and a bunch of egotistically manipulative midwayers. On a planet such as this, I recall thinking at the time, life for the rapidly expanding global human population wasn't going to get much better anytime soon.

What I was unable to anticipate was just how challenging and difficult it was going to be for all life-forms over the next few millennia.

* * *

When Mein Host met Ruth Gordon at the townhouse to negotiate the contract, the actress was already in her late seventies and had just had a great success—and a Golden Globe Award for Best Actress for her role as Maude—in the much acclaimed movie *Harold and Maude*. She had already earned an Oscar a few years earlier for her role in *Rosemary's Baby*. She had been working in films since the early 1930s and went on making movies and appearing on the stage until she died in 1985. Yet for her many successes and a lifetime in films and theater, she has remained one of the lesser-known grande dames of the American theater.

My ward was at his most charming at the meeting, and the old lady—in a business in which charm is coin of the realm—was more than happy to be charmed. She seemed homely and sweetly unpretentious considering her fame; "somewhat like my great-aunt Iris," as my ward said later. Iris, as a genteel old lady of seventy-eight, had launched her career in British films and television, playing—no surprises here—genteel old ladies.

Ruth Gordon, of course, unlike Mein Host's great-aunt Iris and her boasts of "extradom," had a lifetime of acting behind her, having played a wide variety of roles, young and old. Yet both of these old ladies possessed a similar inner sparkle of delight. While they were way past normal retirement age, each was doing what they loved to do, and they would go on doing it until they dropped. It was precisely this sense of barely suppressed childlike excitement that made both of them "such great fun to be with," as he told the others after getting back to the chapter later that afternoon.

After settling down in Ms. Gordon's living room to a cup of tea there was a quarter of an hour of casual chitchat as both parties were hoping to sum one another up—although this is perhaps an oversimplification. While Ruth Gordon must have been seeking to reassure herself that she could trust her house and its precious contents to an obscure religious order, my ward was equally dedicated to appearing as normal and as trustworthy in her eyes as he could manage. I'm sure he would have had no illusions as to how the house would be forever changed by the presence of eight or nine priests—and as many large dogs—rattling around on those light-colored, carefully carpeted floors.

I believe his English accent added the required gloss to his credibility—American ladies of a certain age seem particularly susceptible to their fantasies about well-bred, elegant Englishmen. Thus it was much to my ward's obvious relief (obvious to me, anyway) that Ruth Gordon came to her decision so remarkably quickly. Perhaps she was a little too anxious to rent the house, as she didn't seem especially keen to ask the sort of personal questions, the answers to which might have risked putting her off the deal. So the rental paperwork was completed efficiently and just as fluidly as the whole process of locating the house in the first place had been.

Under the circumstances, it was fortunate for my ward that Ruth Gordon was such a woman of the theater. As an actress she would have been well coached in deceit and artifice or, to put it in its most basic terms, pretending to be someone else. Over a long career, I believe this may have led her to an unconscious bias for the well-acted part, in preference to probing deeper by digging beneath my host's surface charm.

I could see how relieved my ward was at not having to explain how the house would be used by a whole bunch of priests, and he certainly didn't want to get into the subject of pets. If Ms. Gordon wanted to hurry the meeting along and have the contract signed so she could get back to Hollywood, I don't believe he saw the need to introduce the subject of large dogs. As he said later, he didn't want her mind distracted by images of her precious tchotchkes flying off tables and shelves at the mercy of the wagging tails of at least half a dozen incorrigibly enthusiastic adolescent German Shepherds.

The contract mandated a monthly rental of twenty-five hundred dollars and immediate occupancy—an important factor for the group given that they were already bursting out of the two places they were renting on East 38th Street. My ward bid Ruth Gordon good-bye, unaware that he wouldn't be seeing her again.

There was some chaffing at the high rent, but when the price was compared to the few Manhattan rentals that were actually available—a furnished townhouse for rent on the East Side was itself a rarity—the coup was generally acknowledged as miraculous.

Once again, the ease and fluidity with which the property had been acquired by the community was yet another confirmation that they were on the right path.

They knew the Great Gods were smiling on them.

As you will have gathered by now, in spite of choosing to live in a community, there has always been a solitary turn to Mein Host's personality.

He had chosen to be born into a family wherein he would grow up without a father and be an only child to a busy mother, so he'd had the chance to hone his enjoyment in his own company from a young age. In fact, I've come to believe one of the reasons his companion angels are so supportive of his decision to live in a community is that it gave him the opportunity to experience the other side of the coin—and to do it under the most extreme of circumstances.

At this point in his life, as he was about to enter his thirty-third year, my ward could claim to feel as at ease in communal life as he had felt at those times that he'd been on his own—even if his preference was being alone. I believe it was this equanimity—and possibly an unspoken reward for finding the place on 49th Street—that landed him his own tiny attic room right at the top of the house.

Yes, his own! His very own room—while everyone else was sharing. He'd not had his own room for more than nine years—not since he'd joined the community.

It was a tiny space on the fifth floor—a maid's room from another era—with a low ceiling and a small window looking north out over the tops of the trees on East 49th. The mansard ceiling, with its dark-painted, faux-Tudor beams, cut an awkward diagonal across the space from front to rear. Yet my ward clearly didn't appear to mind that at six feet two inches tall he had to crouch in so much of the space.

Not that he was going to see very much of it at the pace the Process was expanding. Within a few months the pressure on him would be so great that he'd be living on four hours of sleep a night, week after week, month after month, barely able to appreciate the room. Yet I'm sure he reminded himself as he laid his head on his pillow that at least it would be four hours of sleep *in his own room*.

Mary Ann and Robert had by now moved from Toronto and after an extensive trip through the American West had bought a large property in upstate New York. Mount Chi, as it came to be called, started as a sprawling rundown bungalow sitting on twenty-five acres of wooded and gently rounded hills. It was located some miles outside the small town of Pound Ridge in distinctly upscale Westchester County.

The house was set halfway up a closely mown meadow that sloped down to a lake, which filled up the bottom of the valley that ran through the property. Although the house itself—built perhaps sometime in the 1930s—had seen better days, the landscape was remarkably well cared for. On that warm spring day in 1973 my ward first saw the place, and I heard him later describe the land as being idyllically beautiful.

The trees were bursting with life and the air was heavy with the scent of flowers as my ward accompanied Mary Ann and Robert on a late afternoon stroll around the lake. The water was dark and placid: it was impossible to see beneath its sheen as flying insects buzzed the obsidian surface, leaving their expanding radiant circles of interacting ripples.

The three of them were walking slowly and thoughtfully, mainly in silence, breathing in the somber beauty of the place. The late afternoon sun was fluorescing the new young leaves into tiny explosions of electric green and then splashing onto the ground in golden puddles.

I was aware that Mein Host didn't yet know why he had been invited up from the city. It was most unusual to have been asked on his own, so he would have been aware that something significant was in the air. He also would have known to keep his mouth shut until Mary Ann was ready to reveal her reasons. If I were to guess what was going through my ward's mind as they meandered slowly along the path that wound through the trees bordering the lake, it would be that he was racking his brain for whatever he might have done wrong this time in the eyes of his Goddess.

Every once in a while there was a sudden glopping sound as a fish broke the surface to snatch an insect from a careless dive. These created yet other sets of radiating waves of somewhat greater amplitudes that first absorbed and then swallowed the ripples of the insects. A golden haze hung over the water's surface. A line of wispy weeping willows bordered the far side of the lake, darkening the water beneath them and adding to the sense of mystery that Mein Host was feeling.

In including these natural details I am paraphrasing a conversation Mein Host had with Juliette after he returned to New York that evening—for it struck me as revealing a telling aspect of his personality. He told her how during that walk he'd seen the lake's surface as an entire microsystem with an atmosphere about three inches high. It was a whole flat world, he said, a constantly shifting, rippling landscape with an ever present danger from below and above, just waiting to gobble up the inhabitants.

It only occurred to me later that this apparent and rather unexpected preoccupation with the lake's micro-world had been a smokescreen. It was sincere enough, but in retrospect it was clearly designed to distract Juliette from knowing more about the visit. Mary Ann had instructed my ward to keep quiet about the real reason for his having been asked up to Mount Chi until the Omega was ready to tell those of their inner circle who didn't yet know about the estate.

Anybody who was invited unexpectedly into the Omega's presence was always of great concern to others of the inner circle, in the constant uncertainty that could have found any one of them excluded and out of favor before they knew what had hit them. Most knew better than to ask him outright, and even Juliette, who knew my ward better than most, hadn't pressed the point when he'd finished going on about micro-worlds.

As they walked and looked back, the house could be glimpsed through the trees, appearing and disappearing until it finally vanished from sight by the time the three of them had reached the far end of the lake. The air took on a dank brooding thickness in the deep shadows of the densely forested hill as they slowed to a halt.

Mary Ann broke the long silence. "Well, Micah, what do you think?"

"The . . . the lake?" I could hear the worry in his voice.

"The lake, the land, the house . . . everything." Mary Ann swept an arm over the property. "Well, what do you think of it all?"

I could feel his confusion . . . What *was* he to say? What was expected of him? Did she simply want the place to be praised? Why would she need him for that? He also knew better than to try to fake her out. She was far too smart to be fobbed off with a superficial reply. And besides, to her credit, she couldn't abide her followers pandering to her and would pounce on offenders, slicing them to pieces with her cutting sarcasm. When she was angry, this was a terrible thing to experience.

Now I can't guarantee this, because at that point I still had no access to my ward's mind—and wouldn't have until we'd started this work—but I believe he must have considered the previous situations in which he had faced a similar dilemma.

I had observed one incident back in Nassau, which I'm sure he must have recalled as well as he paused to gather his answer. Mein Host might have called it part of Mary Ann's dark craft as a Sufi teacher to demand reactions to weighty and often murky issues. When she would throw one of these out in a group situation it frequently created what came to be called an *xtum,* which can best be described as the deer-frozen-in-the-headlights effect. If one of the most basic of human instincts is summed up as fight-or-flight, then the lesser-known option of "freezing" describes an xtum. I have heard my ward speak about the experience of xtumming as "one part terror, one part shame, one part cognitive dissonance, and one part hypnotic fugue state."

Mary Ann, of course, was a master at manipulating the energy she had generated by creating an xtum. It was then that she could take the measure of her followers—as well as using the opportunity to exhibit her power—piling shame on some while raising another person into her favor.

In Nassau, when she'd pitched one such accusation at the whole group—this one heavy with blame—it was only my ward who'd conquered the pall of fear that fell over room and who gave her the truthful, but quite possibly unacceptable, answer.

Now, everyone in the community had seen what could happen to someone who Mary Ann chose to believe might be opposing her opinion or values. As I've watched her doing this over the years, I have come to believe that her choices were mostly arbitrary, or at least subject to her whim of the moment. As such, keeping everyone around her on edge was one of the ways she maintained her control over the group.

Fully expecting to become subject to her vicious anger, I could see Mein Host had been surprised to find himself praised by Mary Ann and held up as an example of bravery and independent thinking to the others. It was the first time that anyone had ever recognized his courage.

I suspected it was this memory that might have given him the courage to blurt out that while the land was beautiful, the house itself was a disaster.

"It's a shame too," he rattled on, when he saw Mary Ann's impassive expression. "It could have been so great. It's set okay in the landscape, but that's it. It's just a very ordinary bungalow plonked on that slope . . . they haven't taken any real advantage of the views, or the sun . . . and it's really dull inside."

Mary Ann gave Robert a meaningful, what-did-I-tell-you look and turned back to my ward. There was still no sign of any anger from her, so he visibly relaxed.

"You're an architect, Micah, aren't you?" Mary Ann asked him pointedly. "Qualified, yes?"

She knew perfectly well that my ward was an architect—he'd designed the interior of Balfour Place back in London for her. I knew this must have been a jab at Robert, who'd never finished his degree in architecture.

"So what would you do with it?"

My ward started listing off the changes he would make, but before he finished she interrupted. "Then go ahead and do it. You're an architect. Start right away."

"But Mary Ann," Robert chimed in, and I could sense a hint of condescension in his tone. "He can't do that. He's an architect in England, but he wouldn't be allowed to practice over here. He'd have to get a license in the States, and that would take ages."

Mein Host was nodding his agreement. I doubt if he really wanted to take on the project, but he clearly didn't know how to get out of it. It was Robert who added that they should both look through some architectural magazines and see if they found a style she liked and take it from there.

But Mary Ann wasn't quite ready to let go yet. "Micah, you worked for an architect in Nassau, did you not?" It was an impatient demand, her well-disguised Scottish burr breaking through. "You worked there . . . *that's* not England!"

There was a moment of embarrassment when Robert and my ward glanced at each other; I imagined both of them were wondering which of them was going to have to say it. Mein Host appeared only too glad to defer to Robert, but I missed any silent signal of agreement that must have passed between them.

"You're getting confused, Mary Ann. The Bahamas were still operating under English law. Of course he was allowed to practice there!"

Mary Ann brushed this aside. By now they had started walking back along the path bordering the far side of the lake. The earth had risen and the ridge above them was beginning to block the sun. A new chill had them picking up their steps, so they were almost back to the house when Mary Ann finally spoke.

"We'll find the right American architect, Micah, and your job will be to coordinate between him and us."

So the situation had stood for a couple of weeks when he received a call from Robert. An architect had been found, and Father Micah was to accompany him up to Mount Chi on the following Tuesday for their first meeting.

It would be a surprise for my ward to know what he didn't until this moment. Norman Jaffe, the chosen architect who was driving them both in his open-top sports car fast up the expressway to the Tuesday meeting, was an incarnate rebel angel who, like my ward, was as of yet completely unaware of his true spiritual identity.

5

A Coming Singularity

Multifarious Pagan Deities, Emerging Cretan Culture, a Deeply Troubled Soul, Mother Goddess, and a Path Less Traveled

As I come to consider the sixth through third millennia before the birth of Christ, I'm bound to warn you that what I observed will be somewhat different from what you might have been led to believe.

The practical reason for this is straightforward: the natural global catastrophes that culminated in the great floods of the third millennium effectively wiped the historical record clean. There were asteroid strikes and shockingly destructive tsunamis; volcanic eruptions and glacial deluges; famines and violent climatic changes resulting in massive desertification, all of which put extraordinary pressures on the ever-shifting global population. The sea level that had been continuing to rise since the tenth millennium had wiped out most of the coastal cities by the sixth millennium, forcing the survivors inland and into conflict with the indigenous population.

Thus by the sixth millennium almost everything that had preceded that time in the long history of humanity, the fine civilizations that had flourished from Lemuria to India to the Land of the Two Rivers, had all but disappeared, leaving behind what has been termed the *Stone Age* and the start of human history as it has been officially taught.

As I am sure you will have gathered by now, I am no historian. The sequence and the precise timing of events in the human realm is of less interest to me than the more intimate incidents I've observed on which matters of significance have sometimes turned. Being a watcher, I have also had the advantage of being able to interact with various celestials, as well as the interviews I have been privileged to conduct with Lucifer and Prince Caligastia.

Apart from describing the ensuing global events in the most general terms, my focus has to remain, of necessity, on what I observed and what I directly experienced. Naturally much will have occurred on the planet when I was elsewhere—on the other side of the world or during those times I was off-planet. We watchers might well be able to travel from place to place exceedingly rapidly, but we certainly can't be in more than one place at a time.

I say this as a warning as much to myself as to my reader, because I regard these next six thousand years as being the most complicated and challenging period of human and midwayer activity to narrate in any cogent order. The global situation was difficult enough to follow *while* it was occurring eight thousand years ago! So much so that I felt I needed to retreat to the world of Zandana more than once during that time when my mind was spinning from what was happening down here.

I admit I'm finding it now every bit as challenging to try to capture in my narrative the many competing threads that contributed to this paradoxical era. I use the word *paradoxical* because that handful of millennia saw, on the one hand, the most rapid development of human resources I had yet observed over a similar period, while it was also a time during which Prince Caligastia and his midwayers were at their most active and at the height of their power.

Of course, I now know what all the hustle and bustle was about. I didn't back then. Such an extraordinary and rare event as the mortal incarnation of a Creator Son would never have entered my mind. I don't believe that Prince Caligastia, for his claims of being God of the World—or any of his midwayers—would have been aware at the time of what was coming. I wonder if they would have behaved in the way they did had they known the degree to which their activities would come to be used by the MA's agents as an illustration of what can occur when Planetary Princes run wild.

So I find myself in another dilemma.

The incarnation of a Creator Son on a third-density planet is such an exceptional event that it could be considered to be a singularity. And then for our Michaelson to have chosen such a hostile and fear-bound world as this for his one mortal lifetime only made it more astonishingly unexpected.

My dilemma lies in finding it next to impossible to now narrate the events I observed over the next seven thousand years without viewing them through the lens of the coming development. This was also a period during which my feelings about the viability of Lucifer's revolutionary proposals were turning progressively sour.

While I still supported the ideal of greater independence for mortals and angels, throughout that time I was witnessing the unfortunate consequences of this new sense of personal liberation playing itself out in primarily the Planetary Prince and midwayer realm. Mortals, for the most part, had little control over their own destinies and were essentially pawns in the games of the rebel midwayers.

I don't want to paint all the midwayers with the same brush. That such a vast majority of the slightly more than fifty thousand midwayers—four out of every five—had aligned with Lucifer and Caligastia suggests a uniformity of intention that never really manifested. If anything it was rather the opposite.

It seemed to me that most of the rebel midwayers were directly competing with one another, and, by manipulating naive and superstitious human beings through the midwayer guise of divinity, they were able to bring their conflicts into the human arena. Over time—through various pacts, some brutal power brokering, and plenty of bribes—many of the rebel midwayers had gathered into a number of ever-changing alliances; from these have descended the more familiar ancient pantheons of Sumeria, Egypt, Greece, and Rome.

Much the same was happening all over the world. As the human population grew and expanded into regions liberated by the receding glaciers, midwayers accompanied them, and a similar pattern emerged. Whether in China, Africa, India, Australia, or in North and South America, these next seven thousand years found many hundreds of these pantheons of so-called gods and goddesses—large and small, conciliatory and warlike, isolationist and crusading—wherever humans were to be found.

I found there was a tedious similarity to these pantheons—midwayers aren't known for their imagination—in the way they capitalized on human gullibility and the existence of worship circuits in the spiritual bodies of humans. While I have heard midwayers justifying their position by saying they were merely keeping the Divine alive, this was evidently a profound self-delusion promoted by Caligastia to give some gloss of spiritual credibility to their shenanigans.

Caligastia's main concern throughout this period seemed to be devoted to attempting to consolidate his power as God of the World. His failure to do this effectively can be deduced from the profusion of independent pantheons that were functioning outside of the Prince's immediate influence.

The truth was that Prince Caligastia, for all his vacuous conceit, had long since lost control of his rebel midwayers. There was a contradictory aspect here to Prince Caligastia's personality, which became more particularly pronounced as time passed. His enthusiasm for personal liberty—which had originally drawn him into Lucifer's orbit—had never been quite so willingly extended to those under his charge. It turned out that Caligastia was every bit as autocratic and bullying as the Multiverse authorities against whom he was rebelling.

The rebel midwayers, accustomed to following his orders and, in my opinion, lacking the imagination to appreciate how far the Prince had slipped into obsession, had been blind to his behavior for far longer than I'd have thought possible. Yet as Prince Caligastia's megalomaniacal delusions became progressively more obvious, his authority over the rebel midwayers had been steadily diminishing. His midwayers, in their turn, had been turning away from him for at least two millennia, creating independent lives for themselves. Knowing no better, many of them hung out their shingles and set up in the religion business for themselves.

Just as human civilizations have repeatedly risen and fallen over the millennia, with humans having to start over again each time, so also do the midwayers have to reassert their influence each time. The period between the mid-eighth millennium and the time of Christ saw their most recent ascension in the form of the multifarious pagan deities. It culminated in what could be called the golden age of the pseudo-gods. It was during this time, with these simulacra of gods and goddesses imposing their terrifying demands and extracting their terrible dues, that humanity was overlaid with many of the superstitions that have trickled down into the modern era.

It was also the sudden disappearance two thousand years ago of more than forty thousand of these meddling rebel midwayers that has made it so difficult for the modern mind to fully grasp why the ancients considered their deities to be so existentially real.

As I've tried to have as little to do with Prince Caligastia as possible, I can't be sure of this, yet from what I observed of midwayer activity over these next seven thousand years, I suspect the Prince was too self-absorbed by this time to take much notice of this gradual exodus of his loyal midwayers. Or if he did notice, he didn't really care. He had steadily become more isolated inside his own bubble of self-delusion, vanity, and pride.

I trust I have clarified some of my attitudes and revealed the nature of my bias as I now embark on attempting to make sense of this troubling epoch for myself.

Of course it wasn't all doom and destruction.

Within the short cycles of a human lifetime there were numerous acts of great courage and noble self-sacrifice. For all the interference of the midwayers, men and women begat their children and raised their families as best they could. Needless to say, by today's standards these were brutal times for most of humanity. Many of the advancements made in previous eras had been lost in the various catastrophes and population migrations, so that most of the Western world had to start again from nothing, with just their ingenuity and a few stone implements.

Yet there were a few places—relatively isolated islands like Crete and Malta—in which a far more sophisticated culture had been emerging while much of the rest of the Mediterranean region was in decline.

I recall following a small tribe—some five thousand years before the time I'm currently narrating—as they made their long journey from the Land of the Two Rivers, across the Arabian Peninsula, and to the Turkish coastline. There they built the boats that would carry them across the Mediterranean, west to the island of Crete. It wasn't an easy voyage; one boat was lost in a storm that blew the other four way off course. The trip—which should have taken only one or two days and been uneventful—ended up by depositing the small tribe, starving, exhausted, and somewhat reduced in number, on the southwestern coast of Crete.

There were a couple of small settlements composed of the descendants of survivors of shipwrecks from the heyday of Atlantean piracy. Apart from these two enclaves, the new arrivals found the rest of the island uninhabited.

Originating in the Land of the Two Rivers, the tribe had a healthy genetic endowment of violet blood. They could also trace their ancestry back to the descendants of Vanu—the Vanites who, with the Northern Nodites, carried the enhanced genes of the Prince's staff—which in itself was among the most dominant bloodlines on the planet.

It is currently unacceptable in the public square to talk of the different races of humanity in terms of possessing inferior or superior genetic legacies relative to one another. I can understand how this has come about after Western science's brief flirtation with eugenics and the terrible abuses that followed in its name. But sentimentality aside, it remains observedly true that some genetic mixes are more successful than others. Certain mixes, of necessity, build on the other's strengths—or compensate for the other's weakness. Others, on the other hand, will have the opposite effect of degrading the resulting genetic line.

I should emphasize for my collaborator—who finds talk of racial and genetic differences as awkward as anyone else these days—that I'm not arguing for racial purity, or for ascribing to certain races some mystical transcendent quality. Far from it! It is only as a product of racial interbreeding that a truly optimized human being will emerge when the dust finally clears.

I'm merely suggesting that my collaborator—and those who may feel discussions about race introduce a murky area—step outside the aura of distaste currently overshadowing the implication of genetic disparities and accept that down through history, for better or worse, racial differences have been an inevitable and unavoidable factor in driving human development.

Obviously, human beings the world over are far more genetically mixed in the twenty-first century than they were ten thousand years ago, so racial differences have become less significant among other forces—like economics, politics, or the demand for natural resources—that power human societies. Yet for all the changes, the degree to which race still plays its part in modern life demonstrates the continuing power of racial identity.

Most of my observations about race are, of necessity, generalizations. However, I hope they serve to show how important genetics and race are to those who oversee the course of human evolution. It's not overly condescending to claim, as some Life Carriers have, that mortals are grown and cultivated much as mortals grow and cultivate their roses.

In purely practical terms, the genetic aspect of racial identity comes down to the individual men and women of different races and how they relate to one another. Early tribal life in the mainland was naturally endogamous, and as a result most racial intermixing was the result of conquest. The men of the conquering tribes did what victors have always done: they raped the women, or they killed them. That raping an enemy's women has continued as a deliberate practice to this day— reported in places such as Bosnia and the Congo—suggests how deeply embedded this behavior is. Although rape under these conditions will be intended as a savage humiliation for the defeated, the unintended consequences were sometimes beneficial for the overall health of the collective gene pool.

It was almost unheard of in that age for men and women of different races to ever bear children in loving relationships (indeed, it remains rare enough today), so what occurred on Crete was an exception to what I was accustomed to seeing.

After some initial cautious encounters between the new arrivals and those living on the coastal settlements, the two races settled into an unusually harmonious alliance. Within five hundred years, and much to the benefit of the overall Cretan gene pool, both races had become fully assimilated—so much so that a single, dynamic, creative, and remarkably peaceful culture was the result.

* * *

Mary Ann's choice of Norman Jaffe as the architect to remodel the house at Mount Chi was as curious as it was prescient. I've no doubt she would have plucked his name from *Architectural Digest,* having seen a few photographs of a house the architect had built in the Hamptons. It wasn't much to judge him on, but Mary Ann prided herself on trusting her gut in such situations.

Norman Jaffe was by no means as famous and successful as he would later become, and in 1972 he was just in the process of breaking away from working for Philip Johnson and setting up his own practice in Bridgehampton, on New York's Long Island. In the 1980s and '90s, Jaffe caught the wave of new money and became the architect of choice for millionaire money managers who were trying to outdo one another with the size and unconventional beauty of their weekend beach houses. He would go on to become the most prolific architect in the Hamptons, with as many as fifty houses to his name.

It was my ward's opinion—which after sharing it with Juliette he kept wisely to himself—that Norman Jaffe was probably an efficient jobbing architect, but he didn't seem gifted with much creative imagination. Now in retrospect, and having had the chance to research Norman Jaffe's career, he feels less justified in his earlier observation. Reviewing the dozens of houses Jaffe designed, it's obvious the man suffered from no lack of imagination. How creative it was is another matter. There are certainly a great many different shapes and styles in the houses he designed on Long Island, as if a score of different architects were battling it out for recognition.

I had better turn to my collaborator—again being a self-described lapsed architect—for his thoughts. Perhaps he'll be more compassionate in his understanding.

He writes that, "considering the sort of people Norman built houses for, it's not surprising there was so little consistency of style. The owners were competing for their houses to look the most important and the most unusual. I think Norman was the perfect architect to serve them. He was exceptionally good-looking and was capable of being quite charming, in a tousled romantic genius kind of way. He was hardworking and ambitious and, having come from a poor background, it was important for him to be seen and accepted as an equal of his super-rich clients, a fellow master of the universe.

"As anyone who has been in a similar situation knows, this is generally an impossibility. It is also a terrible trap for an architect to fall into because the outcome is invariably mutual resentment. The rich will frequently treat an architect like a servant, and the architect will sometimes think of a client as an ignorant philistine undeserving of their genius. Even under the best of circumstances the client/architect relationship is seldom an easy one. It's always a battle of one sort or another. There are surrenders and victories, capitulations and submissions, issues of trust, and personal responsibility. All this and more are occurring in an arena that is about as basic as one can get: the home—which is arguably the most expensive acquisition one will ever purchase in one's lifetime.

"What I came to know about Norman in our months of working together back in the early seventies suggests to me that these pent up stresses and strains must have bent him out of shape over the years of his career. It would have taken a far stronger and more emotionally mature person than Norman not to have been affected by all the pretense and hypocrisy, especially when such large sums of money and trust were involved.

"Finally, just to sum up my feelings about the design of Norman Jaffe's houses, I'd say that, for whatever reason, the man was trying a bit too hard to impress. Having had a chance now to view photographs of the majority of Norman's houses on Long Island, I have to admit they look more interesting than I'd previously allowed from knowing him back in the '70s. I wouldn't rate him as an influential architect by any means, but at least he found a niche profitable enough to ply his craft a lot more extensively than most other contemporary architects. And that, in itself, is a minor triumph."

As it turned out, it was not so odd that Norman Jaffe wanted the job of fixing the house at Mount Chi at that stage of his career. Remodeling, however expensive or elaborate, is never the Holy Grail for an aspiring architect. Yet starting a new practice takes money and—as he shouted over the wind to my ward while they were speeding up the parkway on the way to the first client meeting with the Omega—"beggars can't be choosers."

From his choice of words Mr. Jaffe obviously resented having to compromise and just as likely considered that taking on a remodeling job was beneath him. However, the architect had yet to meet Mary Ann at her most charming and charismatic.

I have heard my ward talking about that first—and as it would turn out—only client/architect conference as an example of Mary Ann's uncanny ability to melt a hard man's heart within twenty minutes of meeting him. And Norman Jaffe was a hard man in the manner of extremely sensitive men who have built a heavily armored persona to protect themselves.

As the discussion progressed it became quickly evident that the meeting was going to be far more about Norman Jaffe the man, and rather less about Norman Jaffe the architect. Under Mary Ann's direct yet sympathetic questions it emerged that the architect was a deeply troubled soul. He'd abandoned his wife and infant child back in the early 1960s to move to New York to work for Skidmore, Owings and Merrill, which he had proudly insisted was the most important architectural firm in the world. Then, a few years later in 1965, his wife was killed in a car crash, and his adolescent son was now living with him. It couldn't have been more difficult, Jaffe said. The boy hated him for abandoning the family and blamed him for the death of his mother. Jaffe the senior felt consumed with the double dose of guilt and the constant thought of how things might have been different. Perhaps she'd not have died so tragically if he hadn't left them, and what with taking the risks of starting a new practice . . . the man was living on his nerves.

The meeting went on late into the evening, and by the end of it Norman Jaffe had his contract for remodeling Mount Chi, and Mary Ann had once again demonstrated her power to strip a man psychologically naked and have him love her for it.

As might be imagined, Mein Host was peppered with questions from Jaffe as they drove back to New York together. There was a light rain, but now with the convertible's roof secured tightly above them they could at least hear each other without having to shout.

"Who *was* that extraordinary woman? Where does she come from? How did she know that stuff about me? Is she psychic? Telepathic? She wasn't a witch, was she? Why do I feel so much better?"

So the questions came, as Norman drove progressively more slowly, obviously anxious to prolong the journey. He was highly intelligent and perceptive, so I could see what care my ward had to use in answering his questions. Mary Ann had long prohibited any talk about her to people outside the community. This situation was an exception, of course, for the architect was one of the few outsiders to have actually *met* Mary Ann, or even knew of her existence. This hadn't made Mein Host's answers any easier as he struggled to appear open and transparent. He needed to be enigmatic enough in his replies to cloak the truth while simultaneously attempting to satisfy the architect's reasonable curiosity.

When Norman Jaffe dropped my ward off at the house on East 49th Street and drove home, he could well have asked himself whether he was really any the wiser about Mary Ann after all those questions and my ward's Delphic answers. He might even have asked himself why it was that he felt so comfortable and uplifted in the company of these strange people.

Robert and Mary Ann had left for an extended visit to the West Coast while the building work was proceeding at Mount Chi, leaving the decisions and details up to my ward to settle with the architect.

Mein Host came to know Norman well over months of design discussions and site visits. Although they were very different by nature and would have been unlikely to have developed a friendship had they not been thrown together by circumstances, they worked surprisingly well as a team. The building was completed on time and within budget, and when the Omega returned to take up residence they were delighted with the result. It was a modest conversion compared to the architect's later work, but the design was clean and open and filled the house with light.

Norman Jaffe, much to his disappointment, never did get to meet Mary Ann again. Additionally, with the construction complete and new demands on my ward's time, neither did the two of them stay in contact.

Norman went on to become successful and wealthy. He remarried in 1986 and started a new family. Surprisingly, as he'd shown little obvious interest in religion when he was working with Mein Host, Jaffe became celebrated toward the end of his life with awards for contemporary religious design.

My collaborator's research revealed that the Gates of the Grove Synagogue in the Hamptons, which Jaffe designed in 1987, was described by Helen Harrison in the *New York Times* as a "masterpiece," and as "one of the finest examples of modern synagogue design in America." More tellingly for the story I'm narrating was the comment of the architectural historian Alastair Gordon that the Gates of the Grove Synagogue was "the jewel in the crown of his [Jaffe's] turbulent career."

And turbulent it was, for deeper reasons than the social and architectural.

I'm writing in some detail about Norman Jaffe's life and career, because for Mein Host it was a path less traveled. Both Norman and my ward shared a similar spiritual heritage as incarnate rebel angels, yet neither was aware of it. Norman would continue to be ignorant of his true nature until his death in 1993, at the age of sixty-one. Mein Host, in contrast, having turned his back on a career in architecture in his twenties, had learned the truth of who he was before he turned fifty.

Norman Jaffe's life was indeed tumultuous. He always worked obsessively hard, frequently to the detriment of his personal life, completing more than six hundred projects in his career—an unheard of number for a single architect. Purely in terms of output he had much to be proud of, while working in a profession known for its disappointments and failed endeavors. His work was recognized and praised by filmmakers and artists and detailed in a scholarly book, *Romantic Modernist: The Life and Work of Norman Jaffe Architect 1932–1993* by Alastair Gordon.

Yet it is impossible to ignore that it was the unusual volume of Jaffe's work, as well as the wealth and the intensely competitive nature of his clients, that allowed him to explore so many styles. During his prime, Jaffe demanded design fees of up to half a million dollars. However, for all of his success and wealth, Norman Jaffe's was a deeply unsettled life and career.

Eight years older than my ward and born in Chicago in the midst of the Great Depression to a poor immigrant family, Norman Jaffe was of a generation expected to tow the line. He joined the military at twenty-two to support the war effort in Korea—in part because it was expected of him, but mostly because he couldn't wait to get out from under the oppressive conditions in which he was living. He was both far more intelligent and more ambitious than anyone in his family—the proverbial swan in a family of geese—and was proud to have become the first of them to go to college, and then to have established a lucrative career in a highly regarded profession.

In worldly terms, Norman Jaffe's life was a great success. It was, perhaps, the American dream made manifest—rising from poverty to wealth and the admiration of his fellows. And there's no denying the effort and self-sacrifice he underwent to make his mark.

Yet as Norman now appreciates—for issues become so much clearer in the afterlife—his career had become a massive distraction that took him further and further away from his true nature. At the root of his "turbulent career" was the internal conflict he fought daily, with a deeply buried part of himself that was trying to reassert itself. This was the aspect that knew he was being seduced away from his truth path by wealth and by the demanding attention of rich men and women. It was inevitable that this inner conflict would be projected out onto others—frequently onto his clients whom he envied for their wealth but simultaneously despised for their insensitive stupidity. This made him difficult to work with, while also adding to the weight of his guilt.

Entering his fifties, Norman had a modest awakening, not, unfortunately, to his true self, but to the damage he'd caused those around him by his obsession with work and his overweening ambition. Later in his life he had sought to assuage his guilt through his generosity to various local and international charities and by donating his professional services for projects such as a children's hospital in Croatia.

While this might have eased his conscience slightly, it did little to bring any real equilibrium to his inner life. As he became more inwardly disturbed toward the end of his life, so also did his need to appear to be the successful accomplished architect—an affable Frank Lloyd Wright, as he liked to think of himself—or so he now tells me.

The stresses of this inner conflict became unbearable by his sixty-first year, and he knew he had reached the end of his tether. His fear of being revealed as an impostor and a fraud—as a sort of makeup person, which was how he had come to think of himself—had started to plague his dreams.

Norman may have had some severe emotional problems, but he wasn't stupid. He knew perfectly well his options were running out fast. His attempts to sustain his persona were sounding increasingly hollow to him, and his film star good looks had worn haggard as age caught up with him.

On a deep level, he was being presented with a simple choice that any number of fifty- and sixty-year-old men and women are presented with: get real, dig for the truth about yourself, and discover who you truly are, or you will continue to suffer in ignorance until you die.

Although Norman is drawing a veil over the incident, I'm sure this choice was on his mind as he strode down the beach at Bridgehampton early one August morning in 1993. Was he still thinking about his choice as he stacked his clothes neatly, well above the waterline, and waded into the rolling breakers of the Atlantic Ocean for his morning swim? He had done this dozens of times before—it was one of the reasons he loved the beach. It was his only chance to be completely alone now that he had a new young family. He dived through the waves and struck out.

It would be the last anyone ever saw of Norman Jaffe.

So was he just sadly overconfident that August morning? Or might he have been trying to get as far away from his inner demons as possible? Could he have been trying to wash himself clean? Or was he trying to prove to himself that despite his sense of moral weakness he could be physically brave? He had only learned to swim a few years earlier and was said to be a far weaker swimmer than he believed himself to be.

Was it, perhaps, more deliberate? A final romantic gesture? Or perhaps it was less consciously deliberate, yet intentional just the same? Had the guilt and self-hatred that Norman revealed under Mary Ann's questioning twenty-one years earlier finally caught up with him?

And in those last moments, when he finally understood there was no returning to the shore, that he was quite alone and being swept farther and farther out to sea and his death was becoming inevitable—what then might have been going through his mind?

Was he relieved to get off the wheel, to stop the pain, or did his eyes open in those final seconds to his abandonment of a second young family?

If I've been overly harsh in my brief analysis of Norman Jaffe's life and career, I've narrated it in this direct manner as a cautionary tale for young rebel angel incarnates as much as for my ward's understanding of what he avoided by nature of the choices he made. And also, what he has just realized for the very first time—his own father's career in architecture, his life, and his early death had followed much the same arc as Norman Jaffe's did a generation later. I'll let him describe his insight.

He writes, "I never knew much about my father. It sure sounded like he'd had an unhappy life from the one letter I received from him. Georgia's been very helpful too with what she's been able to show me and what she has written about my father earlier in this narrative.

"Yet it has taken her pithy character review of Norman Jaffe to remind me of my father and his father, also an architect, and to drive home to me the strength of familial expectations. My father would have been expected to be an architect by his father, as in many ways I was expected to be one too. No doubt these expectations are frequently meant with the best of intentions, but it's the way these projections can impose themselves on young minds that I kicked against. I saw that familial expectations can too easily freeze a young person into a false identity, and if their training is as long as that of a doctor, an academic professor, or an architect, it's much harder to break free.

"I realized I'd broken an essential cycle by turning away from an architectural career at the age of twenty-five and striking out on my own. Although I didn't stumble into my true purpose in this life until I turned my fortieth year, I would never have been able to discover what that was had I taken the easy path.

"So I thank Normal Jaffe, a friend I once knew well, for a reflection of what might have faced me had I followed the easy path."

* * *

The small tribe that arrived on Crete represented one of the finest genetic mixes to be found in the Middle East, and by then isolating themselves on the island they were able to maintain their racial integrity. They were an exceptionally beautiful people—tall, fair-haired, and blue-eyed—who could trace their ancestry directly back to the children of Adam and Eve, the off-world visitors of the MA's second mission.

Their gene pool was enriched by interbreeding with the Atlantean survivors, many of whom were still carrying Vanite Lemurian blood. Over time, this produced an unusually intelligent and hardy race of great creative ingenuity, with a fine sense of aesthetics and a natural spiritual equanimity.

Over the centuries, and then over the millennia, others joined the burgeoning Cretan population; the inherent difficulty in actually finding the way to the island effectively filtering out the faint of heart. So it was that by the eighth millennium, the Cretan culture had become by far the most refined in Europe and the Middle East.

The Cretans were superb mariners and boatbuilders, and yet they were sensible and cautious enough not to spread their knowledge to other peoples. They had little of the naked aggression of many of the mainland tribes, and with both the Atlantean and Egyptian cultures in decline, weakened by warfare and corruption, the Cretans were able to develop their elegant and balanced culture in relative peace.

Much of this can be credited to their veneration of the Mother Goddess. I recall how happy and relieved I was when I first realized this. As an angel, of course, I hold a deep love and respect for the Holy Mother Spirit, and as a result I have a natural affinity for any manifestation of goddess worship.

On Crete, this goddess worship had continued over the millennia in a very pure vein, with the religion growing out of the worship being powerful and authentic enough to prevent it from being taken over by the rebel midwayers. This I found surprising, and I felt I needed to look more closely at how that had come to be in a world so dominated by the machinations of the rebel midwayers.

The most important factor appeared to be the authority and integrity of the belief system itself, which had emerged from the beneficial syncretism of two separate streams of belief. The tribe from the Land of the Two Rivers brought with them a reverence for the Goddess that came from a love and respect for Mother Eve and the religion that grew out of her teachings. As it turned out, this belief was then very favorably augmented by the Lemurian devotion to the Earth Mother.

This indeed was a puzzle inside an enigma.

Why Lemurian? Why not the far harsher solar gods of Atlantis? The survivors of those shipwrecks were Atlantean, weren't they? How could the Lemurian goddess beliefs have survived so long in such a hostile and belligerent culture?

There was a sudden fluttering in the ether next to me, and there was Astar, my sister watcher, who always has a particular interest in all things Lemurian. And in the way of watchers, she frequently arrived when I was groping to understand some imponderable issue. By this time I was no longer surprised when she appeared, so after we had silently greeted each other, she didn't hesitate to dive in.

"It was a complex operation," she said, and I caught a glint of pride in her tone. Then she did surprise me—with an uncharacteristic non sequitur. "No doubt you will have already gathered that this island is one of the sacred enclaves of the loyalist midwayers."

Well, no. I hadn't known that.

I could feel her smiling at me, and I determined not to look at her. In those moments, another picture formed in my mind, of a previous time I had been on Crete. It must have been more than thirty millennia ago when the island was still uninhabited and I was on a mission for Prince Caligastia. Wasn't it then, when I was resting on the meadow at the head of the Gorge of Samaria, that I had become aware of a group of loyalist midwayers?

I couldn't help but break into a grin when I turned back to Astar. So that's what accounted for the harmonious atmosphere on the island! I realized that I had grown so accustomed to the constant conflicting energies wherever the rebel midwayers held sway—which was pretty much everywhere—that I must have shifted awareness of psychic atmospheres to the back of my mind.

Astar broke into my thoughts. "It was the loyalists who arranged the whole campaign . . . and believe me, it *was* a campaign! It took at least a thousand years to play out."

I'm sure I must have felt puzzled to her. What was she talking about? What did she mean by *campaign*? At that point I hadn't been around the Mediterranean basin for more than two thousand years—not since I'd observed the disasters that overwhelmed so much of Atlantis back in the thirteenth millennium. That was the first and least damaging of the three catastrophes that had finally destroyed the island nation.

Astar spoke again. "You're not aware of how deeply subversive Lemurian influence was on the Atlantean aristocracy after the islanders had rebuilt their cities. They kept the solar gods for public worship—yet behind closed doors it was the highborn women who kept the cult of the Mother Goddess alive."

I wondered if the women were doing this to somehow balance out the aggression of the solar deities—but again Astar cut across my thoughts.

"Wait. Listen. No, that wasn't it. And anyway, it didn't stop the aggression. I suspect it was the loyalist midwayers who were actively supporting the women . . . The loyalists were playing a longer game—even then, back on Atlantis. And you know *that* couldn't have been easy!"

Frankly, it sounded almost miraculous to me. I was aware of what strict control the rebel midwayers always tried to assert through their Atlantean solar priests—so how could goddess worship have ever slipped through?

This conjured images of a stream of women—of mothers, grandmothers, and daughters—whispering their love and praise for the Mother Goddess, passing their veneration from generation to generation . . . keeping the belief alive over the centuries *and* keeping it quiet . . . It did seem an extraordinary accomplishment . . .

"In part, you can credit the loyalists for supporting the belief's continuity over time," Astar said. "They also had some encouragement from the Sirians . . ."

I recalled, then, accompanying the dolphin on that rescue mission for the long swim south . . . and what I had learned about the Sirian mission . . . So *that's* what happened after the first catastrophe, after they'd rebuilt their cities and their culture. The Sirians must have returned when I was on the continent—and I'd already learned of their veneration for the Goddess.

"It was the women who were really clever," Astar cut in. "They were the ones who deserved the most credit. You could say the women hid their belief in plain sight . . ."

Astar left it to me to puzzle that one out. Hiding a belief in plain sight? What could that mean? It was certainly true that most highborn women and men on Atlantis lived very separate lives . . . the women *could* have pulled it off, I suppose.

"You're getting a bit warmer!" I assumed this was Astar being playful, yet there was that condescending tone again. I wished she would stop doing that. I didn't know what she had to be patronizing about! After all, we were stuck both in the same situation.

Astar overlooked my petty peeves and answered the puzzle for both of us. "Women's business!" she told me. "They made the worship of the Goddess part of women's business—that's what I heard them calling it. They took advantage of their men's natural distaste for the birth process and their indifference to small children. That's how they kept it sub rosa for so long. Clever, wasn't it?!"

Astar seemed so proud of the women's ruse that she might have thought it up herself. She couldn't have heard my thought because she was hurrying on. "Fathers almost never showed any interest in their newborns . . . They were more than happy to leave the child-rearing—at least for the first few years—to the women."

"So the lads could get on with the fighting." I'd seen this pattern repeating itself in almost all the high cultures I'd observed.

"It gave the women the perfect opportunity," she replied. "The boy children who survived were taken by the fathers at seven years; the girls remained with the women. It was the ideal forum for the Goddess. It's only been in more recent times that goddess worship spread from being an esoteric cult practiced by aristocratic women to the sailors manning the Atlantean fleet."

That brought me up with a jolt. The secret cult of sailors? That seemed something of an improbable jump to me.

"Not as far as you might imagine," Astar said quickly. "Seafaring folk took to it very naturally. The ocean's always been the sailor's mother. Always will be. But don't forget, this was part of the midway-ers' plans."

I knew that the growing Atlantean wealth and influence was based on the copper that was mined in North America and then trans-ported back to the Mediterranean civilizations on the large oceangoing Atlantean merchant ships. Copper deposits on the European Continent were rare, or inaccessible at that time, so what would later come to be called the Bronze Age was almost entirely fueled by the copper mined by Atlantean colonists around the region of Lake Superior.

"The Atlantic crossings took many months." Astar was now reading my mind and answering my unasked questions. "The sailors often trav-eled with their families . . . with their women . . ."

Astar paused, and when she continued I heard a tentative quality in her tone. "I witnessed this just once," she said. "It was only later that I learned the wrecks had happened at least ten times over the centuries. To begin with, I didn't understand what was going on. I admit it."

This was the first time I had ever heard Astar express a personal failing. How about that! This thought earned me a sharp look that immediately squashed any impulse I might have had to gloat. Catching herself, however, she burst into laughter, and when I heard her again there was a new softness in her tone.

"Truly, my sister, it was much like a military campaign. So much trade was plied by the Atlantean fleet throughout the Mediterranean and yet regularly, every sixty years for more than five centuries, one of their large oceangoing boats was conveniently wrecked on the Cretan coastline. And in each case there was almost no loss of life!

"Their good fortune—I recall thinking that, Georgia—the first time I saw it happening. It took three of these shipwrecks before I realized the midwayers must be behind it. It was quite deliberate! Then as I observed more closely, I saw that they were slowly building up small communities of the finest Atlantean stock they were able to pluck from the sea.

"The settlements had grown modestly—they probably wouldn't have survived if they hadn't been replenished every sixty years by a new influx of Atlantean sailors, many with their families. Yes, of course there were a few conflicts; there were bound to be—they were human beings!"

"Probably why they never spread all over the island," I thought breezily.

I realize now as I write these words, just how eager I was to impress Astar with . . . with *what*? With the depth of my insights? The breadth of my knowledge? I think not! Yet for all that, I can now better appreciate that I was simply growing more familiar with the full range of human emotions—these were the darker ones lurking beneath the surface. I recall thinking, perhaps for the first time, that I must be developing a subconscious level to my mind. And it was true. I *had* started to notice that I wasn't feeling quite as in control of my emotions as I was used to—especially the darker ones.

"These were the local people," Astar continued, ignoring my self-concern. But I was confused.

"So let me get this straight, Astar. These local people—the original arrivals—were all these shipwreck survivors, right? It was a couple of thousand years later when we have the tribe from Mesopotamia arriving on the island, yes?"

"Correct. These were the people already on the island who greeted the tribe when they arrived on their boats from the Land of the Two Rivers. And guess what? It surprised us all!"

She paused for a couple of beats.

"It was love at first sight! Imagine that! After everything we've seen on this world! Yet these two quite different races fascinated each other. Almost immediately. Certainly they were a little cautious at first, but there was little real antagonism, and the few conflicts were very minor and easily resolved."

Astar must have felt my change of mood. I didn't know where the thought came from, but it hit me all of a sudden that the ease with which these two very different races had intermingled was how it was always meant to be . . . how it might have been if there'd never been a revolution . . . how it *could* have been . . .

Hurrying on with her account, Astar saved me from becoming

mawkish, which left me wondering whether she might have had much the same thought.

"When they came to interbreed," she was saying, "it was this mix that laid the foundations for what would blossom later into the Minoan civilization. Good genetic stock and a solid, well-developed belief system . . ." Astar suddenly seemed distracted.

As a watcher I understood the sensation. She was getting drawn away by some other necessity. I knew that was all I was going to get out of her for now . . . but before I'd completed that thought, the ether shivered, and I was alone once again with my thoughts.

Astar was right; this *was* a very fine culture.

Even though I was formally still aligned with the rebel cause, the civilization I was seeing developing on Crete, evidently nurtured by benevolent and caring midwayers, was an appealing sight. The Cretans were masterful craftspeople—they were weavers and potters and skilled workers in a variety of metals. More than anything else, they were great builders in stone. Although they no longer possessed the secrets of their ancient Lemurian forebears in shaping and manipulating enormous blocks of rock, their stonework showed a far greater delicacy. It was clear their interests were more domestic than ceremonial. After all, these were a people who had developed a system of plumbing their houses at least nine thousand years before the Romans were erroneously credited for inventing it.

Much can be derived and understood about early Cretan culture from this simple observation. Give human beings a few millennia of peace, a strong genetic foundation, a goddess to worship, and they will most likely settle into lives of peaceful domesticity.

It was inevitable that by the mid-sixth millennium news of the brilliant culture flourishing on Crete would become more widely known. The once thriving Mesopotamian culture was in its final stages of collapse, and many of the more adventurous were migrating west, some to mainland Greece and others to Crete.

Egypt was absorbed in keeping the Sea People at bay through a series of constantly broken alliances. The Sea People—the Atlantean survivors who had rebuilt their fleet after the disasters—were once again threatening Egypt's decaying hegemony. So again Crete benefitted—and this time Carthage too—from the influx of migrants escaping Egypt. These people tended to be the wealthy, the creative, and the ingenious, and they added yet another dimension to life on the island.

Then an event occurred that seemed astonishing in its deliberate nature until I realized that the loyalist midwayers must have had a hand in it. I wasn't present at the Council on Crete when the decision was made, so I can only report what emerged out of the debate. Three hundred seventy-five people were selected—young women and men between the ages of thirteen and thirty—to emigrate to mainland Greece to start seeding the culture with the best of what Crete had developed.

Greece was still relatively sparsely populated at that time, but over the previous two hundred fifty years an increasing number of clans had been leaving Mesopotamia to lay down roots in Greece. Thus when the group of Cretans arrived and settled in the country, they found a natural racial and religious commonality with many already there. It was impossible not to notice that by the turn of the fifth millennium the foundations were being laid for a people who had the potential to become the next dominant power in the Mediterranean region.

Yet it was also equally clear (to me, anyway) that by stepping outside the protective aura of Crete—the widely acknowledged home territory of the loyalist midwayers—the chosen three hundred seventy-five noble souls and their many descendants were once again subject to the wiles of Prince Caligastia and his rebel midwayers.

I say this was clear to me—and I assume to those of my kind who observe mortal life from a broader frame of reference—because it was soon obvious that the immigrants from Crete had little idea of the capacity the rebel midwayers had for making trouble.

I recall thinking there would be some challenges ahead for this nascent Greek culture.

6

Beginning of an End

Biting the Big Apple, ETs and Reincarnation,
the Prince's Plans, Impossible Demands, the
Art of Donating, and the Nature of Envy

I could see matters were starting to get out of hand at the Process chapter on East 38th Street as more and more people were crammed into the Alpha each Saturday evening at seven o'clock for the weekly Sabbath Assembly.

Norman Jaffe's elegant renovation of Mount Chi had been completed to the Omega's satisfaction, and the 242 East 49th Street rental was working out well as the primary residence for the Processeans in Manhattan. However, they needed more work space, and—given the sudden surge of interest that the Chapter was experiencing in the city—Mary Ann determined that a new, much larger, and more impressive chapter house would have to be found as soon as possible.

Normally this would be a task given to my ward, but this time he had been excused because work on the new magazine was just starting to gather momentum. Together with the others on the production team, he was trying to fit the art department into a dark, cramped room on the second floor of the subchapter on East 38th when the news filtered through that the Omega had found the perfect building for the new chapter.

When they heard this they looked around at each other, then around at the tiny room. They collectively contemplated the difficulty of squeezing an operating art department into that little space, and then they burst out laughing with happy relief. Whatever this new building was going to be like, the prospective art department could never be smaller or more inappropriate than the room in which they were standing.

One of the great advantages of the building—as Mary Ann explained to a handful of senior Internal Processeans (IPs) at first viewing—was that so little needed to be done to convert it into a Process chapter.

"It already has the necessary trappings," Mary Ann was saying as they walked around the large four-story townhouse on the west side of First Avenue.

"Look! This'll be perfect for the Cavern." They'd climbed the long narrow flight of stairs that opened into a large room with a twenty-foot-high ceiling. Golden light streamed through tall windows facing onto the avenue, flooding the room with light.

"There's even a kitchen in just the right place," Mary Ann said while walking toward the back of the building and excitedly pointing out its possibilities. And it certainly did appear as if the building would be perfect for them. It was more than large enough for any anticipated expansion: the basement was extensive and well-finished—good for a thrift shop and a printing and art department—and the top two floors were residential, with a lot of space for individual offices.

However, as the little group walked around, Mary Ann evidently saved the best 'til last, which they saw for themselves when they filed into the room at the rear of the building.

It was enormous! What's more, it was completely unexpected! How could a room this large be hollowed out at the back of a narrow New York townhouse? It seemed an impossibility to them. The ceiling was the same twenty-foot height as the previous room—the one that would become the Cavern.

The five of them stood around in silence. There were some gasps of surprise as their heads swiveled around to take in the pure volume of the space. For a few moments it must have felt as if they'd walked into a conjuring trick—or a magical house that appears tiny from the outside and yet turns out to be improbably large inside.

"I get it! Of course! Of course!" Mein Host broke the solemn silence and was laughing in recognition when Mary Ann nodded for him to go on. "You see what they did? There's another house on the next side street up, perpendicular to this one, which backs into it. They've joined the two together here, where they make a right angle . . ."

Robert, who hadn't spoken since they had entered the building, seemed to need to assert his presence, because when he spoke it was to state the obvious.

"See, everyone," he swept his arms around. "We're at the corner of the two buildings, at the nexus. It's why the room's so enormous . . . it's perfect for the Alpha, all you'll have to . . ."

Mary Ann looked sharply at her husband. I could see it stopped him in his tracks. There must have been something going on between them before coming to the building. I had seldom seen him so sheepish.

There was some awkward laughter cut short by Mary Ann gesturing everyone toward the door and back to the elevator. Yes indeed, the place actually had an elevator. Not a very large elevator, granted, so they decided to walk up the long flight of stairs. But, just *having* an elevator seemed to be status enough.

They were laughing and talking among themselves as they followed Mary Ann up to the next floor. She pointed out the well-preserved dark-blue carpet that stretched back through to the rear of the building where a large space was subdivided into a cluster of elegantly designed cubicles. There were a number of well-appointed offices and expensively furnished conference rooms. There were sufficient bathrooms and adequate space on the top two floors to comfortably house the IPs, as well as all those they hoped would join the community.

"It was Bert Stern's old studio complex . . . ," Mary Ann explained after they finished the tour and were gathered outside on the sidewalk, craning their heads to see the whole facade.

"You know . . . the *photographer* Bert Stern!" Then again, louder,

"*Bert Stern!*"—as if volume would suddenly bring name recognition. There were some unconvincing mumbles that Mary Ann broke across with a derisive snort. I'm sure she hoped they would be impressed—and now she had to explain.

"Bert Stern's one of the great American photographers . . . he's world famous. This was it . . . that was his studio . . . at the back—the big room."

It was Malachi who lit up first. "Didn't he direct that Newport jazz film . . . what was it? *Jazz on the . . .*"

"*Jazz on a Hot Summer's Day*"! Mary Ann was looking pleased that at least one of them had heard Bert Stern's name. "He's done a lot in *Vogue;* I'm surprised you don't know him!"

I could tell my ward was flinching at this. After all, Mary Ann had a lot more time to peruse fashion magazines than any of them did. *Why ever* should they know Bert Stern's name?!

But Mary Ann hadn't finished trying to impress them with her inside knowledge quite yet—although I never discovered just how "inside" her knowledge was. Before she spoke, she gestured for the group to get their heads close to make certain they could hear her theatrical whisper over the drone of First Avenue traffic.

"Marilyn Monroe. He photographed Marilyn Monroe . . . just before she died, only a few weeks before. I heard he took thousands of shots of her . . . and then she died. They can only have published a few of them, if that . . . which leaves literally hundreds and hundreds of photos of Marilyn. Think about it. Nobody's even seen them."

Mary Ann drew back, looking from face to face, hoping for . . . hoping for, *what?*

I could feel Mein Host's puzzlement. What on earth was behind her sudden obsession with Marilyn Monroe? Did she think they would uncover a hidden cache of Marilyn photos worth millions? Was it a sign from the gods? Or perhaps the real reason she'd bought the building? As my ward said later, he'd never heard Mary Ann mention Marilyn Monroe so much before. He didn't think it was hero worship. If it was, she had never revealed it.

His confusion was interrupted at that moment when a smart new station wagon drew up curbside. The community had chipped in a few extra hours on the street each day to raise money specifically to buy this shining white, modernistic-looking station wagon as a present for the Omega. One of the Processeans who lived up in Mount Chi with Robert and Mary Ann and worked as their privileged servant and—in this case as their chauffeur—quickly jumped out to open the car's rear door for Mary Ann.

"Marilyn Monroe!" Mary Ann said firmly a couple of times before turning to enter the automobile, followed by Robert, who'd remained in the background following his comment back in the big room. Once inside the car, he wound down the window. He gave a limp wave with his hand and smiled a weak slightly apologetic smile, and then the wagon pulled away, catching the green-light sequence. It accelerated up First Avenue and was gone.

I could feel my ward's discomfort at seeing Robert's halfhearted gesture and his sad, wan smile. He told Juliette when they were alone later that the image had stayed with him for days, framed in the window of the receding car—the car they'd bought for their beloved Omega.

Yet somehow this inconsequential little event had a "strange sense of foreboding," as my ward tried to explain to Juliette. "A sort of rictus of a smile that grew more weirdly distorted reflected in the window as he wound it up . . . and then looking even more outlandish as they pulled away . . ."

He stopped and looked around in what I assumed, from the way Juliette started to giggle, was a mock conspiratorial manner.

"Seriously though, Juliette! You know what it was like? You know that painting by Munch . . . that guy on the bridge who's screaming? Remember? Like *that* . . . only the guy was grinning, not screaming. That's the image that stayed in my mind. A sort of demonic death mask . . . What do you think it means? Does it mean something?"

Mother Juliette wisely did not have an answer for that.

They sat in silence for a while, both of them lighting their cigarettes and leaning back on the ornate sofas in the living room of Ruth Gordon's house on East 49th.

"And another thing, Juliette. On that tour of First Avenue and when we were standing around outside the place afterward, there was not one mention of price! You know that. No one dared ask her how much it was—how much we were paying for the place—and Mary Ann didn't volunteer it. Not that I heard, anyway."

Neither one of them spoke much after that. They quietly finished and then stubbed out their cigarettes before turning in for the night. Mein Host pecked Juliette gently on the cheek and climbed the stairs to the top of the house, to his own little room, to be alone at last.

When they came to hear what Bert Stern's old studio was going to cost them, and what the stipulations of the mortgage arrangement would be, Mein Host had some cause to remember the image of Robert's hopeless, distorted smile framed by the window as the car accelerated away.

There were profound changes afoot. My ward told Juliette he could smell them in the air. What he didn't know was just how profound those changes would come to be, and just how much he would be personally affected by them.

* * *

There are rules in the outer worlds of the Multiverse, of course; yet most of these rules have to function more as recommended codes of conduct because of the difficulty in enforcing them. This generally encourages a high standard of personal and social responsibility among all extraterrestrials, and they will, like all mortals, have access to guidance and counsel from their own celestial guides. It is this highly developed sense of social responsibility that draws so many different extraterrestrial races to keep a friendly eye on a planet such as Earth, which is going through such a radical transition.

Within the inner worlds of the celestials there are also rules, yet because these rules are more aligned with the natural laws and rhythms of Multiversal development, they are seldom broken or abused. That there have only been three rebellions known to have occurred in the long history of this Local Universe is suggestion enough of the rarity of such rules being broken. This is only one reason why the Lucifer Rebellion has attracted the attention of so many celestials from other Local Systems. Like so many of us, however, their function is purely observational, and the practical material aspects of planetary life have to be left to play out for the benefit of all beings' learning.

In the outer worlds, for example, it is assumed that by the time a planetary civilization has reached a point at which it can come and go from its solar system, that civilization will have mastered the worst of its aggressive tendencies. The few exceptions to this—free will being what it is—are confined to remaining close to their home planets by the limitations of their supply lines and some subtle discouragement by other concerned ET races.

Spiritually and mentally healthy planets are either well aware of life on other worlds, or will surely be greeted with joy by the space-faring races if and when they do venture off their worlds. A large major-ity of planetary civilizations choose never to develop their own space programs. Indeed, there are other space-faring races who make travel possible should they choose to do so. A planet such as Earth, in which technological ingenuity has outpaced the moral and spiritual wisdom of its species, will invariably be watched most diligently by other extra-terrestrial races when it takes its first lumbering flights into space.

Although an interdiction against any direct intervention in another planet's affairs is one of those rules shared by space-faring races, it's not uncommon to hear of a satellite or a rocket being "mysteriously" knocked off course if that race is considered dangerous—or too poorly prepared to join the larger galactic community.

As I write these words early in the twenty-first century, it should be evident by now to most intelligent, open-minded people that there has been a fairly continual extraterrestrial presence on and around this planet for many tens of thousands of years. Clues to this will be found in a number of indigenous traditions, with their legends of the "Star People." Extraterrestrials will frequently feature in indigenous Creation myths, or in some cases a tribe will claim that its ancestors came from the stars.

In my own experience, and by no means have I observed everything, extraterrestrials have been intermittently coming and going for half a million years—as long as I've been here—but they have greatly increased their interest since the Industrial Revolution in the West. They have redoubled their interest since the 1950s, after the invention of thermonuclear bombs and the development of space weaponry.

Yet it is equally true that claims of extraterrestrials can be interpreted as evidence of how careful the obvious impact of the ET presence over the past half century has been. As I have previously discussed, this was not so true in humanity's earlier times. Pleiadean arks had evacuated Lemurian survivors, and a group from star system Sirius intervened to aid those drawn out of the first Atlantean disasters. I've no doubt there have been other interactions between humans and extraterrestrials in the Far East, in Australia, and on the American continent that I haven't been able to observe for myself.

Regardless of these dealings, it remains generally true that extraterrestrials have wanted to remain in the shadows over the course of modern history, as they are required to do under normal conditions. Third-density planets exist for the advancement of that particular world's sentient creatures, and not for the benefit of a technologically superior race, however noble their intentions.

In the case of Earth, because of its particular significance to the celestials of the inner worlds, and because there are transcendent plans afoot that would not benefit by some ETs stumbling into the arena and spoiling the fun, this world has so far maintained a hands-off policy for any kind of mass intervention.

At least I can only assume that would have been the MA's general intention. Yet simultaneously there are a number of extraterrestrial races who have been involved with life on this "experimental planet," and who have a significant spiritual investment in individual mortal beings. These individuals will be souls from some of those off-world races who have chosen bravely to incarnate at this particular point in history to help with the upcoming transition.

There is a deeper truth here.

As I previously noted, the MA regards this world as a decimal planet—as is every inhabited tenth planet. It's experimental in that the Life Carriers are allowed to experiment and build on what they've learned over the previous cycle when they planted the original germs of life. However, I have overheard it argued by some off-world races that an "experimental planet" should also permit them to conduct *their* experiments as long as they keep quiet about them. Most of the so-called alien abductions fall into this category—with those humans "abducted" by the ETs having agreed to function in that role prior to incarnation.

This raises the question as to how this could have happened if, as the MA asserts, this Local System—and in particular the thirty-seven rebel-controlled planets—have been quarantined and effectively isolated from normal Multiverse affairs. This is presumed to mean all extraterrestrials have to stay clear. Yet here on Earth, ET hybrids and even some extraterrestrials themselves are living and working alongside you.

As I investigated this apparent contradiction, I found what I believed might throw some light on the phenomenon. I learned that many rebel angels are being required to cycle through a series of incarnations on other inhabited worlds as well as on this one. The star systems and the worlds that I heard were involved with this program were a combination of third- and fourth-density planets with the suggestion that these would function alternatively for individuals. This was described to me as a way of incrementally preparing angels for the stresses of living in the lower frequencies of third-density worlds. I'll use the colloquial names, but in some cases the planets concerned exist on a higher dimension than the star system mentioned, and the name given them merely refers to the general direction in which they can be found.

I've already described the Pleiadeans in some detail. I have also touched on those who have incarnated from Sirius. There are Antares and Arcturus—the beings from the latter system claiming they made their planetary shift—which transformed their home world two thousand years ago. There are Ursa Major and Orion, and for those described as more spiritually advanced, they tell me that Venus is inhabited by a mortal race that exists in the fourth dimension. These worlds I haven't yet visited.

I intend to cover this in more depth a little later in my narrative when I come to describe my second encounter with my ward at a time when he was incarnated on one of the Arcturian home planets. For now, however, I simply wished to lay down a broad context within which to appreciate some of the events that occurred in the sixth and fifth millennia.

On the previous occasion that I had an opportunity to spend some time with Prince Caligastia, I noted that he wasn't in the best of conditions. His actions had become increasingly erratic, and I believe something of the reality of the mess that he'd driven himself into was starting to wear down his spirit. Perhaps there was even a chance that he might hit the bottom of his delusions of grandeur and then bounce back up a better being. But that was before the Prince had successfully outwitted the visitors, sabotaging Adam and Eve's genetic mission and staunching all but a dribble of violet blood. It was this triumph that he believed would give him final control of the planet.

I had heard that Prince Caligastia's victory had fully restored his vigor, so I wasn't altogether surprised, when I encountered him again late in the sixth millennium, to find him back at his most flamboyant and mercurial.

The encounter was after I'd spent time in Crete and then later in mainland Greece to see how the Cretan immigrants were settling in. After that, I'd meandered along the Mediterranean coastline to southern Turkey, just allowing myself to be drawn along lines of subtle energy, when I felt a familiar tug that, frankly, I didn't altogether welcome. I had to quickly mask any distaste I was feeling before I found myself once again in Prince Caligastia's presence.

I'd taken my time as I was drawn inland, west over fertile plains and gentle, forested hills to a series of hilltop structures that I had never seen before. Later times would call this place Göbekli Tepe. Its great age wouldn't be recognized by modern archaeologists until excavations began in the 1990s.

I have to admit that it was most impressive. It featured large enclosed circular structures—some roofed, some open to the air. Others of various different circumferences interlocked with the larger structures; some even had small fountains, and their floors were finished with a substance that sparkled in the sun. I had been impressed by many of the buildings in Crete, but they were delicate in comparison to what I was observing here. I hadn't seen such massive monolithic stonework since Lemurian times, although these surfaces weren't dressed quite to those impeccable Lemurian standards. But they were impressive nonetheless.

What got my attention were the large, megalithic T-shaped pillars, many of which were freestanding and sunk deep into the ground. They were richly decorated with carved bas-relief and supported the roofs— most of which were also covered in carvings. As I moved closer to examine the pictograms I felt a shudder in the ether beside me, and there was the somewhat indistinct form of Prince Caligastia gesturing for me to share his frequency domain.

I downstepped my energy until the Prince became more fully resolved into material focus. I could immediately see that he'd been reinvigorated, and, from his effusive greeting, I might have been deceived into believing that he was actually pleased to see me.

The Prince and I have not had an easy relationship. I know he has never really trusted me, although as a watcher there was nothing I could have done to subvert his plans, and I certainly wasn't spying for anyone. Yet I've noticed it is in the nature of autocrats and tyrants—mortal or celestial—to demand absolute agreement from their inner circles. Mortal dictators tend to ruthlessly eliminate or exile any hint of opposition. The fact that the Prince had neither the authority to administer such punishments upon a watcher, nor the power to uphold them should he try, has never deterred him from issuing such threats. He thought of himself as God of this World, after all.

I can't speak for Astar or any of the other watchers, but I never wanted to be the one to puncture the Prince's delusions. Although he can neither eliminate me nor drive me any farther into exile than I am already, I saw no personal profit in angering him or challenging his delusions of grandeur.

In retrospect I can appreciate that this was my cowardice rearing its head again. At the time, I believed I was merely being sensibly expedient to humor him, to let him be. I'm a watcher, not a therapist! Having become more familiar with the depth of feeling available to mortals I now have a better understanding of the nature of moral integrity, of challenging power, and of standing up for what I know is right, regardless of the consequences.

But that hard-earned wisdom is something that I understand *now*—this was *then*.

I'd like to make believe that I had some prescient insight that Prince Caligastia's grandiose dreams of divine power would inevitably collapse, but I didn't.

I did, however, manage to resist his charm and his seductive offers of privilege in his new religion, and I listened with as much detachment as I could summon in the face of the emotional density of Caligastia's outsized ambitions.

* * *

Mein Host wasn't involved in the negotiations that procured the new chapter on First Avenue for the Process Church, so he was as delighted as everyone else in the community to move in to the enormous building and to finally manage to set up an art department with ample space for all the equipment. It was a delight that wasn't going to last very long.

The move from East 38th Street was completed within a couple of days. All the Chapter members wholeheartedly threw themselves into it and worked around the clock to get the new chapter up and running. Quick! Quick! All was abuzz getting the Cavern open and ready for customers—unpacking the cartons of books and magazines for the street sellers, settling the senior IPs into their offices, ensuring that the junior IPs weren't arguing over their ascribed bedrooms, and everyone demonstrating that they were working that little bit harder than anyone else.

The pressure to bring in money—to not lose a day out on the streets—always weighed heavily on them. I think they must have suspected—some with more dread than others as they scuttled around the echoing halls and offices of the First Avenue Chapter—that buying a building as outsized and as expensive as this one was going to stretch everyone to their very limits.

It would break some of them too.

I would like to believe I have not been too harsh on Mary Ann and Robert and the mystery school they inspired and nurtured through its brief and controversial existence during the 1960s and '70s. I may have had my own criticisms and skepticism, but I've had to admit that the Process Church has provided the best training and preparation for what Mein Host would come to do later in his life.

I can see now how limited my understanding must have been when I believed my ward had given away his life to an unscrupulous and manipulative woman, when all the while his companion angels seemed to fully support his involvement with the Process. Of course, his angels had the advantage in that—prior to my ward's incarnation—they participated with him in planning the broad outlines of his life to come. In my capacity as a watcher, I didn't have quite the same privileges. His angels would have known the overall purpose of his stint with the community in a way I could only attempt to determine over my years of observing him as month followed month.

I confess, it was at this point in time, when everyone in the community was scrambling to get the First Avenue Chapter fixed up and ready for the public, that I probably feared most for my ward. I could see the implications of the albatross that Mary Ann had hung around their necks, even if he couldn't. To expect a small group that seldom exceeded twenty people, however dedicated and hardworking, to raise forty thousand dollars a month—*just for the mortgage!*—was going to be impossible. And this was before the other normal monthly expenses, together with the sizable cut off the top that always needed to go "up the line" to the Omega!

I recall thinking at the time that the building was just another of Mary Ann's grandiose conceits, and one that would be sure to entangle her followers in an endless cycle of grubbing for money. Whether such thoughts passed through my ward's mind I was unable to know, but I suspect not. He was still completely devoted to Mary Ann, and, like the others, he appeared to settle unquestioningly into trying his best to accomplish this ridiculous task of scraping together a small fortune each month for the mortgage.

The only sure way they had of making money was to sell their magazines and books on the street and practice the Art of Donating—I'll get to the explanation of the term *donating* and *donators* a bit later— for all hours of the night and day. It was effective and quick, and the end result was ready cash. If necessary, donators could be sent out for as many hours as needed to fulfill their quotas, which in some cases stretched far into the night.

A top donator—and there were only two or three in any one chapter—might bring in two or three hundred dollars a day, while an average one would be in the range of fifty or sixty dollars, depending upon how long they were out working in the street. It was not uncommon for a poor donator to return clutching their few dollar bills, red-faced and protesting their determination to do better next time. And indeed there was an unpredictable volatility to the art—even the best donators had bad days just as the worst dreamed of having their good days. And who might randomly be blessed to receive the occasional fifty- or hundred-dollar bill was totally up in the air. It could always be the next person that one approached . . .

The word *donating* (others might call it *panhandling*) had been adopted by the Process to give some class to the act of asking a complete stranger for money. The choice of using this word allows some insight into the community's mind-set. While *donating* is certainly a more generous word than *panhandling,* the meaning of the word as applied by the Process was quite the opposite of what might be expected. The donation was not the money given. Indeed not! It was the Processean who was donating his or her *time* and healing energy to the fortunate stranger in return for money proffered (or not) by said stranger. The *Processean* was the donator.

The Art of Donating—and I'm assured by my ward that it *was* an art—was one of those innovations that was pioneered inadvertently by Mein Host and which then came to be adopted by the community. This discovery had occurred, as I've previously noted, back in the 1960s, when Mary Ann, Robert, and their inner circle were in Los Angeles and believed themselves to be out of money. Knowing Mary Ann as I've come to, I doubt if this was altogether true—she was not a woman to leave herself without options. However, broke or not, within the small of group of seven or eight people it was generally understood that they had spent their last few dollars on two rooms on the second floor of a rundown Hollywood motel.

They had no books or magazines to sell and were sitting around the Omega's motel room involved in one of their endless discussions. It was late afternoon, and Mary Ann had been using my ward's talent for selling magazines on the street as a cudgel to berate the other less successful Processeans. At one point she wagered, more as a sarcastic crack than with any serious intention, that my ward could go out on the street with nothing—no magazines, no books, no nothing!—and he would still come back with more money than the lot of them with their armfuls of unsold magazines.

Since I was unable to enter Mary Ann's mind and read her thoughts I couldn't tell how contrived this situation might have been. Panhandling was not unknown, but in the 1960s it was generally restricted to down-and-outs and hadn't yet been adopted by sects like the Hare Krishnas or cults like Reverend Moon's wide-eyed followers.

Yet for all that, I'm inclined to believe Mary Ann's taunt was authentic. It was made in the moment and not preconsidered, for it was very much part of Mary Ann's armory to carelessly—and sometimes unknowingly—provoke a wholly unexpected consequence. She would have thought of this as her intuitive genius. Although whenever one of her throwaway challenges failed to bear fruit, its casual nature allowed her sufficient deniability—implausible though it might be—

to blame and mock those who had failed to fulfill her wishes.

There was a story she liked to tell that revealed this attitude. J. Edgar Hoover, so she said, always insisted on receiving his typewritten memos at the FBI with borders of a specified width that allowed him to write his comments there. A memo arrived on his desk one day with wider text and far thinner borders than he demanded, so he scribbled a hasty *"Watch the borders!"* in one corner of the memo. A few days later the United States–Mexican border was crawling with bewildered FBI agents, their seniors having been unwilling to query Hoover's orders.

Apocryphal or not, Mary Ann always took great delight in telling the story. It was clear that it was J. Edgar Hoover with whom she identified, and it was the poor dupes too scared to question their boss who received her harshest scorn.

My ward still isn't quite sure what propelled him out of the motel room that afternoon and onto Hollywood Boulevard to ask people for money. But he does recall returning to the motel a few hours later with a surprisingly large number of one-, five-, ten-, and even twenty-dollar bills, as well as pockets swollen with small change.

And that was that. Everyone was then expected to be able to do it— to go out on the street and brazenly approach people for money with nothing to show for it but their persuasion, their charm, and the force of their personalities.

I will say this now, although Mein Host wasn't aware of this dynamic until much later, there were a number of people in the inner circle who deeply resented him for his so-called discovery of donating. They wouldn't quickly forget those hundreds of hapless hours they had spent out on rainy city streets hopelessly hustling for quarters, nor would some of them easily forgive him for it.

I don't say this critically, because this sort of emotional cut and thrust is one of the most valuable aspects of living in such intimate communal circumstances. In such a close-knit group every person has to face and deal with the best and worst—but most usually the worst— aspects of their nature. This is because typically one is dealing with people who are very different from oneself. If the community has a unified sense of purpose that transcends the personal, each person will have a more meaningful investment in staying in the community and facing the truth than they will have in leaving. This investment might be emotional, mental, spiritual—or all three, as it was in the case of the Process. When a community has also placed an emphasis on clear, open communication and an honest expression of emotions, then everything will come out in the open sooner or later.

Envy, however, seems to be one of the more shameful of the human reactive emotions, as it's also one of the most disguised from both self and others. It can come in many colors. Envy can come cloaked in flattery; it can appear in the guise of emulation, or in hero worship; or it can provoke a need to discredit—or worse. In Australia, my ward adds, envy has instigated the "tall poppy syndrome," in which the best and brightest students are cut back to size.

Another characteristic of the envious is that they can't wait for the envied one to fall from grace. Isn't it a deep-seated envy that creates an audience for celebrity magazines and expresses itself in the secret pleasure that's felt when seeing the mighty fall? Heroes might be lauded for their heroism, celebrities applauded for their talents and gifts, the rich admired for their successes and the religious for their holiness, yet beneath the surface will invariably lurk the twin thoughtforms of envy and resentment.

I've observed that in human terms—whenever there is a wide gap between the "haves and have-nots"—in almost every field of human activity envy is frequently one of the most common and unrecognized emotions in the public square. It is also one of the most destructive. Sadly, the general public's capacity for envy is titillated by corporations in their marketing, given that envy can be pushed by politicians to manipulate voters. The very idea of "keeping up with the Joneses" is based on an envy of others.

It was for good reason that I said envy is one of the most destructive yet largely unrecognized emotions in the public square. Envy can affect everyone individually to the extent they buy into it. Envying another, for example, for what a person feels lacking in the self, can deprive that person of the deeper impulse to seek within the self their true and unique purpose. In the spiritual world—as mortals will discover for themselves in the afterlife—a person's inability to find her or his true purpose over the course of a lifetime is regarded as one of the tragedies of a human life. I can't vouch for this personally—it feels good to use that word *personally;* it makes me feel more like a person!—but I have heard there are spirits in the afterlife who claim that failing to find a mortal's true purpose is wasting a lifetime, and those souls will simply have to repeat the experience until they do find their true path.

The emotional dynamics of the Omega's inner circle were largely governed by who was in or out of Mary Ann's favor at any given point. As this changed frequently and unexpectedly, all of them found themselves at one time or another raised to the bosom of the Goddess and then, for some perceived slight, thrown into the depths of misery by being separated from their Goddess. It was when a person was in disgrace that everyone else was able to pile on and express their feelings, some of which had been repressed or hidden until that particular person's fall.

While this might sound like reprehensible behavior in a normal social situation, the value of being flung from the heights of joy to the depths of despair was that it would greatly strengthen the emotional body of the one being flung. The risks lay for those who'd become emotionally exhausted or those who had given away their power, much as subjects under hypnosis do. It also pertained to the weaker ones who were driven, in a few cases, to possess what could be called a mild but persistent case of post-traumatic stress disorder.

I believe what had allowed Mein Host to remain relatively free of these psychological disturbances was the thick skin he'd formed under harsh conditions while attending Charterhouse, an English public school. At such time, he'd refused to scream out when he was being formally thrashed by an out-of-control senior monitor. He had also exercised his willpower and determination when sitting in the jungle outside Xtul for as long as it took after having been ordered to leave by Mary Ann. In fact, through the various agonies and ecstasies of serving his Goddess—and there were plenty of those—what was really happening was that he was stretching and flexing his emotional body, as well as growing more familiar with exerting his will.

I have heard my ward claim recently that it was in this period that he learned how to bounce back from failure and despair. To quote him, if I may—because this is outside my emotional range of experience—he says: "It's in being prepared to sink to the very depth of misery that I discovered that the proverbial bottomless pit did indeed have a bottom. If I summoned the courage to make myself feel even worse, as bad as possible, then I could use the bottom of the bottomless pit as an effective trampoline. This led to a credo that Alma and I published in the *Bozon Interplanetary Gazette:* 'It's not how you fall, it's how you bounce that counts.'"

I have listened to my ward referring to community life, borrowing from Georges Gurdjieff, as "a path of accelerated evolution." The trick, he tells me, is never to get caught in community life for too long. It's important to know when to bow out.

So perhaps he did know, somewhere deep inside him, what was awaiting him in a few months' time.

7

Temple of Death

Caligastia's Diminishing Influence, Secrets of Göbekli Tepe, Enter the Four, Natural Energy Grids, and Political Maneuvers

I have previously made note of Caligastia's increasingly unrealistic demands, which led me to believe he was coming to see that the revolution had not turned out as he had hoped.

He firmly believed, for example, that because I'd accompanied him on his mission to the planet almost half a million years ago, I should therefore treat him as my superior. He thought this way even though technically he had no authority over the angels who functioned alongside the mission.

Caligastia was well aware that my primary allegiance was to Lucifer—whom I considered my *true* superior—and I could tell this irritated him. It had become a delicate issue for both of us. He knew that I knew he couldn't argue with my loyalty to Lucifer without betraying his own will to power, as I knew I could always pull that string if he became overbearing with me. This arrangement largely protected me from the worst of his bile, but there was little doubt that he resented me for what he saw as my outwitting him. On the rare occasions we encountered one another, the Prince could assume an unctuous tone of mock subservience—calling me names like "Commodore" and

"Admiral" and touching his brow in a cynically sloppy salute. I refused to let myself be riled at this, and after he'd exhausted his options in trying to push my buttons (I thank my ward for that phrase), we had settled into an uneasy truce.

I didn't know at the time how the other watchers had worked out their relationship with the Prince—and how they'd handled Prince Caligastia's unreasonable demands—so I made a mental note to ask Astar about this the next time she appeared.

I had been able to keep a relatively amiable relationship with the Prince prior to the uprising, although as an independent observer I never considered myself subordinate to him—and back then he didn't try to control us. Subsequent to the rebellion and Caligastia's increasingly erratic behavior I'd been able to detach myself to some extent and pay close attention to keeping out of his way. This was one of the reasons I avoided going anywhere near his palace, which was in a frequency domain contiguous to the settlement of Salem in southern Palestine.

When I encountered Prince Caligastia at Göbekli Tepe, I didn't yet know he had recently relocated the center of his operation to Turkey.

Caligastia must have heard my last thought, because he was laughing and gesturing around at the splendid circular structures beneath us while he was greeting me. I was surprised to find him at his most charming and benevolent, and I recall thinking at the time: "also probably at his most devious." Yet as our interchange developed, I wondered if I might have misjudged him. It seemed all he wanted to do was to impress me with this new third-density manifestation as an example of his growing power on Earth.

"Naturally you will wish to know how I achieved this magnificence," he said, his voice ringing in my mind with renewed confidence.

He was right, of course. How *had* he pulled it off?

A moment later we were standing side by side in one of the circular roofless chambers before one of the massive T-shaped limestone columns. A carved rock basin stood against the enclosing dry stone wall at one side of the court, gathering water leaking down from where a natural spring trickled out between two carefully shaped rocks. The spillover from the basin fed water into two channels in the floor that ringed the space and led off into the darkness of an intersecting roofed chamber.

Although I'm unable to detect or experience the temperature or barometric pressure in third-density reality, I can generally read the tell-tale physical signs. Here I could observe the evaporation rising off the water in the channels, and I realized this system must be dramatically cooling the interior spaces.

Three massive, freestanding T-shaped columns stood triangulated in the center of the enclosure. I saw the Prince now peering intently at a group of carved, embossed pictograms that covered the flat side of one of the columns, and it came to me that he wanted me to puzzle out his cleverness for myself.

Really! Sometimes the Prince could be very gauche! He was like a child proudly showing off an elaborate card trick and then urging me to tell him how he'd done it.

I am sure you can appreciate my predicament. I was caught between a rock and a hard place (if I may pull that much-loved cliché from Mein Host's memory). The Prince would be sure to know immediately if I was humoring him, yet I needed to maintain my own integrity and detach from the Prince's authority, which I had taken such care to establish.

I moved closer to the column to examine the pictograms.

"Mostly different animals," I thought out loud. "Look, there are insects and that's a fox, isn't it? And a lion . . . and I can see a snake over on that column over there . . . They must be the animals that are hunted around here. They're hunting magi . . ."

Caligastia cut me short, as I'd hoped he would. "No, no, look closer watcher, not just animals. Yes, animals, but these," he said, pointing to some more enigmatic pictograms in one of the top corners of the lintel. "What about these? These aren't animals."

I squinted my eyes and traced the raised sculpted forms with my astral fingers. As I did that, another image floated in front of me, and for a brief moment I was back in the Gorge of Samaria admiring those enormous glyphs that appeared carved into the canyon's sheer walls. As the panoramic image of the gorge's massive petroglyphs flickered in my mind's eye, I gradually came to see that they had a curiously similar quality to the much-reduced hieroglyphs on the lintel. I recalled then how I felt I was being shown that those sculpted petroglyphs in Crete were, in fact, the work of the loyalist midwayers.

Then of course, it dawned on me. I put it together. It must be that the pictograms on the lintel were the sigils of the rebel midwayers. It followed that the various animal figures were more likely clan and tribal totems . . . with the positioning of the sigils and totems on the columns showing the nature of the relationship between the midwayers and the tribes they'd adopted. As we moved around the complex together I saw that this held true on many of the original columns, with some of the most recent carvings evidently carrying more complex meanings.

In those moments I had a wholly unexpected sensation—I caught a glimpse of Caligastia's true brilliance. Yet while I was admiring his achievement, I simultaneously felt a wave of terrible sadness and regret that this hadn't always been so. It frightened me. The feeling was too honest. It revealed too much. I sincerely hoped that the Prince hadn't picked it up from me. The feeling was freighted with what might have been had the Prince maintained his integrity.

After all, he'd created this temple complex by getting his rebellious midwayers to stop their continual bickering and competing with one another. In this, they'd been able to collaborate on this project. This in turn evidently had the effect of uniting the various nomadic tribes, who then provided the enormous manpower needed to quarry, transport, and erect the limestone megaliths.

However, if the megaliths were massive, they were still somewhat modest when compared to the smoothly finished granite monoliths that the Lemurian builders used in their temples. Another contrast I found with Lemuria was that the Göbekli Tepe megaliths were obviously quarried and finished with crude tools—such as stone axes. In the case of the sculpted bas-reliefs, the soft limestone had been finished with copper chisels.

I'd become lost in the glyphs while admiring some of the enigmatic midwayer sigils before I became aware of Prince Caligastia growing increasingly impatient beside me.

I guessed I must have passed the test. I'd worked out the puzzle for myself—or at least enough of it to satisfy Caligastia's vanity—because he clearly couldn't wait to boast about both how he had created this place and his plans for the future. It became a long and varied diatribe that he continued as we moved through the different temples. The Prince only broke off to point out the different glyphs with their meanings and their attributions, so I'll compress and paraphrase what I heard from him that afternoon at Göbekli Tepe.

He told me that only after he had vanquished the visitors and diluted (or crushed) their teachings—and after he had dispersed their followers—had he started to have the temple constructed. These dispersed followers would have been the tribes that migrated first to Egypt and then later to India. They would have been the steady trickle I'd seen earlier moving in to Europe and fighting battles like the one I'd witnessed on the banks of the Somme River.

The Prince said that after the cataclysms of the thirteenth and twelfth millennia there'd been a revival of the religion and the teachings the visitors had promulgated, which Caligastia believed had threatened his absolute authority. He didn't put it in quite those terms, but he evidently needed to exhibit his power directly in third-density reality.

I knew his mortal power base had been steadily eroding ever since the natural physical disasters of the thirteenth millennium. To my astonishment, he openly admitted that his influence over humans had nearly disappeared in the millennium following the floods and rising sea levels, which had wiped out coastal towns and cities the world over and caused a massive die-off. He said that sometime in the mid-twelfth millennium he had started to put his plan into action.

Populations invariably surge in numbers after serious natural disasters, and the Prince said he had taken advantage of this rapid expansion to put his stamp on the emerging culture. Göbekli Tepe was the material symbol of his power—as well as an example to all beings of his continuing ability to harness the rebel midwayers and the mortals to his singular demands.

I must have appeared puzzled, because the last I'd heard of the rebel midwayers they were running amok and trying to establish their independent identities. The Prince went on to explain how he'd expedited his plan—how, by operating through his midwayers, he had amassed the huge numbers of people needed to realize his hilltop temple. He made sure to stress that these were nomadic tribes so I would appreciate the difficulties he must have overcome. This had taken many centuries, with the structures ultimately continuing to increase in volume as subsequent cultures built over earlier ones during Göbekli Tepe's long tenure of more than three thousand five hundred years of existence.

Something in his boasting tone must have tipped me off. I suddenly understood what he was trying to do. I knew the Prince had always been envious of Lemuria's great cultural success—largely because he always spoke so rudely about Vanu and Amadon and how they were dastardly traitors who had betrayed far too many of the secrets of nature. Neither he nor his midwayers had ever been able to penetrate the inner workings of the Lemurian culture, and I'm sure this must have always been a thorn in the Prince's side.

He clearly wasn't happy with the direction my thoughts were taking me, because he broke across them, telling me more than he probably should have if he'd followed the code for which he'd so bitterly criticized Vanu and Amadon for breaking.

"You see only the structures, don't you, watcher?" There was that old sarcastic tone of an assumed superiority again. It came to me in that moment that he only used that particular tone when I'd demonstrated that I was interested in what he was showing me—when he felt he had me finally caught on the hook.

He didn't wait for my reply before continuing. "You cannot not appreciate the true purpose of my creation. It is indeed a material witness to the power and majesty of the God of this World, which will be self-evident when I have completed my plan."

Now this did get me curious. A plan? Prince Caligastia? I had never seen much sign of long-range planning on his part in the past—at least not since the uprising. He appeared to operate almost entirely on momentary reactive impulses and on his latest whim. And now he was planning?! *Really?*

By this time I'd given up any attempt of masking my thoughts from him. It took too much energy. Besides, he well knew what I thought about him. In light of that, I was amused to see that my attitude was actually provoking him to further satisfy his vanity.

"You desire to know what I'm really doing? Isn't that correct, watcher? You desire to see the true brilliance and power of your Planetary Prince. This is why you are here in my magnificent Temple of Death."

I knew then that he wouldn't be able to resist telling me his great secret. He was cunning, there was no denying that, but he was also compulsively boastful.

"And I have plenty to boast about! You have no idea, have you, watcher? Well, let me astonish you. I'm about to override my world's natural grid. Do you understand that? I am going to reimprint the energy to serve my own divine purposes! Do you know what that means? Have you any idea of the power that will give me?"

With Caligastia it was always difficult to separate the bombast from the reality. Regardless, a shudder ran up my spine at his words, so perhaps I really *did* know what it meant.

Once again I found myself fearing for the future of us all—mortal, midwayer, and watcher alike.

* * *

Of course it was an impossible task.

Everyone in the First Avenue Chapter was working all hours of the day and night to bring in the money needed to support their white elephant of a building. Donating was producing more money than ever—given that donators were increasingly spending longer and longer hours on the street. Yet as week followed week, it was never enough.

Mein Host was splitting his time between leading a small army of donators into the Manhattan midtown fray and starting work on the next issue of the magazine. Because he clearly both enjoyed donating and loved designing for the magazine, he tells me that the next couple of months in that summer of 1973 passed very happily. He also appeared relieved not to have been given any overall responsibility for the Chapter. He hadn't been involved in the negotiations for purchasing the building, and although his common sense must have told him the place had to be expensive, he was happily ignorant of the true state of affairs.

Given that the Process had grown in size—there were now thriving Process chapters in half a dozen North American cities—there had been some recent changes at the top of the community's hierarchy. If I were to hazard a guess as to what Mary Ann's true motives were in setting up a committee of four of the most senior Processeans, I'd have to say she was setting them up for failure. The plan was apparently for these four people to take over the day-to-day operations of the rapidly expanding organization. As well, they created an additional buffer between the Omega and its followers.

Now known as "Luminaries," these four senior members of Mary Ann's inner circle would have the privilege of living at Mount Chi—in a wing of the Omega's house in Westchester County—so they would be close to the center of power. They would come to be known eponymously as "the Four," and, for a few months during the summer of 1973, I believe this new system may have given the appearance of working fairly well. You may remember their names from their occasional appearances in my narrative. There was Father Aaron, my ward's traveling companion throughout the United States and Europe; Fathers Paul and Christopher, both of whom played cameo parts in the Xtul saga; and Mother Cassandra, who appeared earlier as Wendy (they changed their names from time to time) as, squeezed into a Jeep, they'd bumped along together on the way to Xtul.

However, when an autocrat sets up a committee to handle business, it rarely involves a concomitant delegation of the autocrat's power to that committee. Had any one of the Four been disloyal enough to express a true opinion, he or she might well have questioned whether Mary Ann may have had another, perhaps less obvious, reason for creating the Luminaries. As the months passed, her intentions would become more obvious, but at that point no one in the community knew just how intractable was the rift developing between Mary Ann and her husband.

The troubles between the couple had been brewing for some time, with Robert playing less and less of an important role in the affairs of the Process. He'd written no books for years and mainly appeared to occupy his time penning articles for the magazine—which were so plentiful that many had to be published under the names of other Processeans. But apart from the writing, he seemed to be becoming increasingly irrelevant as Mary Ann became progressively more dominant.

The Omega had recently returned from London. There they had lost the court case in which the Process was suing the English publisher of Ed Sanders's book *The Family* for the removal of an incendiary and libelous chapter that tried to connect Charles Manson to the Process. A couple of years earlier, the matter had been settled out of court in the American case to the advantage of the Process, so I've no doubt Mary Ann was confident the group would have similar success in the English courts.

Mein Host knew nothing of this at the time, and I, in turn, didn't attend the trial in London, so much of what I know about this matter resulted from my ward's research into the court records many years later for another book: *Love Sex Fear Death: The Inside Story of the Process Church of the Final Judgment*.

However, if my ward wasn't aware of the details of the English case until after the Omega returned with the three senior Processeans they'd taken with them, he says it was obvious from the sadly deflated atmosphere that something had gone very wrong in London. But just how wrong was hard to pin down, as no one was talking openly about it.

In fact, as it turned out it was a complete debacle. As such, it was the result of a series of miscalculations by Mary Ann that were so arrogant that she really deserved to lose. I can only assume she must have forgotten the intensity of the hostility the Process had stirred up before leaving England five years earlier, because every move she made only worsened the situation. Her single most cavalier act was to prevent Robert from testifying ("Robert should not have to descend to defending himself!") at the trial. Another mistake was having one of the other Processeans speak for him—someone who was clearly unprepared and ill equipped to make an effective presentation. This only further weakened their position.

The court records also contain a number of suggestive remarks about Mary Ann's "sexy boots" that she chose to wear during the trial. Surprisingly, these comments were made by the pompous elderly judge who appeared to have something of a foot fetish.

Although I doubt if there's much truth in this, I wouldn't put it past Mary Ann—with her contacts from her previous life, many in the corridors of power—to have done her homework. If she wore her sexy boots intentionally to pander to the old judge's fetish, then it seemed to evoke from him only a schoolboy reaction of bemused disgust. If she wore such ostentatious footwear to an English courtroom without understanding the impression she created, I can only believe it was due to arrogance. Had she become so used to being seen as above criticism by those around her that she'd lost touch with how she might be perceived by an archaically conservative court?

It really should have been a clear-cut case. In the English edition of *The Family,* the publisher had left in the libelous chapter—the very chapter they had agreed was a concoction of lies and which had been removed from the American edition. The case had already been made; surely it was a done deal! But there was no accounting for the English system of justice.

While what occurred in the courtroom over the days of the trial couldn't really be called corrupt, it was laughably unjust, and the result was arbitrary and punitive. The judge clearly loathed the Process and everything the community stood for and made that obvious in a most biased way from the start of the proceedings. Possibly he'd been tipped off beforehand; the English ruling class feared and hated any social innovation that threatened its authority. The Process had been extremely strident in its criticisms of the English sacred cows before they'd turned their backs on the country—only to then flourish in the States. Having such a success in America after having been so critical about England must have hit a raw nerve in any full-blooded, patriotic Englishman—especially one old enough to resent the swagger of the American troops in England during World War II.

But this wasn't limited to just older people! My ward discovered this to his surprise when his friend—the English writer and polymath John Michell—made a crack about rats leaving a sinking ship when they were talking about my ward's life in America. John was a man of similar background and education, and only a few years older than my ward. He had chosen to remain in England and make his career there in a world with which he was familiar.

His remark was said mostly in jest, of course, as having the common sense to leave a sinking ship couldn't be denied. As well, neither disagreed about the ship sinking, but there was a bite to the comment that told a deeper story.

They had been friends for more than thirty-five years until John died in 2009, my ward making sure to meet with him in London whenever he was there visiting his mother. In fact, over the years, Diana and John had formed their own relationship. John had become enchanted by my ward's mother's intelligent interest and her "English lady" charm. Diana, in turn, was delighted and flattered by the attentions of such an erudite and attractive man.

John and my ward had many interests in common—from Earth mysteries, cosmologies, and sacred sites, to simulacra, geomancy, and the mystery of the extraterrestrial presence—yet their approach to these subjects was very different. John Michell's first book, *The Flying Saucer Vision,* came out in 1967, but it was his 1969 book, *The View over Atlantis,* that sealed his reputation as an elegant writer and a brilliant, independent mind. He was prepared to challenge scientific dogma, and he clearly took particular pleasure poking holes in questionable orthodox scholarship wherever he found it. My ward—along with many other independent thinkers—credits John with providing the intellectual foundation for the modern Earth mysteries movement in his writings and research.

My ward's approach, as you will have gathered, has always been more experiential. He prefers to throw himself into experiences, and the material in his books is largely derived from what he has discovered from his personal explorations. His literary output has been extremely modest compared to John Michell's forty books and booklets—and his numerous articles and newsletters—and he has nothing of John's richly deserved, worldwide reputation. Yet what they'd discovered when sharing stories shocked them both.

It's a standing joke among most writers that when they get together they will talk as much or more about their sales figures as they will about the content of their books and their ideas. What took them both aback was the vast financial imbalance between a successful book in America when contrasted to one published in England. It must have been something of a rude awakening for John to learn that just one of my ward's seven books had sold more copies than John's entire life's work of more than forty books.

I write this not to laud my ward for his success—and certainly not to imply any comparison of the relative importance of the two writers—but merely to emphasize what John called "the enviable advantages of leaving a sinking ship."

As Mein Host observed later, it had to be this harsh financial reality that added the sharp edge to his friend's bite.

Returning to the English court case, it is my ward's belief that the judge was simply a confused, opinionated old fool. He considered him "an old fool from the old school"—an old man at the end of his career who had allowed his prejudices to cloud his judgment in a case that he evidently hadn't cared to take all that seriously.

Regardless of whether the verdict in the case was unfair or whether the judge was biased, I noticed that Mary Ann and Robert completely ignored their own bedrock teaching of total responsibility at the core of the community's belief system. My ward says he never once heard the question mooted as to why they needed "to pull in" such a disaster. The responsibility that Mary Ann and Robert should have taken for creating what was, in reality, a shockingly unexpected slap in the face had never been seriously questioned.

It was in the magazine meetings that my ward attended after the Omega returned from London that I could see beneath this blatant hypocrisy a resurgence of the demon of anger lurking in Mary Ann's emotional body and progressively growing in virulence over the course of the meetings. During the ensuing weeks, this barely suppressed fury started taking a form—so that before long it was Robert who had "screwed everything up in London." It became one more of Robert's disasters in his long trail of failing in Mary Ann's eyes. He had utterly failed to ignite a crowd on the two occasions he had tried to speak in public; he had failed miserably to be the messiah of her outrageous ambitions; and he had failed to fully and unconditionally support her more outlandish schemes.

I am unable to pinpoint the exact timing of this, but it was at some point over these few weeks that I believe Mary Ann realized Robert's essential irrelevance and began to plot to displace her husband. It wasn't going to be easy. Robert was still the public face of the Process; expensively shot, full-page photos of him were featured in every issue of the magazine. He was the Teacher, the figurehead, the first prophet of the Process Church. He was generally loved and respected by everyone in the community, more so perhaps by the junior members who had never met him and thought of him as a Christ figure.

No. Indeed it was not going to be a simple matter to oust Robert from the church of his own making, and Mary Ann would need to go about her plans in an exceedingly careful manner. She would have to slowly build a case against him until she could finally pounce and expose him. She was cunning enough to know that she couldn't just chuck Robert out. She would have to be able to justify it in the eyes of her inner circle and move her husband along—all while making it appear to be his choice to leave.

It was a tricky and challenging situation, but, to a woman of Mary

Ann's undoubted skill in the dark arts of subconscious manipulation, it would doubtless present little problem.

Much of this political maneuvering at the Omega went over Mein Host's head. Like others in the New York Chapter, he was far too busy to notice the gathering storm. The magazine meetings weren't unduly turbulent—although my ward might have noticed that Robert was more subdued than usual. The real problems, as far as Mein Host was concerned, were the ones erupting in the First Avenue Chapter.

Each of the Four had done a stint in leading the Chapter and trying to see what could be done to increase the income. Each of the Four, in turn, had failed to inspire more than a marginal increase in overall revenues. After all—they would argue in their defense—there was only so much even the best donator could make in a day, and top donators were rare enough. An average donator, while proud of the sixty or eighty dollars a day they brought in, was only contributing a pittance when set against the constant demand for the fifty or sixty thousand dollars necessary per month. And as it stood, they had no other way of bringing in money.

It was indeed looking to be an impossible task.

* * *

I was aware of the natural energy grid that crisscrosses the planet, because we were informed in our Jerusem lectures that every inhabited planet possesses a subtle energy matrix. Although this natural grid has both electromagnetic and gravitational characteristics, its overall bandwidth is so broad that it spreads well into the finer frequencies within the subtle energy realms. It is this that allows a reciprocal relationship whereby the material world is interpenetrated by the higher frequencies of the etheric realms . . .

". . . And therefore the entire grid can be influenced by modulating energies at the higher end of the frequency spectrum. You got it," said Caligastia, finishing my thought for me while relishing his own cleverness.

The Prince and I had moved in to one of the larger roofed circular chambers of the hilltop temple complex at Göbekli Tepe. While we were talking about the energy grid, he was showing me another of the limestone columns and proudly pointing out the various clan totems along with the midwayer's sigil. He was explaining how his midwayers had worked through the various nomadic tribes they'd adopted and how in this way they had provided a continuity of purpose over the many centuries that were needed to complete the project. But that still didn't answer what the temples at Göbekli Tepe had to do with the subtle energy grid.

In the Jerusem lectures all we were ever told about this grid was that it had multiple purposes and that its primary function was to keep an overall planetary equilibrium by constantly balancing the many energetic systems which support the biosphere. Really not much more than that . . .

"Exactly!" the Prince jumped into my line of thought. "And that was because the MA refrained from telling you the grid's true purpose—as they held back and deceived us about so many things . . ." I will leave out the next few minutes of his vitriolic rhetoric—blaming the MA for the ills of the world . . . *his* world!

"What they *never* told you," Caligastia said, ending his harangue, "what they never *trusted* you with was the higher function of the energy grid. The real purpose of it. Think about it. It's obvious."

I thought about it. And then I thought it better to simply let him tell me the answer since it was so obvious!

"As above, so below," he said, his tone turning didactic. "As below, so above. As the grid constantly moves toward achieving equilibrium in the material realm, so also do the higher frequencies hold the energetic balance necessary to facilitate the mortal ascension process. The MA held that little gem back from you; can you see that now?"

Caligastia's tone became singsong, almost playful—and there was that triumphant child again, gloating in his secret knowledge. The thought crossed my mind that there may have been a very good reason why the MA had kept the workings of the ascension process to itself!

The lecturers always made sure to impress us with the fact that any interference with the mortal ascension process was absolutely taboo. It was also true that the lectures had never made any connection between the grid and the ascension process. That was completely new to me.

Having let the cat out of the bag, Caligastia couldn't stop telling me the details. I wondered whether he had anyone else to whom he felt he could boast so freely.

"I tell you these secrets because there is nothing you can do to interfere with my plans; there is no one you can tell about them who is powerful enough to stop me . . . Besides, I enjoy having a witness. And I like you, my dutiful watcher. I have some respect for you. You have been with me from the start of this grand adventure. Did you not join with me unhesitatingly back at the time of our great revolution?"

Not quite true—I'd had *much* hesitation. Anyway, I joined for the sake of Lucifer and only tangentially for Caligastia—but this wasn't the time to press that point. I didn't want to stop the flow, and although I wasn't taking the Prince's talk of his plans too seriously, there was always a chance I would learn something I didn't know.

"It is for these reasons I choose to share with you these hidden matters," he continued, too filled with self-admiration to notice my skepticism. "I want you, Georgia, to be special to me . . . I want you to understand my most brilliant strategic stroke."

I didn't like the sound of that! Why had he selected *me* for this? I had to tread carefully. Yet I was also almost painfully curious by now. What *was* I to do?

He had tried to seduce me back into his fold before with his flattery, so I listened to him with some caution, intent to give no sign of any overt reaction. However, when communicating with a telepathic being this is no simple matter. Indeed, I had to pay so much attention to cooling down my emotional reaction to what I was hearing from the Prince that afternoon in the temple that, as I write these words, I find I can't guarantee that I have his idea as clearly expressed as he would have hoped.

"They would have told you in your lectures," I recall him saying, "that it is in the nature of the grid to create specific locations of material power. These are the nexus points where the telluric currents and subtle energy circuits intersect. What is important to know is that every major point of intersection will then produce a powerful vortex with the vortical energy flowing at a ninety-degree angle to the grid. They didn't tell you about *that* in your lectures!" He paused and turned to look at me, a triumphant glow on his beautiful face. "Those are the places, those vortices," his tone rising in intensity, "*those* are the locations I am interested in. Those are the places where I'll build my temples. That is how I will gain my access to the grid."

Was this delusionary? I simply didn't know enough to judge either way, so I nodded my interest. After a few thoughtful moments, I stated what I'm sure he wanted me to understand for myself: Göbekli Tepe was obviously one of these major vortex points.

Encouraged by my interest, his hopes and ambitions started spilling out of him, and I thought, yet again, how the poor creature must have had no one in his entourage with whom he could share his dreams. Where did Daligastia stand in all this? Wasn't he meant to be the Prince's right-hand guy? Wasn't he the Prince's confidant? It was no secret among us watchers that the relationship between the two Planetary Princes had always been fiery—despite both fully supporting the rebellion. We knew they sometimes spent many centuries at a time incommunicado and avoiding one another. I'd even heard it recently rumored that Daligastia had finally lost confidence in his Prince and might be setting up in opposition.

No matter—Caligastia waved aside my thoughts, and when he continued he appeared to be thinking his concept through as he was relaying it to me.

"This is the first of my nodal structures," he said. We'd risen above the temple complex by this time, and the Prince was pointing to where he was planning an additional building. "This place you see beneath us, this is the location of the primary vortex. It will be from here that I will link with the other nodes and . . ."

I could no longer make out his words in my mind, for my attention had been taken by our speed as we rose up and away from the planet until the curve of the globe filled my vision. When I heard the Prince again, he was saying, ". . . and when I have completed the matrix I will have fourteen functioning structures at major vortex points in the grid, each one in a different part of my world. You will see, watcher, it is in the precise location of those fourteen vortices that will allow me a controlled and balanced access to the grid. The MA won't even know I have interfaced with it until it's too late! I will have complete control of the ascension process, and there is nothing the MA can do about it!"

Caligastia was glowing with pride, and as we leisurely circled the globe he pointed out some of his nodal points and what he was considering for each of them. His plan for most of these structures, but not all, was pyramidal. A few, like Göbekli Tepe, were evidently going to be circular.

"With my fourteen conduits in place I can finally protect my world from the MA's aggression. It will teach them not to interfere . . . and it will give me the leverage I need to keep my world free of the MA's meddling! If I can control the mortal ascension process, you see, I will never have to lose my human children. I will have them living again and again on my world, serving my divine will.

"I will seal off my world so that no human can ascend to the higher realms and thus leave my bosom. My love is too great for my precious children that I should allow them to fall into the MA's judgmental hands when they pass from this world. I will give my children what they desire most—the chance for another life on Earth."

Now I started to understand the terrible logic of his plan. By overriding the natural ascension process whereby a mortal passes over and moves on to their lifetimes in the higher realms, he would sabotage one of the fundamental reasons for the MA's investment in third-density worlds. The MA has always been dedicated to nurturing the billions of souls who start their eternal Multiverse career on planets such as Earth. It is then the MA's function to guide those souls through the many levels and lifetimes within the Local Universe—to finally launch them on their journey to the Central Universe.

If Caligastia could do this—if he could *really* short-circuit ascension—I realized just how serious this could be. He wasn't just going to deprive mortals of their rightful due as spiritual beings to ascend—he was going to turn people, lifetime after lifetime, into his servants and slaves. I had a moment of utter horror. My heart dropped at the thought that this was what our great revolution for personal liberty was coming to, and I quickly tried to choke this back before the Prince picked up my doubts.

I needn't have been concerned. It seemed the Prince was too consumed with his horrifying plans to have noticed my reaction.

"With the true isolation of my world," he continued, "I will finally fulfill the promise of complete independence that was pledged to the Planetary Princes, and which my Sovereigns—Lucifer and Satan—have been notably unable to deliver."

I couldn't fail to notice the petulance along with the pride in Caligastia's tone, and it came to me that in his grandiose delusions he wanted to outshine and humiliate Lucifer and Satan, his direct superiors. He further confirmed this in his next statement, which I heard almost as if he was mulling it through for himself. It made me additionally nervous.

This is what I heard him think: "And when I have finished the grid modification—when I have the cycles of mortal reincarnation running smoothly here on Earth—then surely the other Princes will want to emulate me; they will see the great good I am doing, and they will have to acknowledge my genius . . ."

I had to strain to listen to his next statement, because I don't think he really meant for me to tune in to his further thoughts. Regardless, caught like a politician unaware of an open mike nearby, I overheard him thinking much along the following lines.

"The princes will see the wisdom of my path. They will know for certain I am their leader. That I, Prince Caligastia, *I* am the true leader of our noble revolution. Then . . . and then . . . we will be ready to challenge the Sovereigns for . . ." and his volume dropped away into telepathic white noise. He must have suddenly realized that his contemplation was taking him in a dangerous direction. His tone was much louder when I heard him again—as though he was trying to obscure the direction his seditious thinking had been taking him.

"But most importantly," he was almost shouting in my mind, "it will give me complete control of my midwayers. They will be forever indebted to me for the gifts I will bestow on them. They will know never to oppose me again."

We slowed to a halt, both momentarily bewitched by this pearl of a planet turning slowly beneath us. The ice-capped North Pole was a flash of white against the velvet darkness of the void.

The Prince drew himself up to his full impressive height and turned to me with a curious mix of emotions on his face. There was pride of course—that seldom left his presence—yet there was also a sense of hopelessness too, as if this might be his last chance to assert his divinity. I had a quick glimpse of what I believe was his profound insecurity—and his desperate need to be loved and worshipped to the point of adoration. It horrified me to think that he needed his so-called children to keep returning again and again just to boost his wilting pride. Is that what this plotting and planning was about?

Perhaps Prince Caligastia was aware of what his face was betraying, because when next I heard him—and just before we parted ways—his final question revealed his true state of mind and required no answer from me.

Caligastia said, "So now that you have heard my plans, my dear watcher, can you still think so poorly of your Prince?"

And that was that.

As he was disappearing, the last I saw were his eyes—and for a moment I was floating helplessly in a pool of resentment and thwarted ambition, of pride poisoned by self-doubt and shame.

Whatever was I to make of his claims? I didn't know enough about the workings of the grid to say whether the Prince's scheme was possible. I hoped Astar would be drawn in by my curiosity—she is more analytical than I—but no such luck. Perhaps later she might pay me a visit,

I thought—after I'd spent more time observing Caligastia putting his reincarnational plans into action.

The more I thought about the possible consequences of the changes he was plotting to impose on the grid, the more I realized the brilliance of the move—*if* he could actually make it happen. It would ensure his dominance and omnipotence in a way in which he had always dreamed. Mostly it would confirm for him his claim of being the God of this World.

Whether the other rebel Princes would be quite so admiring, I rather doubted. Even if they copied his system—I had already come to think of it as the "Reincarnation Express"—they certainly wouldn't want Caligastia as their leader! And their leader of *what*? Was he really going to attempt to freeze Lucifer and Satan out of their prominent positions in the revolution?

This seemed most unlikely to me, but, if nothing else, the encounter with Prince Caligastia exposed me to some of the rifts I'd heard were starting to appear among the higher echelons of the revolutionary junta. Yet what shocked me most deeply as I pondered what I'd heard was the Prince's proposed betrayal of the most fundamental principle of our revolution.

If I understood what he meant, he was intending to trap mortal souls in an endless cycle of human lifetimes—depriving them of their right to ascension. This would ensure that—while in mortal form—the soul would come to owe its allegiance and its progressive servitude to a false divinity of Caligastia's fabrication.

What's more, knowing how the Prince worked, I had no doubt he was going to promote reincarnation as an accepted belief system among some groups. For other belief systems, he would implant a denial of previous lifetimes, thus ensuring that reincarnation would become a bone of contention between different religions. He never could resist the malicious pleasure he derived from his compulsive need to divide and conquer!

Yet beneath the Prince's maneuvering was the undeniable fact of the imposition of his autocratic will on those for whom he had originally arrived to uplift and free from the dominance of their animal natures.

Now he was planning to ensnare those souls and condition them over lifetimes of subservience to serving his will. He didn't really care what mortals would call him. If he was able to accomplish his plans—whether he would be worshipped as a trinity by some or a singular divinity by others—he was determined to establish himself, once and for all, as the highest god.

This was such a blatant abuse of every principle of personal freedom and self-determination we stood for when we had turned our backs on the MA's rigid theocracy. I couldn't believe he was going to be permitted to get away with it. But then, of course, I realized that Prince Caligastia's free will would also need to be respected, and therefore the MA was not likely to intervene. This was especially true, I thought ruefully, because we had placed such an emphasis on the sanctity of personal liberty.

It was a horrifying prospect for another reason. I wasn't fully cognizant of this at the time, yet the thought of what would become of us watchers must have been playing on my mind. This was betrayed by my immediate and lasting antipathy to Prince Caligastia's plans for his Reincarnation Express. If souls were going to be locked into multiple cycles of mortal lifetimes, would there ever come a time when watchers such as myself would be able to enter mortal incarnation? Would there even be space for us? And if we could squeeze in, would we then always be the renegades—the outsiders? Would Caligastia's reimprinting the grid—should he really succeed in doing it—benefit us watchers? Or might it delay our incarnations? Or worse, could it inhibit altogether any possibility of a future mortal lifetime?

As self-concerned as those questions may have been—and happily they were barely whispers in the back of my mind—they would serve to demonstrate the state of my consciousness at the time. I trust you can tell I was facing this new worry with deep concern.

I'm surprised now to be reminded as I write these words that it was over the course of this interchange with Caligastia that I had my earliest hints of a future incarnation for watchers!

I have previously mentioned rebel angel incarnates a number of times in other contexts over the course of my narrative. Yet I believe this encounter with Caligastia must have been the first time I actually entertained the idea of a mortal incarnation as applied to myself—even if it was no more than a fleeting hope at the time.

In retrospect I find it intriguing that an insight of such personal value—however momentary—might have come to me during Caligastia's bragging of his illicit machinations. Had I given more credence to this insight at the time, I might well have saved myself the doubts that had increasingly been plaguing me. As I look back over this unsettling period of history, my regret is that what is so clear to me now was so opaque to me in those desperate times—when, frankly, I could have used a dose of authentic certainty in the future.

If Prince Caligastia was to succeed in subverting the mortal ascension process, I couldn't imagine what the results might be. Would this act be criminal enough to bring the whole weight of the Multiverse Administration down on the Prince's head? Would the MA really permit such a radical dislocation of the mortal ascension process as it has been practiced on third-density worlds for all time?

Perhaps I should have known better by that point.

8

Condemned to Watch

Collaborating with a Mortal, Gene Frankel's
Sad Story, the Consequences of Suicide,
and Spiritual Technology

It should be apparent by now that I hold a deep affection for Mein Host. Not only have I known him through a number of his previous incarnations, but I have also made sure to remain close to him throughout this current lifetime. My hope was always that we would have the opportunity to work together on deconstructing the history of my half a million years on this world. I was delighted when he agreed to allow me to use his biography—and what I've observed of his life—as a down-to-earth example of what it means to live the life of an incarnate rebel angel.

When we started this work together, what my ward valued most was discovering all the activity going on around him of which he was unaware. These events were impacting his life deeply. This continues to hold true, he tells me. Yet I feel as I write these words that a new emotion—which he describes as "embarrassment"—has entered our relationship. He says that when he agreed to have his story told for the purposes of this work he hadn't realized I would be covering it in quite such detail. He tells me what I already understood—that he wasn't fully aware of his spiritual heritage as an incarnate rebel angel (although he had his suspicions) until I confirmed this for him over the course of this narrative. His embarrassment appears to have been caused by what he describes as my disproportionate focus on him and his exploits, to the detriment of those around him.

"I'm not writing a novel here," I tell him. "I don't need to fill in the backstory of everyone you encounter. In the case of other angelic incarnates who've played their part in your life, if there is a relevant point to be made, I've been sure to share what I know.

"Like it or not," I tell him firmly, "it is *your* story I'm unfolding, and this is no time for false modesty. You appear quite happy when I describe your most serious screw-ups. [True, I learned a lot from them! —T.W.] And yet you become a lot more reticent when I write of your successes."

I am aware, of course, that Mein Host is somewhat shy and retiring by nature. He has never shown any desire to be the center of attention and obviously dislikes it when he finds himself in that position. If it seems odd that such a shy man could throw himself into a confronting activity like donating—with such evident success—I should add that from an early age my ward developed an extremely effective counterphobic strategy. He simply used his will to push through his fears. Indeed, he once willed himself to climb along a crane jib swaying hundreds of feet above the streets of London to rid himself of his fear of heights. This "willed personality switch" had become easier over the years, but each time my ward went donating or had to speak in public, he still had to push through his fears in a process he called "girding his loins."

Now he'll need to gird those loins and face some of the better angels of his nature. I remind him that—at the time I'm about to describe— he was still completely unaware of the role that angels were playing in his life. Consequently, perhaps he can be grateful to them in retrospect for his successes. And lest he starts feeling unduly special, he needs to know there have been three other mortals I have also attended over the course of his lifetime. I have done this with the intention of developing a special relationship with one of them, should Mein Host be unable to work with me as I'd hoped he would during the latter part of his life.

Fortunately, the necessity for this has not occurred. I haven't needed to make any last-minute switches. Yet there was a moment in my ward's thirty-third year when my dream of collaborating with him in this work hung very much in the balance. I will get to this trepidatious moment soon, but the weeks and months that led up to it played their part in bringing matters so sharply to a head.

I mentioned earlier that the only way the community had of generating any substantial revenue was either by selling PROCESS magazines and their newsletters or by whatever could be brought in by donating. It was soon clear to those in a senior position in the New York Chapter that this would never be enough to cover the oversized monthly nut with which they'd been lumbered. New streams of income desperately needed to be found, or they would default on the mortgage. Humiliated, they would be out on the street.

The first opening of the money lock was more symbolic than lucrative. It provided a welcome boost to their wilting spirits, and in their world of signs and portents it served to demonstrate that they were on the right track.

Mein Host was in his office on the third floor of the Chapter when Gene Frankel was ushered in. The man looked to be in his mid-fifties and was obviously in a state of extreme agitation. Unable to sit still, he puffed hard on the cigarettes he chain-smoked throughout the meeting.

Gene Frankel had a broad face with high cheekbones and a weathered, leathery quality to his skin. His eyes were small and intense and perpetually squinting away the smoke rising from the cigarette clutched between his nicotine-stained fingers. His hair was gray and unruly, and it was swept back from a broad forehead in two wings that then inched down over his collar. He was small in build, yet he seemed physically larger because of his manner of thrusting out his chest like a rooster and strutting around the office while speaking. His well-cut suit of a fawn-colored, lightweight fabric—that had once obviously been expensive—was now rumpled and creased with use.

When he spoke, he'd run his hands nervously through his hair, but his voice crackled with the ferocity of a man used to being in command. Yet behind this intensity lay a terrible sadness.

If Mein Host had known more about the underground art scene in the city, he would have been aware of Gene Frankel's reputation as a cutting-edge director of many Off-Broadway theatrical productions.

However, my ward knew nothing of this—but he clearly decided that he liked the man immediately. Gene Frankel was gruff and forceful and a little abrasive in manner, but he was honest and straightforward in his dealings—even if he was quite obviously desperate to close the deal.

And what was the deal? He wanted to create a theater in the Alpha, the cavernous room at the rear of the building that used to be the photographer Bert Stern's studio.

The story as to how Gene Frankel had come to be in my ward's office was a long and sad one. It's too long to ask Mein Host's recording angel to help me reconstruct, so I will briefly précis what I heard that afternoon.

It seemed that for all Gene's theatrical triumphs his career had been fraught with challenges and setbacks—in a profession known for its challenges and setbacks. He'd had some early successes. By the time he won an Obie Award for Best Play in 1961 for his production of Jean Genet's *The Blacks* at St. Marks Playhouse in Greenwich Village, he had already been awarded two Obie Awards for Best Director—for *Volpone* in 1958 and *Machinal* in 1959. Gene was evidently most proud of this production, which he said ran for more than fifteen hundred performances— research shows it was actually fourteen hundred and eight—and earned the cachet of being the longest-running Off-Broadway play of its decade. The production of the play and its unusually long run appears to have been thought significant enough to have been identified in Wikipedia as "a crucial production in promoting African American theater during the civil-rights movement."

He had directed some of the great actors of the day: Stacy Keach, Viveca Lindfors, Eli Wallach, Cicely Tyson, James Earl Jones, and Godfrey Cambridge, among others—but he explained to my ward that he most enjoyed directing African American plays and actors.

The most recent disaster of Gene's life had occurred only a week earlier. The Mercer Art Center, with its complex of small theaters in a residential hotel in downtown Manhattan, had represented his dream—the very summit of his career thus far. This was a situation over which he could exert total control.

And yet a week earlier, he said, he had been rehearsing some actors in one of the theaters, when the entire roof had collapsed on them. A few people had been killed, but Gene and the other actors had been able to get out relatively unscathed. Now he had no theater and a vitally important production—almost everything with Gene Frankel was vitally important—that was currently well under way and which badly needed a home.

It's much to Gene Frankel's credit that he never once mentioned the part he'd played in rescuing those actors from the collapsing building. My ward only learned of this much later in his life.

Apparently Gene noticed the ceiling and walls starting to buckle just in time to lead the actors out of danger. For his quick action he was deemed to be heroic.

If my ward had known of this act of courage as he sat in his office that sweltering August afternoon with Gene Frankel—talking and strutting and squinting through a veil of smoke—he wouldn't have been altogether surprised. As he told the others in that evening's meeting, Gene was "an extraordinarily fierce, forceful, and determined man, with something of Attila the Hun about him."

Once again—as has happened before to Mein Host in similar situations—neither he nor Gene had any conscious awareness that both of them were incarnate rebel angels. Yet they clearly recognized one another in a way that neither of them would have been able to explain at the time. After Gene's death in 2005, I've no doubt he now has a far more developed understanding of his spiritual nature.

Over the years, Gene would produce and direct shows in a theater that his construction people would miraculously build in a matter of days, yet in every negotiation he and my ward would bargain and haggle over every detail as if the whole enterprise was depending on it. It was in both of their natures to fight for every tiny advantage. However, they invariably emerged from their forays liking and respecting each other all the more.

They both were well aware that such a ferocious negotiation was expected of them; it was also clear that is what they expected of themselves. Besides, each in his own way was desperate—Gene because he had a production in the works but no theater; my ward because this was an opportunity to wrestle some meaningful additional income from the very best rental agreement he could extract from the deal.

It turned out that that it was Gene Frankel who blinked first. He ended up signing a contract that may have served his immediate needs but was financially much to the benefit of the Process. Not only was Gene's rent a significant sum to add to their monthly cash requirement, but the Process got well-built bleachers on three sides of the central stage as well as a full set of professional theatrical lighting for their Celebrations and Midnight Meditations—all on Gene's tab.

The construction of the theater having been completed in record time, Gene's first production was a great success. The play brought a lot of new people into the Cavern to eat and drink before and after the performances, some of whom even stayed for the courses and classes the Process was starting to conduct.

All in all, the arrangement with the Gene Frankel Theater was considered workable and to the advantage of both parties. As such, it was considered something of a coup that my ward had been able to make it happen. Not only did it bring money and people in, but having the Gene Frankel Theater in the headquarters of the Process Church was also prestigious in a way that was always important to Mary Ann in particular. She never met Gene—and I very much doubt if she ever would have heard of him or approved of his choice of plays if she had—but it was enough that he was a famous director.

I never actually witnessed this happening, but from her past performances it wouldn't surprise me if Mary Ann hadn't used Mein Host's success, modest though it was, to beat up on those members of the Four who'd already tried and failed to bring the Chapter's income up in any real way. I imagine it would have been hopeless for any of them to protest that it could have been any one of their offices Frankel walked into that afternoon. Father Micah had just been lucky. Any of them could have negotiated a contract, probably a better one too . . .

I doubt if anyone tried to complain. Those close to Mary Ann would know better than to express their resentment and envy of another Processean in such a barefaced manner—unless, of course, it was Mary Ann herself who was unloading on that person.

I was aware—in a way that Mein Host was not—that though the envy and resentment directed at him by those close to Mary Ann was unlikely to have been voiced in front of the Omega, it did not mean that those negative emotions were going to go away. For my ward, this whole state of affairs was only going to get more difficult as additional innovations of his proved to be successful.

Note: An event just occurred as I was reading through and revising what was written about Gene Frankel yesterday and—as has occurred previously with Donyale Luna, for example—in popped Gene, drawn by the energy and needing to say a few words. He wanted Mein Host to know he was extremely sorry for blaming him for driving such hard bargains that he, Gene, had convinced himself led to the demise of his theater. He said he was particularly apologetic about trying so baldly to manipulate my ward's emotions, for trying to make him feel ashamed for taking advantage of him when he was in a desperate situation.

Gene said he now knows it was wrong and irresponsible of him to blame Father Micah. He said he never stopped liking and respecting him, but as time went on he said he just couldn't stop himself from holding Micah responsible for making it impossible to succeed.

He said he understands now that Micah had pressures on him to strike the best deal he could. He said he had never known the real financial situation of the Process—he'd bought the hype and believed them to be fabulously wealthy. This had just made it worse, he said—and more unfair—and it confirmed his opinion that all churches were the same. They gouged the last penny out of their flocks.

He wanted Mein Host to know that he no longer held these negative emotions and that he was sorry for any distress he may have caused by projecting his own psychic pain onto my ward. He asked me to include this brief interaction in my narrative—both for Father Micah's illumination and for the benefit of others who may have found themselves in my ward's position.

After several moments of standing quietly beside me, two spirits arrived, and Gene moved off between them feeling, I could see, much lighter than when he'd initially introduced himself.

It was true that the later mood between the two parties wasn't as buoyant as it had been in those first few months. With the passing of the years, as the Gene Frankel Theater and the Process Church both started to flounder—each for their own reasons—the relationship became more strained. It was then that Gene began unraveling—although my ward tells me that Gene's attitudes toward him never really rose to the level of bothering him. Gene's blaming him was such a transparently obvious projection, and his manipulative attempt to make my ward feel guilty was so silly and misplaced that my ward says it was more endearing than irritating.

Regardless of how Gene felt, throughout the turbulence of the following years Gene insisted in dealing only with Mein Host. It required all of my ward's patience and ingenuity to maintain as balanced a relationship as possible throughout Gene's ranting tantrums, his shameless pleadings, and his laughable attempts at making my ward feel guilty.

Whether or not anyone else in the community could have managed to deal with this volatile man—a man accustomed to being the toughest, cleverest, and the most commanding person in the room—with quite the same panache was totally irrelevant. Apart from the fact that Gene refused to work with anyone else, as they came to know each other better Gene started to display some of the psychological acuity that made him such a fine director. Although he had become extremely fond of Mein Host, he could get very caustic and bitterly critical of those Processeans who had treated him in an offhand way—or the few who were openly contemptuous of his plays taking place in *their* sacred space.

Gene Frankel was a passionate and thoughtful man, but he was not a religious one. His sarcastic complaints about the Processeans who resented him—and the presence of his theater in the building—touched on an internal conflict within the community. This had been bubbling along largely hidden, but occasionally showing its head—and biding its time.

However, for now, with the theater operating at full capacity and Gene happy and relieved to have pulled off the impossible, the griping of the purist faction at Gene's profane productions faded in light of the income produced by his presence.

It was thus with a renewed confidence—and Mary Ann's blessing—that Mein Host was now able to pursue the task of radically increasing the Chapter's income.

Let me take a break for a moment, as it amuses me to report—with my ward's permission—on a small incident that occurred only a few minutes ago in real time.

My ward had gotten up from the keyboard to go to the kitchen to get himself a packet of cigarette papers to find only one left. Now, I've spoken of my ward as an ingenious man, and in certain ways he is. He likes to surprise himself. If he buys rolling papers, for example, he'll buy four or five packets at a time and secret one of those packets in a different place in case he runs out. In this case he then has a rush of pleasure and surprise at remembering his one emergency packet. He does this with other things too—simply for the pleasure of his own forethought—so I've no wish to paint him as only preoccupied with the half a dozen or so smokes he rolls for himself while he's working.

So far, so good.

Yet a spiritual lesson is always waiting to be learned, and pride can poke its head up in the most modest of situations. In this case I was able to help him, because we maintain such close contact while we are writing, and I hadn't left his mind when he went to the kitchen.

So what was it in his mind when he went to check that his emergency pack was safely in place? He was congratulating himself on his cleverness, of course! This immediately brought up another thought, one that had persisted in puzzling him ever since he was first accused as a child of being "too clever by half." His child mind rationalized that this must mean that he was one and a half times as clever as other people. It soon became more of a private joke when he was disabused of this notion, but the phrase itself had remained as puzzling as ever.

Whatever *did it* really mean, *"too clever by half"*? Of course he had no problem understanding the meaning his elderly critic intended. If I'm now reading his nine year-old mind correctly, his final position was that the phrase *"too clever by half"* must apply to those people who could figure out that it was really an unintended compliment.

It was when he looked at where he'd put the rolling papers that he found—to his surprise—that there was no packet. He swore he'd hidden one away in this very spot the last time he'd bought a batch. Bless me if he hadn't forgotten the last time around to single out and hide away his emergency packet.

It was when he straightened up with a look of bemused shame—at the arrogance of his presumption of cleverness—and broke into laughter that I was able to give him his answer after all these years.

I told him, "Being too clever by half, my dear one, is to be clever enough to *think* of a clever idea, but not always clever enough to *fulfill* it."

My ward giggled all the way back to the computer.

* * *

I remained looking down at the lazily spinning planet long after Prince Caligastia had disappeared. I found that I'd been made extremely nervous by what I had heard of his plans to redirect the grid so as to enslave human souls in an endless cycle of third-density lifetimes.

I am not proud to admit that my compassion for those poor, trapped souls paled beside my concern for myself. It was going to make life even more unpleasant for humans, of course, but my fear for myself was more elusive and worrying. It was hard to pin down at that time. It was only later that I realized I must have been emotionally reacting to what I was not yet able to understand with my mind. I wondered whether I was becoming more familiar with some of the emotional ambiguity of a human being's life.

To be frank, I wished Prince Caligastia had not shared his wretched plot with me—curious though I may have been. It really was not a scheme I needed to know about, thank you very much! It was still hard to believe that the Prince would have buttonholed me—I love the words I find in my collaborator's vocabulary!—if he hadn't had some nefarious and hidden purpose. I'm not, in *my* opinion anyway, one of the Prince's most loyal watchers.

The more I mulled this over, the more unreasonable it seemed to me that—if his meddling with the grid was as radical as he'd claimed—he would not have discussed it with those close to him. Perhaps they would have tried to talk him out of it! Could it really be that he didn't have anyone in whom to confide? Or was the Prince setting me up for some future personal disaster? I wouldn't put it past him. Or perhaps he was just making a fool out of me, a simpleton—a mere watcher—who would believe any silly old story?

I was not a complicated being at the time, certainly not as complicated as I am now—or will be when I enter mortal incarnation (if that is my destiny). I used to become numb when I was faced with such imponderable puzzles. The issue that was troubling me would then fade away. This is, in fact, what eventually occurred in the case of this particular dilemma presented to me by the Prince. It was helped along by the beauty that I watched unfold beneath me as I floated motionless, high above the slowly turning planet.

It was through half-closed eyes that I could begin to discern subtle energy flowing through the global grid in great sinusoidal waves. It was lovely to watch. As my eyes adjusted, Mother Earth appeared wrapped in a constantly flowing, rippling, wriggling, open-weave tapestry of snaking waves darting and shivering with the nervous electrical energy of the northern lights. The primary meridians ran parallel to the equator. Other meridians streamed at right angles north and south, yet energy would leap—often in sheets—at different angles from meridian to meridian in a seemingly arbitrary fashion. Then, as I watched, the beautiful shimmering vision of the natural grid started to grow dim before my eyes and faded out completely.

It was such an unusual sight that I knew I must have been afforded the privilege of this vision of the global grid for a reason—although I had no idea what that could be.

It had been a long time since I last viewed the planet from this distant perspective. Mother Earth in her third-density glory—her gleaming oceans and ice caps, the smudged dun and green of her landmasses peeking from behind a fleece of white clouds—all possessed a diaphanous translucency I'd never had the chance to witness before. I would never again be able see Mother Earth as merely a solid chunk of dulled matter, having now seen her dressed in a coat of many colors—even if only for just those few glorious moments.

Mixed with that knowledge was a nagging feeling of impending doom should Prince Caligastia ever manage to turn the grid to his own purposes.

Gloriously beautiful though the planet may have been, I couldn't stay up there forever. Earth always calls me back to her. Even when I travel to Zandana—or one of the other worlds I've been permitted to visit—I feel a small part of me is left there, and it always tugs me back. I think of it as "spiritual gravity"—a force that positions and holds spiritual beings in our rightful places—just as gravity holds the planets in their orbiting journey around their suns.

The thought of Zandana reminded me that I had been promising myself a visit there ever since the first of the serious Atlantean disasters in the thirteenth millennium. I'd even set out for the Seraphic Transport Center (STC) on the West Coast of the North American continent—only to become distracted before I had even reached it. Spiritual gravity drew me down to South America. In that case it was to observe what had become of the descendants of the Lemurian diaspora subsequent to their having settled on the high plains of the Andes.

After that, my proposed visit to Zandana seemed to have faded from my mind.

As a watcher, my function is to observe. I watch. That's what I do. That's how I'm created. Even if I have inadvertently overstepped my function a few times—luckily for me, so far only on Zandana!—I am, if you like, *condemned* to watch. It's hard to draw an analogue because of the different ways in which the senses operate, but perhaps if you had no choice but to listen with complete concentration to everything you hear—day after day, without any way of turning it off—this will convey my experience.

I say I feel "condemned to watch" because the downside is that everything I observe tends to become uniformly interesting. If I describe this sensation in terms of my ward's experience, it's as if I observe everything I see at a similar level of focused involvement that I find in him when he is drawing or writing; in other words, when he loses himself doing what he loves to do. The difference between the two experiences is that my ward can turn off his concentration and go about his day while I have no choice but to watch with the full essence of my being.

This may sound all very well, and I certainly wouldn't deny the deep satisfaction that observing the activities of angels, mortals, and midwayers has brought me. Yet when everything I observe is so uniformly engaging there can come a certain flatness of response—an ennui that can set in to a watcher's consciousness—which a human being might feel, for instance, in an art gallery featuring only the world's masterpieces.

These were the kind of thoughts that were in my mind as I descended and returned once again to the temple complex at Göbekli Tepe. After hearing of the Prince's plans, I wanted to see for myself whether I could discern the energy nexus he'd told me about. I hadn't noticed any such confluence of energy when I was in Göbekli Tepe earlier, and there was always a possibility that Caligastia may have been deluding himself—or me for that matter.

Moving slowly around from temple to temple I felt nothing out of the ordinary. I even meditated in one of the larger open spaces hoping to reproduce my state of mind at the time I had my glimpse of the overall planetary grid, yet still nothing. Try as I might, I could neither perceive nor feel any of those beautiful streaming energies I'd seen so briefly from afar.

As you might imagine, this resolved nothing.

Watchers are not all-seeing. Our senses are primarily tuned to our frequency domain in the fifth dimension, just as a human being's sensorium is correlated, in the main, to the frequencies found within the third dimension. As I have noted previously, the finer frequencies interpenetrate the grosser ones in a manner that allows me to observe mortal life without being detected. Yet because I normally observe from the higher astral realms of the third dimension, there is a lot happening on an energetic level within the frequencies of the third dimension of which I'm not aware.

So I'd learned little of value. I had merely succeeded in becoming all the more anxious when it occurred to me that Caligastia was quite capable of implanting the brief vision I had of the global grid as a posthypnotic suggestion. I have already remarked on how unusually pleasant he was when I encountered him this time. I wondered if I'd let my telepathic guard down without realizing it. The Prince was notoriously tricky to deal with—especially when he was playing extra nice.

He was certainly right about one thing. There was absolutely no one I could turn to for advice. Nor could I tell anybody what he had shown me. And if I could, what could I say when I wasn't even sure what I had seen myself? I had no way of knowing whether the Prince's plans for his Reincarnation Express were merely impotent dreams, an early indication of a cunning disinformation strategy, or a real and terrible prospect for all human beings born after Caligastia had successfully reimprinted the grid.

These thoughts and more were whirling around in my mind—my somewhat simple mind—when I finally left Göbekli Tepe. There seemed to be no possibility of an immediate resolution, and I felt I needed a major change of scenery to clear my head.

It was then that my thoughts turned naturally back to the planet of Zandana again, and the peace and sanity I had once found beneath the tree in a forest grove on that amiable world. I recalled how deeply disturbed I had been at that time—it was immediately before Caligastia's North African atomic war had broken out—because I was just starting to grow more troubled by the Prince's actions. I remembered how caringly that tree had drawn off my troubles—down into its roots—and how warm and nurtured I had felt afterward.

So, in a sense, the decision to go to Zandana again made itself.

Looking back, I fear I'm more suspicious now of the ease with which this decision was made. I was a little too willing; a bit too anxious. Or perhaps I convinced myself I was simply emotionally and mentally exhausted at having to constantly worry over what to make of Prince Caligastia's idiosyncratic behavior and how it might concern me—immediately, or at some point in the future.

Now I am more inclined to believe it was the demon of cowardice that has beset me from time to time. A little trouble and I go scuttling away. Naturally, in the moment, I always believed I had reasonable justifications—which I then used as rationale to convince myself of the rightness of my actions.

Yet there is no getting away from the truth. I believe it was moral cowardice and a betrayal of everything we had hoped for in our rebellion. I know now what I didn't then: that in all those many millennia since the uprising, it would have been far more advisable never to have left Earth on my interplanetary jaunts. I'd thrown myself behind the rebel cause for Lucifer's sake, and yet here I was, saddled with a Planetary Prince whose actions were becoming increasingly brutal and self-serving.

I must apologize to my patient reader if I sound like I'm whining or harping on about Prince Caligastia's injustices. However, it is important for me to recognize the dynamics of those times when I may have exercised my right to speak truth to a power. I think that was my true cowardice. Even if my truth had made no difference whatsoever to Caligastia's decisions—it wouldn't have—I am now sure speaking out was the correct action I should have taken.

One of the kinder comments made about the rebel angels in the MA's record of the events concerning the Lucifer Rebellion was a claim that we lesser angels were too much in thrall of our superiors, that we couldn't accept that such brilliant angels might be misleading us. Possibly there was an element of truth in that. However, it strikes me now in retrospect that our weakness was less that we were dazzled by the brilliance of our superiors, but rather that we lacked the moral courage to challenge them. Furthermore, having made that crucial misjudgment at the very beginning of our revolution—whether or not any of us would have been actually capable of speaking out—resulted, at least in my case, in setting a perpetually awkward stamp on my relationship with the Prince.

This insight also helps me to understand why Prince Caligastia was constantly trying to assert his authority over me. And why, more importantly, I'd found it so hard to tell him my truth when I was sure beforehand that he wouldn't appreciate hearing it.

All of this is much clearer to me now, which I attribute to my growing sense of personal independence and confidence. In turn, I also give due credit to this narrative and the closeness I feel to my collaborator for much of my new sense of self and for what it means to take responsibility for my beliefs and actions.

It also confirms for me that it is only in confronting my shortcomings in this fashion that I can contribute my part to the spiritual recalibration of the planet that is currently under way.

* * *

It wasn't long after the masters and priests of the Process Church moved into their house at 242 East 49th Street that they found out where their celebrity whoring had gotten them. The owners of the houses on either side of them turned out to be wealthy, world-famous film stars. It was an irony that went unappreciated at the time, but I have heard my ward since refer to it as being akin to the inadvisability of "pissing on one's own doorstep."

The buildings on the south side of that block of 49th Street had been built originally as a terrace of uniformly similar townhouses of a somewhat modest appearance. They were painted in various different earth tones. Each house had been painted—and repainted over the years—to presumably try to match its neighbor's shades of brown, and each had failed in its own way.

There were many other streets like this one in the city, and in most cases the townhouses—once built for Victorian families—had long since been broken up into separate apartments. Not so on the south side of this particular block of 49th Street. There was no multiplicity of doorbells—or little ladders of name tags that climbed up beside the front doors. There was just one simple bell or knocker on each door. It was the only way of telling from the outside that all was not as it seemed on the inside. Here the rich had discovered the advantageous anonymity of ostentatious modesty. A quick look inside any of those houses would prove the truth of this.

New York City has always been like that. I'm told it's one of the reasons so many celebrities choose to live there. They discovered that the actor Anthony Quinn lived next door to them at 240 East 49th Street, although they seldom saw him coming and going. On the other side—at 244 East 49th Street—lived Katharine Hepburn, whom my ward in particular came to know during that autumn of 1973.

They had first met when each was raking up the leaves in their neighboring gardens, exchanging pleasantries over the garden wall. My ward had not known that Ms. Hepburn was living next door until then. However, she was close friends with Ruth Gordon and Garson Kanin, the owners of the house that the Process was renting. She had evidently heard about the Process community from them.

It was fortunate that my ward had had such extensive experience in courting celebrities. In this, he was able to return her greeting without betraying that he was aware of who she was. He had clearly learned a valuable lesson from his long conversation with Robert Mitchum some years earlier at Hugh Hefner's Chicago Playboy mansion. On that occasion he hadn't known to whom he was speaking. What he did know was that most celebrities, especially ones with world-famous faces, really enjoy the rare novelty of being treated like a normal person.

It must be that there is a point in the arc of fame when celebrities no longer feel the need to introduce themselves. If the person with whom they are speaking has an obvious English accent, is an admirable listener, and is considerably younger than they are, the celebrity would sometimes take advantage of her or his presumed anonymity to speak unusually honestly.

In Robert Mitchum's case, the actor chose to use his assumption of anonymity to talk remarkably openly about his pot-smoking troubles with the law. In Ms. Hepburn's case—although she claimed to be an atheist—she obviously appreciated an animated discussion about God, the Universe, and Everything; from a safe distance behind the garden wall, of course.

Mein Host would later say that it was an odd friendship, if it could be called that. It was perhaps more of a series of interlinked encounters. She was a brittle woman of hard angles and chiseled surfaces, with a flat voice that was all head and no heart. Her intelligence too was sharp and hard, as well as being emotionally detached in the manner of people who are repressing their psychic pain.

It so happened that Katharine Hepburn's personality was remarkably similar to that of my ward's mother. Diana was another independent, ambitious, and emotionally repressed woman of a similar age and world-view. My ward commented later that this sense of familiarity did a lot to smooth the way when the famous actress started reaching out to him.

In her midsixties at the time—and clearly still weighed down by the death of her lover Spencer Tracy six years earlier—the actress was torn between desperately wanting to believe in the afterlife and her rational-ist denial of life after death. There was nothing much my ward could say to this for—from what I could gather—he didn't give much credence to the afterlife either. He told her how his experiences with LSD-25 and mescaline had shown him that reality was not what it appeared to be on the surface—which had made her curious. He had added, however, that he couldn't be sure if that meant there *was* an afterlife.

She was obviously a thoughtful woman, although her brusque, self-assertive manner pretended a certainty that any glimpse of her emotional body would prove demonstrably untrue. She did appear to soften somewhat over the course of their little talks, but her wounds were too deep and her social persona too polished to let my ward in very far. She had achieved a level of fame awarded to very few people, and she protected her privacy with a ferocity that had permitted almost no one to get anywhere near her. These over-the-wall encounters which appeared to happen by chance—with a young Englishman who seemed not to know who she was—became atypical events in her life.

I don't believe my ward was aware of what was really going on an emotional level with the actress at the time (He wasn't! —T.W.). I could perceive, for example, that she felt she was able to shed something of her hard persona and reveal a little of the tremulous and insecure young girl who'd never had the opportunity to mature in any real way. I could see she had received a terrible shock when she was very young from which she'd never recovered. Clearly it was serious enough to have made her resolve never to let herself become overwhelmed by her emotions. I'd no doubt it was her facility in controlling her emotions that had enabled her to become a great actress. Yet it also created a hard carapace around her which—at the age of sixty-six—she was just starting to recognize as being counterproductive.

It was only when my collaborator was researching Ms. Hepburn's life for this book that he discovered that when she was fourteen she had come across her older brother—whom she was described as "adoring"— hanging dead from a beam.

Then, my ward says, things started coming together. No wonder there was such a similarity between Diana and the actress. My ward's mother had lost her father to suicide as a young girl of almost exactly the same age, and—like Katharine Hepburn—had used the shocking event to become a strong and independent woman.

However, there was an unanticipated downside to this for both women. They couldn't help falling in love with emotionally unavailable men—men who were too egocentric or too needy to threaten the emotional vulnerability of the women. Katharine Hepburn and my ward's mother had each married only once when young, divorced within a few years, and preferred to live on their own for the rest of their lives. They'd had a number of lovers, yet only one man had ever managed to penetrate their soft centers. Both women had been so profoundly hurt at a tender age that their unresolved psychic pain had irrevocably shaped them. One of the offshoots of this was that they both had put their careers before their personal lives.

To make matters worse, in both cases their families denied the reality of the suicides—never speaking about it in Diana's case, and pretending it was an experiment gone wrong in the suicide of Ms. Hepburn's brother. Neither young girl would have had any real opportunity to process and release her grief, and would carry the unresolved pain for the rest of their lives. Yet each in her own way turned out to be a determined and strong woman who carved out a successful career from repressed pain; in so doing, acting perhaps more like a man in a man's world. And both would sincerely claim as old women that their lives had been happy ones.

Although my ward would be the first to shrug off any possible beneficial influence he might have had on the actress as a result of their talks, it was no coincidence that Katharine Hepburn used a two-hour TV interview with Dick Cavett in October of that year to present a more personal side of herself.

To say that life in the house at 242 East 49th Street was not entirely free of stress would be an understatement.

It was a beautiful house inside, no doubt about that, even if a little old-fashioned. The seven current occupants were now working such long hours at the First Avenue Chapter that they were spending less and less time at the house—just returning to grab a few hours' sleep before starting all over again the next day.

Adding to the tension in the house was the constant need for vigilance, given that seven large rambunctious German Shepherds—generally well-trained though there were—were quite capable of erupting in a moment of fury at some perceived slight from another dog. Even when the dogs were happy, wagging tails could easily send

Plate 1. *Convolutions of Time*. Collaborative prismacolor pencil drawing by Timothy Wyllie and June Atkin. An Australian Aboriginal insight claims that time moves in two directions simultaneously—from past to future, and future to past—with perceived reality at their intersection.

Plate 2. *Galactic Grid*. The apparent disorder in the physical world so evident in lower dimensions resolves into the ordered patterns of the higher dimensions.

Plate 3. *A Welcome Sight.* There will come a time, most likely when we least
expect it, when we will open our hearts and minds and find ourselves
welcomed back into the galactic community.

Plate 4. *Tulpu Emergent.* A form emerges: Can a beneficent thoughtform, a tulpu, be created by focused visual intention?

Plate 5. *Planetary Mitosis II*. Has the global shift already started?
Could the recent emergence of the mysterious
Mandela Effect be a precursor of the shift?
Is this the way of the future?

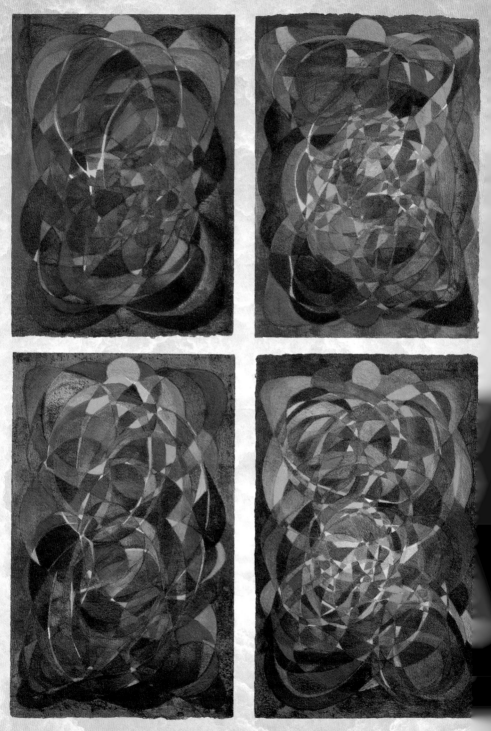

Plate 6. *Angelic Quatrain*. Deep in the dark mysteries of the fifth dimension, light momentarily coalesces into form before dissolving back into the darkness.

Plate 7. *Cosmic Transparency*. Angels have observed that the workings of
the Multiverse are sufficiently simple and straightforward and that they can
be understood by an intelligent twelve-year-old.

Plate 8. *The Progenitor's Song.* Collaborative prismacolor pencil drawing by Timothy Wyllie and June Atkin. The transcendent music of Creation spreads through the Multiverse like the expanding ripples of a rock dropped on the placid surface of a lake, animating dormant matter.

elegant end tables laden with Ruth Gordon's tchotchkes flying—until lessons were learned and the trinkets were hidden away.

One night, after another exhausting day, Mein Host had hurried back to the house and flopped into bed. He was in his little room at the top of the house, in his bed—a box spring and a mattress on the floor—and his dog, Ishmael, asleep beside him.

When the explosion occurred it was almost comical to watch both man and dog simultaneously thrown off the bed, both looking equally bewildered as they lay on the floor in a tangle of sheets. It was an extraordinarily loud explosion. The blast had shaken the house so violently it pitched the two sleeping mammals right off the mattress.

It must have taken man and dog a few moments to realize that they were still alive and that the house hadn't collapsed around them. It shouldn't be surprising that it was Ishmael who was able to pull himself together first, but then only to squeeze himself as far as he could into a corner of the room where he crouched, wild-eyed and panting. Throwing on his clothes, my ward—followed by an excited hound now over his funk—ran out into the street, expecting the worst. The explosion had been so violent and so loud, my ward said afterward, that he thought half of New York had blown up.

Nothing. Everything normal. Could it have been a dream?

Ishmael was pulling to the right, so my ward went with the flow and they ran together down East 49th Street to the corner of Second Avenue. Looking right he saw thick black smoke billowing from a large building on the east side of the avenue, a block south between 47th and 48th Streets.

It was three or four in the morning, but—in the city that reputedly never sleeps—the avenue was still busy and a small crowd was rapidly converging on the sidewalk opposite the crumbling building. Getting closer, my ward could see that the facade at the top of the building had blown away, and smoke and flames were pouring out.

The fire brigade hadn't yet arrived, and the little crowd was buzzing with that strange excitement mortals appear to feel in the face of a disaster that doesn't directly affect them. People who would never talk to each other under more normal Manhattan circumstances were chattering away, pointing and laughing nervously, comparing this disaster with other disasters they had witnessed in their lives. Mein Host, not to be left out of this opportunity for some gruesome gratuitous schadenfreude, turned to the man standing next to him to wonder aloud if anyone had been hurt in the explosion.

Kurt Vonnegut, in his bathrobe and slippers, had been staring up at the flames with a curious expression on his face; a mixture of sadness, horror, and a hint of a smile. He had obviously leaped out of bed—if he hadn't been thrown out of it like Ishmael and my ward—and he looked as unkempt and ill-dressed as a homeless man.

My ward told the others afterward that he reckoned Kurt Vonnegut must have gotten pitched back in his memory to the horrors of Dresden, just like his hero—what's-his-name—in the novel.

"*Slaughterhouse-Five!*" one of them said. "Billy Pilgrim. He was the guy kidnapped and put in a zoo on Tralfamadore, remember? With that girl? The film star . . . whatever's her name. Weren't they were both naked? All those Tralfamadorians crowding 'round the cage watching 'em at it!"

Everyone sitting around the kitchen table as Mein Host later recounted the day's big event must have read the book, because they laughed at the memory.

"He didn't have much to say," my ward was telling the others while he poured himself some coffee and lit a cigarette. "He kinda mumbled a few words I didn't catch . . . He was only half-awake—he sure looked pretty bewildered. He was one street closer to the explosion than we were, so God knows what it must have sounded like to him!

"No, he didn't stay that long," Mein Host added. "He left before me, shuffling off in his fuzzy bedroom slippers. We didn't really talk much. He was out the window; there was no point. When you mentioned Billy Pilgrim and the Tralfamadorians," he nodded to Juliette, "it made me laugh. Know what Kurt Vonnegut said to me? Just as he was leaving, he turned and looked right into my eyes with that strange half-smile . . . know what he said?" Mein Host was clearly spinning this out for effect.

"Vonnegut said, 'So it goes!'"

9

Generalists' Ascent

Purists versus Generalists, First Psychic Fair,
Ambivalent Undercurrents, Boring God, and
the Challenge of Psychism

There came a time in the New York spring when there were no more leaves to be swept up and no more conversations to be held. Ms. Hepburn retreated back into the privacy of her home, not to be seen again. And by that point, my ward had other far more pressing matters on his mind.

His success at securing such a favorable agreement with Gene Frankel had allowed him some additional credibility when it came to ideas for making money. There were plenty of wild and unrealistic proposals from different Processeans, but it seemed that my ward was on a roll. His suggestion to use the theater—which was up and running by this time—to mount a series of conferences and lectures that would appeal to the public at least had the advantage of being actually feasible.

While this may sound an obvious solution to their money problems, the point about appealing to the public raised some hackles among some of the senior Processeans of a more purist bent. They didn't believe their job was to "appeal to the public." They expected the public to appeal to them!

There was always an undercurrent of this fundamental difference of opinion within the community that would rise to the surface every once in a while. To put it in the baldest terms: The "purists" insisted the priority must always be the teachings and the dogma of the Process Church, and anything else was thought to be pandering to the public. Those whom my ward would come to call—himself included—"generalists" were the ones who believed in intriguing the public, drawing them in, and introducing them more gradually to the Process teachings.

This schizophrenic undercurrent had surfaced before, but it became more openly expressed as the Process grew more successful in purely worldly terms. This conflict would also ultimately lead to the implosion and collapse of the Process as a mystery school when Mein Host and fifteen of his colleagues broke away from the main group in the winter of 1977.

This internal conflict was not an unusual phenomenon. It must occur to some extent in every small committed group of people with a message they want to share with the world. If this ambivalence is acted out—as it was in the case of the Process Church—the result will often be wild swings of focus.

In the Process, for example, the purists might well first set the appropriately austere scene—preaching and teaching only the obscure dogma of the four "Great Gods of the Universe." However, being *told* to believe in beings such as Jehovah, Lucifer, Satan, and Christ would soon prove unpalatable to all but a very few members of the public. The chapters started floundering, the coffeehouses emptied out, the courses and classes were ignored, and the public stayed away from Saturday Celebrations and the weekend Midnight Meditations in droves. After all, no thoughtful person appreciates being told what they *must* believe.

The generalists would then gain a temporary ascendancy, bringing in audiences for films and lectures on subjects of real interest to the public, though not directly related to the beliefs of the church. The generalists were just as devoted to their gods and dedicated to following the teachings of the Process as the purists, but they offered their teachings as something people *could* believe in—if they so chose—rather than something in which they *must* believe (or risk being "lost"). The chapters would then fill up again with more people coming to the services and meditations and wanting to join the community. At this point, a lot more money—always a key criterion—would be pouring in.

After a time, some crisis invariably arose in which the success of the generalists would be challenged as being profane and irrelevant in the face of the imminent End of the World. And back again would come the purists for a time to frighten the people away with the church's confusing and idiosyncratic cosmology. Soon enough, the emphasis would start swinging back to the generalists, as the need for money provoked their more flexible imaginations to devise ingenious and effective ways of attracting the public—even if to do this they had to push the limits of relevance in the eyes of the purists.

It would then often depend on how financially rewarding the generalists' projects were as to how long they would be permitted to continue before the purists stepped back in to take over. In many ways, it was this wild series of ideological swings over the years that contributed, in part, to the confusion and mystery with which the community's beliefs are still regarded.

However, as that summer of 1973 turned to fall, we found ourselves at the start of what would soon become a gathering wave in the ascendancy of the generalists. The New York Chapter would reshape itself into a thriving spiritual center, widely known for its provocative lecture series, its cutting-edge conferences and seminars, and for what would become the first of its many psychic fairs.

Mein Host is probably too modest to claim it for himself, but the concept of collecting a whole bunch of psychics together for a day in which they could give short introductory readings was his—although he says the idea grew naturally out of the community's interest in the psychic realms.

Psychic fairs came to be much emulated as the New Age movement gathered momentum through the late 1970s and '80s, but the very first one was dreamed up and organized by my ward and held at the First Avenue Chapter. He would have said it was such an obvious solution, since the community always laid such an emphasis on psychic development, and many of the Processeans were themselves proficient psychics. Why, the idea could have come from any of them. One of the workshops they always made sure to run in every chapter was one titled "Telepathy Development."

The psychics working in the first couple of psychic fairs were drawn mainly from the junior IPs; yet, as the news got out, more and more professional psychics and mediums asked to join them. The fairs were an immediate success. The public poured in and seemed to take particular pleasure in juggling three or four short readings with different psychics; perhaps first a tarot card reader, followed by an astrologer, then a throw of coins for an I Ching interpretation, and finally with a Chinese face reading as a chaser. Some people made it their business to get a reading from all twenty-five or thirty readers working at the fair—or as many as time allowed.

The professional psychics loved the fairs, of course. It was ready cash, and if they were good at their craft they could pick up clients for longer, deeper, more profitable sessions at their homes or offices. The general public expressed their enthusiasm by coming in hordes—and when the psychic fairs became regular monthly affairs, each event was filled to capacity.

Within the higher regions of the Process hierarchy, the reaction was more complex. There was no denying the money the fairs brought in—which was split fifty-fifty with the psychics—and no one had seen so many people in the Chapter at any one time. Yet naturally the purists had to argue what this "mumbo jumbo" had to do with the Great Gods of the Universe and the End of the World. And it was true; there was something personally upsetting for many Processeans when they watched these large crowds of people seeking their narcissistic satisfaction in such trivial pursuits as tarot cards or numerology while they showed almost no interest in the more deeply serious teachings of the Process.

It shouldn't be a surprise that the Four—the four senior Processeans in the Omega's inner circle who'd been chosen to administer the growing organization—were of a purist nature. Each had failed in turn to make a success of the New York Chapter with their purist idealism, so they wisely kept their criticisms quiet. Or if they shared their complaints with one of the others, I noticed it was in muted tones—in deference to the income being generated by just these "trivial pursuits."

I found it more interesting to observe Mary Ann during this period. She was obviously thrilled at the money pouring in and enjoyed using it to belittle the efforts of the Four—just to keep them in line. Yet she would also be the first to turn the tables on the generalists when their success started grating on purist nerves. She would then become the purist par excellence.

It seemed to me that for her this was a manipulative power game, a way of keeping her people in play and on edge. To those around her—in her inner circle—she could appear completely unpredictable from time to time. She might support the generalists with passionate enthusiasm for a while, and then, for no obvious reason, she would switch to the purist viewpoint and the emphasis would switch again.

I've commented earlier on this ambivalent dynamic I'd already observed in Mary Ann, although under slightly different circumstances. In this situation, while she obviously relished the money—the Omega's cut, skimmed off the top, was rising rapidly along with the soaring overall income—it seemed that their success could never be allowed to go too far. This happened with the album the Version made in the Toronto recording studio and were just about to take public before Mary Ann pulled the plug on the project.

I knew Mein Host was aware of this. He'd already commented on it to Mother Juliette in one of their off-the-record discussions. At that time they both believed it must be part of the mystery school's teaching. They said they thought it was a *real teaching*—one that could only be learned through direct experience. To be able to maintain the enthusiasm and dedication felt in the most successful of situations as equally as under the most difficult conditions was not a lesson that could ever be taught. This had to be felt to the very bone. Learning to be neither carried away by pride when successful, nor crippled by humiliation when failing, was a lesson that would serve my ward well in future years.

When I previously mentioned this ambivalent dynamic of Mary Ann's, I framed it as a probable consequence of the instructions she might have received from her "handler" in the intelligence services on entering America. Were the Process Church ever to become too successful it might well attract undue attention from the press. Questions would be raised as to how a woman with convictions for prostitution in England had ever been permitted to enter the States—not once, but many times. And, of course, once exposed she would then cease to be of any value to "them."

Mein Host was completely ignorant of this covert aspect of Mary Ann's intentions until I introduced the possibility of her betrayal in the course of this narrative. Although he had heard this theory before and hadn't given it much credence, I know that my suggestion of her likely complicity with MI5 in England—and then presumably the FBI or CIA in America—had introduced another troubling layer to the enigma at the heart of the Process.

I admit I saw no direct evidence of her duplicity, but this would be unlikely anyway because I seldom had a chance to observe her in action unless my ward was present. There were no secret meetings, no drop boxes, no chalk marks on the walls, no slinking about in disguise—so I have based my opinion on what I knew of Mary Ann's personality and her previous life. I have never judged her harshly for this perfidy, as I've no doubt she'd been given a choice she couldn't refuse.

While whatever arrangement she may have had with the intelligence services might have facilitated her movement in and out of the United States, it appeared to have little influence on the day-to-day activities of the group—with this one obvious exception. The Process Church could never be allowed to become too successful or too threatening to the powers that be.

I believe it was remarkably fortuitous for my ward and the others that the demands imposed by this secret agreement of Mary Ann's happened to be so closely aligned with such a rare and hard to obtain spiritual lesson as handling both success and failure with the same equanimity.

It could have been far worse!

* * *

I'd always had a deep love for the planet of Zandana. I have often thought I must love the place more than Earth—although I've always known my real function has been here on my home planet. That's the way I like to think of Earth—as much my home planet as yours, my patient reader—at least for a while. It's just that my "while" can be somewhat longer than yours.

I'm not claiming Zandana hasn't had its problems over the ages—what world hasn't? Both Planetary Princes aligned with the Lucifer Rebellion, yet the approach they had chosen to organize their world subsequent to the uprising was entirely different from the choices made by Prince Caligastia and his minions on Earth. Call me sentimental, but regardless of the widening gap between the development of mortal cultures on these two, third-density worlds, I still think of them as sister planets.

Such were my thoughts after I had taken my place in the generously large waiting lounge at the Seraphic Transport Center. This time there had been no distracting impulses to take me off to South America or China or anywhere else. I had even managed to shrug off the demon of cowardice that had beset me on my previous visits. This time I wasn't running away from anything. Yes of course I was horrified by Caligastia's plans for trapping mortal souls, but—as the Prince had confidently predicted—there wasn't much I could have done about it. That seemed to alleviate any guilt I might have otherwise felt. For the first time in a long while I felt relatively psychically clear.

The lounge was crowded. In one corner I noticed a small group of Melchizedek Brothers in their dark-blue robes who must have been waiting for their transport back, I assumed, to Jerusem. They seemed to me to be exhaling an aura of spiritual nobility that spread around the brothers like a mist, so that while I was watching them huddled in discourse, no one in the lounge dared to approach anywhere close to them.

Transport Seraphs (TS) came and went, and the crowd thinned out accordingly. At one point all the Melchizedek—appearing to respond to a telepathic signal inaudible to the rest of us—got up as one from their chairs and filed out of the lounge toward the escape chambers.

Seeing these exalted brothers set me to thinking about the planetary Seraphic Overgovernment, whom I assumed they had been visiting—and I wondered, not for the first time, where they stood in relation to Prince Caligastia's activities. Did they condone them? Were they unwilling to intervene, or were they unable to? Of course they were aligned with the MA's policies, so what was the part they were playing in what was occurring on the planet? Since the rebellion I had seen almost nothing of the overgovernment—my only contact was when I needed permission for the multiplanet trip I'd been advised to take. But since then, nothing.

I was lost in these thoughts when I sensed a presence close behind me, and there was my friendly Transport Seraph Eleena, waving at me and beckoning me to accompany her to one of the smaller escape chambers. It had been busier than I'd ever seen the transport lounge on my previous travels, and I could see there was an urgency in her gesture. However, when I rose to greet her I found myself unusually moved to see that we evidently knew each other well enough to embrace. Her hair smelled of wildflowers—I remember that. How the scent lingered. It was a fond embrace, but as she drew herself away she smiled and appeared to deliberately wrinkle her delicate nose. It took me aback for a moment before it hit me how much she disliked what she described as the odor given off by the rebel angels . . . then we both burst out laughing.

Apparently I had managed somehow to transform the indelicate odor that had so troubled her previously—or perhaps she'd simply acclimated herself to it. Regardless, Eleena's embrace was strong and sure, and she was evidently at ease enough to joke about it.

The exit chamber was in use when we arrived at the gate, so we sat together and shared a jug of a very decent, fermented fruit juice that I couldn't identify. When I copied Eleena and swirled the juice in my crystal goblet it underwent a pronounced color change—from an indigo-violet to a translucent lavender—and it happened before my eyes.

But it was when I lifted the goblet to drink that I saw the reason Eleena was smiling in happy anticipation. Where the liquid met the inner surface of the crystal there was the distinct glow, a ring of luminescence that, when I took my first sip, gave my lips a pleasurable tingle.

The last time we'd had a serious conversation, Eleena had asked about the mysterious telepathic "voice" we rebel angels had heard, giving us strength and courage to follow our choices at the time of the rebellion. I'd suggested I thought it may have been the Mother Spirit, which Eleena had soundly rejected on the basis that "the Holy Mother Spirit is stainless." That was the phrase I remember her using. We'd hit the block I'd encountered with some others when I'd brought up the business of the Mother Spirit's participation in the rebellion. They were unanimous: It was impossible for her to have played a part in encouraging the rebellion because she was perfect. And then they would want to drop the issue.

As I remembered our previous conversation, we'd just reached that point when we were both called away. Of course, there was always a chance I might have overstepped the mark with Eleena—it was unthinkable that any angel who remained aligned with the MA would question the perfection of the Holy Mother Spirit or the Creator Son. And I mean just that. Most of them were simply unable to think about it. It wasn't even that they couldn't countenance the idea or that the very idea was preposterous. It was that they seemed to block out any possibility of such an inconceivable concept. It came to me then that they might not even have been wired for the thought.

I now think of this mental block as not dissimilar to a man of the sixth millennium BCE who would not be wired to think "telephone" if he chanced to stumble on a small, flat, silvery device that might buzz or even sing at the puzzled paleolith as he fiddled with it. This perspective makes the mental block somewhat more understandable, but at the time it was still a puzzle to me. However, what I'd found interesting about Eleena was that she was a loyalist seraph who had at least been able to take in and absorb the idea for a moment or two before rejecting it as impossible.

Yet here she was again, embracing me and smiling and now sitting quietly next to me, no doubt listening to my thoughts.

She laughed aloud at that, and then I heard her soft voice in my mind. "I know you watchers believe we are incapable of independent thought . . . that we have an automatic, unthinking reaction to any talk of a blemish on the Holy Mother."

I tried to respond that it wasn't quite that, and, besides, I really had found Eleena different—but then I realized she knew that from listening to my earlier thoughts.

She said, "To show you I have been giving the matter some consideration, allow me to repeat to you what you were thinking before we were separated on that last occasion." Eleena continued, "You were going to propose, I believe, that you . . . *had observed enough examples of cruelty and indifference in the natural processes on Earth—of strangler vines and wasps that lay eggs in the paralyzed bodies of small mammals so their hatchlings can eat their way out of living flesh, which surely spoke to cruelty and violence being deeply imprinted into the evolutionary processes of any dog-eat-dog world. And didn't the design of biological systems fall under the general aegis of the Mother Spirit?*"

She had reproduced my thoughts of that day with an admirable precision.

She said, "That was going to be your argument, wasn't it?"

"I realize it's only an inference, Eleena, but it might be a clue. I don't want this to come between us. You know how much I value your openness and friendship. Understand that I'm not proposing the Holy Mother has done anything wrong or bad. I hope you know that. I'm merely suggesting that she might have had an honorable motive for encouraging us to hold firm in our rebellion."

"How can there ever be an *honorable* motive for a rebellion?" she asked somewhat smugly. I don't think she really expected a reply.

"First," I told her, "I never said the Holy Mother actually supported the rebellion. What she said helped give us the courage of our convictions. There is a difference, Eleena."

She looked a trifle impatient but didn't interrupt, so I decided to share more of what I'd been thinking.

"But let's say that in doing this, in giving us the courage to make our individual choices, she was in fact supporting the rebellion. What then? Let's see what might be considered an 'honorable' motive—as we know and agree that the Holy Mother Spirit is free of all blemishes. So what would be a *good* reason for her so-called support of the rebellion?"

Eleena appeared to grow thoughtful. It had clearly never occurred to her that certain actions that might be thought as wrong or bad in the moment might actually be necessary for an eventual resolution—a resolution that would succeed in elevating both sides of the former conflict to a new level of coherence and cooperation.

This time she spoke more slowly. "That thought *is* new to me, Georgia. You are correct in that." Then, more slowly, more thoughtfully, "But if that *is* true then yes, you're right, it would account for some of the anomalies I've seen in my travels."

Now that *was* interesting. A loyalist seraph telling me she had noticed there was something a little strange going on behind the scenes, which was being masked from us. I thought I would take the opportunity to explain what I was starting to believe could be a rational explanation for her anomalies.

"Just think about this for a moment, Eleena. We know the MA runs a pretty tight ship." She smiled at the metaphor, and I realized she hadn't heard it before. I continued, "Not much happens that isn't intended to happen. We know that. And yet here we have the rebellion—and not the first one I might add—and the MA's reaction is to vilify us. They called Lucifer insane, and they ostracized us for following the rebellion, for simply wanting more freedom. I think there's something a bit strange about that, don't you, Eleena?"

She retorted, "You mean all this . . . this . . . this chaos and this hatred is something that was intended to be? How's that possible? That's awful! I don't want to think that, Georgia."

I explained, "You have to think of it more as a grand theatrical piece, with the actors (us) playing our parts. To do that we have to be totally committed to our parts—otherwise we'd learn nothing from it. We *have* to believe it is absolutely real. The good people need to believe they are *absolutely* good, and the villains have to feel *absolutely* justified in their villainy so they can glory in it."

"This is sophistry, Georgia. Pure sophistry. What you're saying is that there is no good and bad, no difference between being kind or being cruel. You know *that* can't be true. That's plain silly."

"That's precisely what I'm *not* saying, Eleena. Of course there are good and bad acts; of course there's a real difference—especially for those concerned. What I am saying is that it's all part of the show—the courage and cowardice, the kindness and cruelty, the love and the fear—everything we do we make happen on the Multiverse stage. We're actors who believe we're acting naturally!"

That got a little laugh from her. She was softening up.

"Listen, dear sister," I said, pursuing my advantage. "Have you heard the phrase 'We are all here to entertain the Most High,' or possibly 'The only crime is in boring God'? I wonder if you have a thought about what these aphorisms actually mean."

I felt I had her attention now, so I took the next cautious step in revealing my thoughts.

"So we've established two truths: one is that everything that happens is intended to happen, and, second, we are all actors in a cosmic drama—though we may be on different sides of a conflict."

Eleena nodded her agreement. So far so good.

"Now, let's switch approaches. We've both agreed that the MA runs a tight ship and that anything as significant as an angelic rebellion couldn't have happened unless it had been intended. We know this intention must exist on a level that we, as actors in the drama, cannot know—or it would spoil the show. Do you see now, Eleena? If we spoiled the show we risk boring God.

"But there's more. What if the angelic rebellion served yet another function—one which is more relevant to the dynamics of the Local Universe? What if the rebellion, Eleena—and the apparently negative polarization it has produced—has actually been serving a higher purpose? If that were so, then wouldn't the Holy Mother Spirit's encouragement of the rebels become one of your *honorable* motives? That wouldn't be a blemish, would it? It'd just be something that happened over our heads; something we didn't understand at the time."

Eleena seemed struck numb by the logic of this. I hoped I hadn't overwhelmed her. As a watcher—a rebel angel "condemned" to watch the outworking of my choices—I can forget how coarsening this experience has become. Seraphs are inherently tender and delicate creatures, which made it that much more intriguing that Eleena had even cracked open the door to what must have sounded to her to be a terrifyingly radical thing to think about.

I wondered later if I should have stopped right there. I could feel that the poor creature was already reeling from the many contradictions I'd introduced, so I knew I needed to back off and lay somewhat low.

I said, "My point about those apparent cruelties I've seen in nature—the ones you repeated so precisely just now—is only that they demonstrate a preparedness for the Life Carriers to embed extremes of polarity so deeply within the evolutionary process."

"So what you're saying," Eleena appeared to have finally marshaled her thoughts, "is that whenever an exaggerated polarity manifests on the third-density world, it will raise the chances of a rebellion?"

I looked at her in admiration. So she *was* made of sterner stuff! At least she could consider the concept without blanking out. As a Transport Seraph she would have come to know a variety of beings serving on hundreds of different worlds. Like the masters of the great caravans that traveled across the landscape of the ancient world connecting far-off places, she would have seen and heard things that must have opened her mind.

"Exactly!" I said. "How could it not? I might even take it one step further. The purpose of polarity must be to ensure subsequent conflict. Do you see? At best, it can produce varying degrees of creative friction—or a competitive dynamic that can accelerate social and technological development. At worst, this polarization has to produce conflict and warfare.

"But I believe the direction this polarization takes—either toward creative ingenuity or toward mutual hostility—is less important than the opportunities both paths open up for creative resolution and reconciliation."

I felt Eleena trying to puzzle this out. I had to remember that she—as a loyalist seraph going about her duties—wouldn't have the need for a developed sense of right or wrong, or good or bad. She simply followed her purpose and fulfilled it as well as she could. This is the way of angels.

As a sister seraph, I was the exception here. I was the one who was facing the choices demanded by such extremes of polarity. How could she ever understand that if she hadn't actually experienced it herself?

"It would exhaust me," she said, looking exhausted at the very thought. "I couldn't do it. But at least I think I now know what you were trying to explain. I don't really understand it, you're right—like I didn't understand why you aligned yourself with Lucifer. But I see what you're getting at."

We sat there quietly together. I was wondering whether it would be a good time to introduce the crux of the concept I was developing—that any good drama requires protagonists committed to their opposing views and beliefs—when Eleena arose, gesturing to the exit chamber that was now available.

Soon I was wrapped once again in Eleena's embrace, only this time it was to be securely enclosed within her heat shield. Next came the pleasant sensation of rapid acceleration, the rising tones of her shield's frictional music of subspace, and a warm, somnolent feeling of well-being spreading through my body.

I was finally on my way to Zandana.

* * *

The New York Chapter was abuzz with activity and excitement. There was suddenly a sense of possibility after the fog of depression that had clouded the previous few months of financial struggle. They really might be able to cover the mortgage.

Among most of the Processeans—a number of whom had performed as psychics at the events—the psychic fairs were unanimously popular.

This was mainly because they brought such a palpable feeling of busy success to the Chapter.

Given that organizing the psychic fairs fell under Mein Host's aegis, it fell to him to take on the task of testing the outside psychics before inviting *them* to participate in the fairs. While to some this might sound the most enviable of assignments—"all those free readings about *me*!"—I didn't observe my ward deriving much pleasure, or information, from those many sessions.

He might have thought of himself as a "sensitive" at the time—had he ever considered himself in those terms—but no, not particularly psychic. For example, he made sure never to do readings at the psychic fairs. He was certainly not cynical about psychism—after all, he'd successfully psychometrized the Italian count's jewelry a few years earlier—but this unusual new function was not quite as straightforward, or as intriguing, as it sounded. Listening to so many different psychics telling him so many different so-called truths about himself sorely tested what he described to Juliette later as his "skeptical neutrality."

"I soon realized I couldn't judge the psychics on their accuracy," he'd gone on to say. "Who's to know about that! Although I *did* turn away an Indian palm reader who told me I was going to die in a few months. I thought that was a bit rich! I didn't want him going around telling little old ladies they were going to fall off their perches at any minute."

Juliette asked the question that must face every psychic from time to time. "Supposing the little old lady really *was* going to fall off her perch in a few days or weeks?"

"Even if it's true," he'd answered, "I don't think he should be saying that. I mean, what good would it do? Would it make *her* any happier?"

Juliette interrupted. "Wouldn't *you* want to know if *you* were going to die soon? It'd give me time to say good-bye to my friends, get stuff in order—you know, prepare myself."

When my ward replied it was in a condescending manner. This happens when he gets impatient and clearly there were times when Juliette's assumptions irritated him. "First of all, Juliette, you'd have to really, *really* trust that the psychic was right. Even if you didn't totally trust her, you'd still be going around wondering if it's going to be a car crash, or whether any moment someone's going to creep up on you and slit your throat. You'd be throwing yourself flat at every car's back-fire, Juliette!

"And what if the psychic's wrong? What do you do *then*? And when do you decide the prediction's wrong? Do you go around for the rest of your life thinking you're going to die any minute? It'd be hellish."

Mother Juliette was thoughtful for a moment. "Yes, but if you *really* did know you were going to die say next Saturday *and* you knew how it was going to happen . . . *and* if you knew it wouldn't hurt much, that'd be okay, wouldn't it?"

"That's an awful lot of *ifs,* Juliette. Anyway, it's not the issue. You're never going to be *absolutely* sure the psychic's right, are you? Life is tenacious. That part of you—the bit not completely convinced you're gonna die—that'd fight like crazy to keep going."

"If I knew the day and time," Juliette insisted, "I'd just climb into bed and compose myself and wait for it to happen."

"The point I'm making," my ward said, and I could hear the impatience rising in his tone again, "is apart from that sort of thing, I was saying I couldn't judge the psychics on their accuracy. Frankly, I didn't much care if they were right or wrong. So I just had to go on their empathy. Were they caring people? Did they genuinely want to help others? That sort of thing. Or equally, were they just in it for what they could get out of it for themselves? There were very few of these ones, actually. I was surprised at that. I thought there'd be more poseurs, yet almost all the psychics who turned up for the interviews were good, compassionate people. I got on quite well with them."

"So you *did* enjoy doing it?" Juliette amusingly queried.

"I thought of it more as a spiritual exercise . . . remaining neutral, you know—and open at the same time. Like in those exercises we used to do back in Wigmore Street, remember?"

That set them reminiscing about the old days in London when it was so much clearer that they had joined a mystery school. There was no longer any time for the exercises in contact and communication which had allowed them to develop an almost telepathic level of interplay between them—which they'd found so valuable. Now it was all about organization—about the money and the numbers of people who passed through the Chapter in a week. These had become the priority. Times had changed.

They weren't really complaining, they assured each other—no, indeed not. "Life moves us all along," Juliette said in a singsong voice—as though it was an aphorism from her South African childhood. "Now we're putting what we've learned into action; we're teaching what we've learned. Isn't that what we're meant to be doing, Micah? Passing it along?"

And soon the talk of testing psychics, and of dying, and the business about the fairs was set aside when they had to hurry off about their business.

I'm aware that in writing that phrase about psychics—*being in it for what they could get out of it for themselves*—I am making my collaborator feel a little awkward. It seems he had never previously considered the obvious hypocrisy of checking out his psychics for the very offense of which he was guilty. I'll let him speak for himself.

"You're right, Georgia. I hadn't given it any thought. I'd never seen it in quite that light before. I was totally focused on making money, I admit it. I'm not justifying it—we had different priorities, that's all. The psychic fairs weren't doing any harm that I could see. They seemed to be making a lot of people happy *and* they were generating a fair amount of cash. I didn't think it mattered much whether I believed in the value of a psychic's accuracy—as long as they were decent, kind people. Frankly, I thought of it more as putting on a show. If it helped people, great. We never had any complaints!"

"And now?" I ask him.

"Now? Yes, I *do* see it differently. Put it this way: I'm not sure I would do it again. Perhaps I've become more of a purist than I used to be! Not that preaching Jehovah and Satan at people would have ever paid the bills! But at least I now know better than to promote something for the wrong reasons . . . or something I don't really believe in.

"I think in retrospect I'd fallen into a trap so common in cults, the old 'us versus them.' We could always justify the means—within reason, anyway—because our ends were sacred and noble. I'm sure that approach must have doomed us from the start."

I'm not going to continue this dialogue except to say that he is essentially correct in this—especially in an area as sensitive as psychism in which the gullibility of simple souls is at stake.

More importantly—from the Processean point of view anyway—too much of this pretense, however noble the motives are believed to be, would ultimately lead to a fracture in the psyche. This is the classic "divided man" syndrome that has become a feature of much of modern life.

Ten years after leaving the community—when my ward first visited those fellow Processeans who had moved to Utah to start the Best Friends animal sanctuary—he found almost all of his old colleagues caught firmly, yet unknowingly, in this precise trap. The religious beliefs they had so avidly espoused—and to which they had given their lives—had evaporated. Their rituals were empty and automatic, and their group prayers were vacuous and purely mouthed by rote. By the time of his second and last visit fifteen years later, his old friends had dropped any pretense of religiosity and devoted themselves solely to caring for the animals they'd taken in to the sanctuary. My ward described the state he found his former colleagues in as "empty inside," and said that "they seemed to be acting out just another irony in their long history of ironies."

He said, "Of course they love animals. Most people do. And good for them for caring for the dogs and cats and the other domestic animals who were cast aside or injured. I don't think badly of them for this. Of course not. They do a great job. And I'm not even going to bring up the obvious disconnect between an ambitious and committed religious community and a group that now merely spends its time taking care of animals. Personally, I think it's a bit of a comedown, isn't it? I'd have thought it was something of a disappointment. But that wasn't the irony that amused me.

"The real irony is how they got there, the reason the group settled on creating the Best Friends animal sanctuary," he continued. "During the street donating we did, we discovered that the most lucrative cause that people would always give money to was the animals. Back then it hadn't seemed to matter very much that the only animals being cared for were our own German Shepherds! After all, our *ends* were noble.

"Earlier we'd written a book about the horrors of animal vivisection, which was sold on the street until the print run elapsed. We found even with no books for sale it was just as profitable to ask for money for animals, and, of course, it saved on the printing bills. Well before the creation of their animal sanctuary, I'd heard they even dressed some of their kids in bear costumes and sent them out to stand in airports for hours at a time collecting money! Do you really think any of that money went to an antivivisection society? Or that it ended up anywhere other than in the coffers of the Process?

"I heard one of them joke that they were caring for animals *because* they'd given up on *people*. I've no doubt this is true—the seeds of that attitude toward the general public had been present when I was in the group back in the seventies.

"So for me, looking from the outside and over a gap of the thirty-five years since I left, the final irony, in my opinion, lies in the way the group has become trapped in a web of their own expedience. These were people who had set out when we were young to change the world; we'd planned to live openly and honestly in a new utopian paradigm; we had hoped to investigate new ways of being and of seeing the world; we were explorers of consciousness, and we believed we were making wonderful new discoveries.

"And yet here they are now, with all that spiritual yearning long gone and forgotten. Taking care of animals—because they love them, of course. Yet I find there is something very sad when such a magnificent dream—a cause that drew us so closely together almost fifty years ago—has dissolved. It was a noble dream, but one that was shattered by the lure of easy money, which became a life of animal husbandry."

I stopped my ward at that point.

I was surprised he had so much to say, but I also understood he'd never had the opportunity to express his sorrow at what had become of the community that he'd had such a hand in creating.

I reminded him there would always be sadness in mortal life; that utopian dreams, magnificent or not, have a way of shattering; and that taking care of hundreds of animals wasn't the worst fate that might have befallen his old friends, most of whom were now in their seventies—some already dead.

And finally, I pointed out that because the very name chosen for the group was the Process, he'd best view his thirteen-year interlude in the community as exactly that—*a process*. As he had always been the first to admit, it was a process that had proved a perfect training for what he was later to take on in his explorations and writings about non-human intelligence.

I had even once heard him half-jokingly say that when all was said and done, the Process might have been made just for him. The lessons were so valuable in the depth and variety of the opportunities and experiences offered—few of which would have been possible had he followed a career in architecture.

The psychic fairs were an immediate success. However, the conferences were a lot more complicated and were going to take longer to organize. Yet they too would pack the house.

Another phase in my ward's life experience was about to begin. Yet the lad was becoming progressively more and more exhausted. He was down to four hours of sleep a night—if he was lucky. There was no time off—no relaxed weekends, no longer any free Thursday afternoons and evenings, for him, anyway. There was always more work to be done.

Something was going to have to change, or the rejected Indian palm reader's prediction—that my ward tells me he'd completely forgotten about—might well have happened after all.

* * *

Ah! Zandana! The psychic atmosphere was as clear and vibrant as I had remembered it. And it was so different from Earth. Its two suns—one large and half obscured by the ridge of the distant mountains—glowed in the azure sky.

After waking me up from the pleasures of a transport sleep, Eleena dropped me off in Zandana's Transport Center and turned right back, having picked up another traveler. It was getting even busier on Zandana, and this world was even more of a "backwater" than Earth.

I'd hoped to continue the conversation with Eleena, but with my transport sleep and the need for my TS to turn around so quickly, I realized that she must be needing this time to assimilate what we'd discussed earlier—which must have been somewhat unsettling. I was surprised and touched that she had opened up to me.

Of course I wasn't trying to convert her—or even persuade her of the rightness of the rebel cause. I simply wanted her to know that I wasn't acting on a whim and that the rebellion had a deeper purpose yet to emerge. I needed her to know that I believed there would come a time when the conflict that had embroiled the Local System for the past 203,000 years would reach a resolution.

It wouldn't be a compromise—all to make an awkward peace—in which both sides would resentfully give up aspects they'd been fighting for. It wouldn't be a reconciliation in which each side would throw up its arms in despair and make an attempt to coexist.

No, this would be a true resolution. Every participant would be required to search their hearts for a deeper understanding of all they had done, and all that had been done to them. It would be when each individual would search themselves with an open and self-forgiving mind. At this point, the deeper truth would emerge, and all beings would grow in wisdom, courage, and compassion.

I'd moved out of the STC by this time and had found my favorite place amongst the trees on the promontory just outside the Transport Center. The lights of the city of Zandan were just starting to twinkle on the other side of the bay as the larger of the two suns disappeared beneath the mountains.

Thus began the magical time—beloved of Zandana—when the second sun, now soon to set, started to cast a ghostly, reddish half-light. This appeared to flatten the perspective in a way my collaborator suggests might resemble the composition of a Chinese landscape painting.

This might be a somewhat fanciful notion, I admit, but thinking back, there *was* something of that quality—as though I might be able reach out and touch the mountains on the far side of the bay. What was more difficult to describe was this crepuscular, otherworldly ruby glow that suffused the landscape and seemed to seep into the very pores of Zandana's people.

Now remember, I was observing this from the fourth dimension and from Zandana's mid-astral realms, so there was always a certain amount of visual distortion that we learned to compensate for under more normal circumstances. This brief period—before the body of the planet rose to obscure the red glow of the second sun—could never be described as normal.

I believe now that the sun's rays had fallen primarily into the lower infrared frequencies of the spectrum. But as I sat on that grassy knoll overlooking the bay—the sleek flitter-boats scudding home before the long night fell, and with the calling of the night birds in the trees above me—I might as well have been there in the third dimension, sharing the physical glories of the material realm with the women and men of Zandana.

The atmosphere, the air itself, had become tangible. Each minute water molecule hanging suspended in the evening mist was refracting the light, bending and slowing it farther still. The effect was like living in the heart of a gelatinous ruby.

This sensation of allowing myself to sink into the lower regions of Zandana's astral realm for this materially palpable experience brought home the profound and terrible difference between the two worlds. The mid- to lower regions of the Earth's astral realms had long been intolerable to those of us of a more sensitive nature. The constant wars and violence on Earth—and the inhumanity with which humans treated one another—created lower astral compensatory realms that were dark, wretched places to be avoided if at all possible.

Here on Zandana, with its long and peaceful history—and its people's emphasis on seeking peaceful solutions to even the most belligerent of threats—the atmosphere in the lower astral had a clear, sparkling quality that made me want to bathe in it.

When I tried to work out how long it had been since I'd last been sitting on Zandana, I was shocked to realize it must have been nearly sixteen thousand Earth-years. Surely much must have changed over that time.

What I couldn't have known was just how *much* had changed.

10

Pulled In

New Consciousness Movement,
UFO Conference, Travels on Zandana,
Lake of Glass, Interplanetary Secret Agents,
and the Center Folds

The undeniable success of the psychic fairs in the New York Chapter, while not beginning to cover the impossibly large monthly nut, opened another not inconsiderable source of revenue. More importantly from Mein Host's point of view, it tacitly allowed him a free hand to put into action whatever ideas and subjects for conferences and seminars he chose.

What a privileged opportunity! How rare to have the chance to create an arena that would allow him to pick the brains of the most brilliant men and women working on the leading edge of the subjects that interested him. But how to go about it? What would induce these busy, highly paid (in most cases) experts, at the top of their fields, to participate in a small (by their standards) conference—and to do it pro bono?

Putting on conferences would never have passed muster with the purists in the community—especially the Four—if money was seen to be flowing out of the coffers. It was the wrong way.

As we know, Mein Host has a cunning side to him which had served him well (as he sees it) when he was at school. It's not that I'd observe him setting out to be cunning, but the solutions he arrived at—to problems such as this—are often the product of an ingenious imagination. If I describe the modus operandi that he arrived at to produce a series of one- or two-day conferences on subjects as varied as alternative medicine, Tibetan Buddhism, the extraterrestrial enigma, and noninvasive cancer treatments, we will find this cunning in full display.

I'll paraphrase what I heard him telling Juliette when she asked to know how he was able to do it. It wasn't complex, he said. Choose a subject you're interested in and want to explore more. At the cutting edge there will invariably be one or two brilliant people with different approaches or ideas about the subject at hand, and who would like nothing more than to declaim their theories in the presence of their rivals. And from an audience's point of view, there's nothing richer than having the chance to listen and question dueling experts.

A little research would quickly reveal at least one of these experts. In most cases they lived and worked on the East Coast. My ward said what surprised him was how willing almost all of them were to talk to him over the phone and then to come in to meet with him to discuss the proposed conference. The next step, he explained, was to subtly encourage the man—and it *was* most often men—to feel that it was *his* conference, *his* chance to expound on his theories. He would be flattered by this, and would soon reveal the names of his main rival or rivals, and, if he was wise and not merely riding his own hobbyhorse, he would likely welcome the participation of an intelligent adversary in his field.

Next came the call to the adversary, who would be almost certain to jump at the opportunity to confront and question the great man, as well as to explain his own theories. The reason generally given for what would seem their unusual readiness to participate in the events were the conditions under which they worked professionally. Time and again one or another would complain about the rigid and restrictive constraints of their profession or university and how their theories had been cavalierly rejected by the old guard. The conference would be a chance for them to speak freely.

In some cases this might lead to putting together a panel of second-tier experts and researchers, people who were more than happy to volunteer their time to listen to and question their heroes.

It was in these panel discussions that my ward was able to put into practice much of what he'd perfected in holding the First Progress. It had been the introductory evening for all those curious about the Process, and it had been a great success. In choosing to facilitate the panel discussions—which also included the active participation of the audience—he was able to draw the best out of both the experts and the audience so that everyone left the conference feeling they'd been heard and understood.

My ward was in charge of organizing these events, designing the posters and leaflets—and frequently having to create them too, which was a time-consuming affair before the advent of Adobe Illustrator. He also had to train the junior Processeans involved with the conference logistics, while simultaneously arranging a weekly evening lecture series on subjects from parapsychology to metaphysics. This was becoming progressively more exhausting for him. He was given secretaries and assistants, but that simply invited even more work—for it took more time to explain to them how and what he needed than to just do it himself.

Given that the eminent speakers were contributing their time freely—and that the Process was collecting the money at the door—the speakers required some extremely deft handling. A number of them needed to be put at ease and reassured that they were contributing to a good cause. Others were so focused on their research, or their unusual abilities, that no reassurance was required before they agreed to give their lecture at the Process Church.

This led to many fascinating discussions as my ward wheeled out his charm and his natural curiosity to facilitate the favor as fluidly and as gently as possible. In a few cases, these initial conversations led to lasting friendships, as was the case with Itzhak (Ben) Bentov and Earl Hubbard—and with the mens' wives, who, in both these cases, outlived their husbands and maintained their friendships with Mein Host. In particular, Jacqui Heriteau, Earl Hubbard's widow, was most encouraging when she read the manuscript of my ward's first book.

The very breadth of the subjects covered in the lecture lineup gave Mein Host the chance to absorb the concepts and theories that were just starting to blossom into the New Consciousness movement. These were the people exploring areas such as the intelligence of plants (Paul Sauvin), pyramid power (Max Toth), near-death studies (Kenneth Ring), Kirlian photography (Thelma Moss), alien abductions (Bud Hopkins), the mechanics of consciousness (Itzhak Bentov), psychokinesis (Matthew Manning, Uri Geller), space exploration (Earl Hubbard), and the list goes on to include many of those pushing the accepted limits of scientific thinking.

Mein Host also had the chance to further his interest in ETs and life on other planets. This interest had been sharpened considerably by a strange encounter he'd had some seven years earlier with a young man who my ward had been intuitively convinced was an extraterrestrial. The first conference Mein Host chose to organize was one titled "The UFO Conference."

It was in coming to know the UFO abductee Betty Hill—and by inviting her to appear as the featured speaker at the conference—that ensured the attendance of other serious ET investigators. My ward saw no point in including the more conventional naysayers and skeptics. This was because their arguments were well-known and predictable, and were invariably held with an irrational degree of certainty. He wanted people who were open to the concept of extraterrestrial life, and who were prepared to make their acceptance of this possibility the starting point of their explorations. By featuring Betty Hill—a woman who, with her husband, Barney, had arguably been the most thoroughly investigated "alien abduction" to date—he was clearly signaling to both experts and audience alike that there would be no time wasted on talk of Venus or marsh gas or lenticular clouds.

Betty and Barney Hill's late-night encounter with other intelligences in 1961—which resulted in the couple's having spent three hours aboard an alien craft—was the first widely publicized case of alien abduction. And that it occurred to a multiracial couple—Barney was African American—who were simple and honest people with no previous interest in UFOs only made their encounter that much more authentic.

The facts of this case—for those who haven't read John Fuller's 1966 account of the Hills' experience, *The Interrupted Journey,* or seen the later TV film, *The UFO Incident*—are readily accessible these days on Wikipedia. However, most people will have heard about Betty Hill's "star map," a diagram of the stars that one of the ETs had shown her when she'd asked where they were from. In 1968, a math teacher and amateur astronomer by the name of Marjorie Fish announced that she had deciphered Betty Hill's drawing of what Betty had recalled of the map under hypnosis. Marjorie had concluded that the aliens came from a planet in the double-star system of Zeta Reticuli.

It's an interesting insight into what my ward calls "the blindness of unconscious terra-chauvinism," to note that Ms. Fish claims to have tried thousands of matches before it occurred to her to look at the map from the aliens' viewpoint. It was only then—when she assumed the primary star shown on the map would be the aliens' home star—that she found a match.

Let me take a moment to use Betty's star map to show why I believe my ward was correct to leave the skeptics out of the mix. Of course the authenticity of a star map—originally seen by Betty in a dream some days after the abduction and confirmed later under hypnosis—is going to invite every sort of critical debunking. Carl Sagan, a man who would have given his eyeteeth to have been the first to encounter an extraterrestrial—yet never really gave any credence to alien life—was not the only "expert" to dismiss the map as just "a random alignment of chance points" in an article in the December 1974 issue of the journal *Astronomy.*

Yet what the skeptic seldom considers is the overall context. This was a star map drawn by a woman who observed it when she must have been in an extraordinarily bizarre and unexpected situation, and no doubt recalled under equally stressful circumstances. The star map wasn't a diagram cooked up out of nothing, an event isolated from the other key points in the couple's encounter. In a sense, the accuracy of Ms. Fish's interpretation of the map becomes less significant when placed within the context of Betty and Barney's complete experience. What was truly significant was that she had been shown the map at all!

Although the star map was a central feature of Betty Hill's presentation at the UFO Conference, no one had yet managed to decipher it. But when Betty described her entire series of experiences—the dreams and the hypnotic sessions—it became impossible to believe this modest little woman would have concocted this whole event. And as it happens, while many attempts have been made to discredit the Hills in the past fifty years and dismiss the encounter as a hoax or a delusion, they've failed to meet the challenge of Occam's razor.

In getting to know Betty Hill—Barney had unfortunately died in 1969—and in the conversations they had together, my ward received the first real confirmation of the existence and presence of alien life from someone he clearly trusted. As I overheard him telling Juliette when the conference was ending: "It's one thing reading about ETs by people who are trying to figure it out; it's quite another sitting down with someone whose actually been in a craft! You could feel the reality of it."

"But did Barney have the same experience? Did he see the star map too?" Juliette asked.

As with almost everyone else in the community, she hadn't attended the conference. The Processeans were kept busy constantly and would have had other, "far more important," tasks to accomplish as the conference was happening. There was also, invariably, a sense in the air that they were somehow above that sort of nonsense. Mother Juliette was more open than most IPs and probably would have liked to have gone to the conference, but even she felt the need to try to pick holes in Betty Hill's story.

So my ward retorted, "What a difference it makes actually being in the presence of someone who's had that experience! Seriously, Juliette, I felt I was there with her when she told her story. It was if I could see through her eyes. It was completely real! I could *see* it."

Juliette didn't appear convinced.

"Of course it's difficult to grok, Juliette. It's just so damn outlandish that people simply can't take it in. And no, to my knowledge Barney didn't see the star map. In fact he was far less conscious and tuned in to the encounter than Betty. He struggled with it much more than she did. I don't think he ever had the dreams that Betty did—which is what alerted her to what had occurred ten days earlier. They were really elaborate and intense dreams that sounded to me like replays of the abduction. And they only happened for those five days; she said they'd never reoccurred. They put a needle through her navel in one of the dreams. This was extremely painful, but the alien apparently just waved his hand in front of her face and the pain went away immediately."

"So did Barney reject her version?" Juliette queried.

"Not quite, although Betty said he wavered a lot. He never completely disbelieved it, let's put it that way. It was more like he wasn't terribly interested. Surprising that! But a black man saying he'd been on a flying saucer wasn't going to make his social life any easier. Apparently, he said at one point he thought he'd developed a mental block about the whole business. Yet he was able to recall, without hypnosis, when he was watching the craft before the abduction—and this was through binoculars—and he said he could see these small, "not quite human" figures who were watching him through the windows of the craft!"

"Good God!" Juliette exclaimed—and I could see from her emotional body that the reality of alien life had suddenly dawned on her. "That'd blow anyone's mind!"

What Mein Host couldn't have known at the time was that Betty and Barney Hill's encounter with extraterrestrials would pale beside an experience he would have in a few months—one that would change his life forever.

* * *

Long after both suns had set I sat there on the soft violet grass overlooking the sweep of the bay. The lights of the city of Zandan were sparkling in the lucidly clear air and reflecting so clearly in the silk-smooth sea that it seemed another city lay inverted and sparkling beneath the waters of the bay. As I stared at this charming spectacle—amusing myself wandering through those underwater caverns measureless to man—I felt the unremitting mental confusion I lived with on my home planet lifting from my mind.

Something much like this had happened before on one of my earlier visits, but, profound though it was at the time, the experience was mild compared to what I was feeling sitting there on the promontory. Zandana had always been a peaceful place for me. Even when the world was going through a turbulent period, being there lifted my spirits.

Sometimes a little too much, I admit.

I'd overstepped my position once, when I became an active participant in discussions with Zandana's Planetary Princes about an imminent invasion from another island power. I have to confess I was excited to see my suggestion to mobilize the women of the southern continent taken up with such enthusiasm—even though I knew I'd transgressed the law we watchers live by.

This is what I mean: I was excited not so much by breaking the rules, but by seeing that I'd actually had an effect on happenings within a third-density reality. At the time, my excitement had been somewhat muted by my nervousness at what I'd done. Now, so many millennia later, I found myself viewing this whole event through what I hoped were more mature eyes and with a new clarity of mind. It occurred to me then that my excitement was probably similar to what mortals must feel when they've accomplished a task, however modest, that creates an actual change in their world.

I was pondering this with my new mental clarity—and hoping my momentary lack of appropriate behavior might be understood within the context of my best intentions—when I felt a slight movement in the ether behind me. Being as familiar as I am with the psychic density of the lower astral regions that encompass Earth, I had mistakenly allowed myself to drift down—as I think of it—too far into the lower astral of Zandana. By that I mean the astral realms of this planet were so sparklingly clean that I wasn't aware how far I had descended until I felt the trembling in the ether behind me.

Turning, I saw it was Unava, Prince Zanda's chief of staff, whom I'd observed but never met at the time of the crisis. He was in what he would have called an out-of-body state. He was clearly practiced and familiar with this state of consciousness in a way he hadn't been the last time around—which is why I said we'd never formally met. He seemed supremely confident and greeted me warmly, courteously overlooking my surprise at his sudden and unexpected appearance.

"Sister watcher, we welcome you. My Prince Zanda heard news of your arrival, and, through me, he sends his greetings. He wishes you to know you are well remembered for your contribution at Zandana's time of need."

I must have smiled awkwardly; this wasn't what I really wanted to hear. I'd hoped this so-called contribution of mine would have been lost to Zandana's history by now. But then again it felt rather pleasant to have been remembered this long—thus my awkwardness.

"This is known only to the Princes and their staff," Unava said reassuringly, reading my confusion. "Prince Zanda required me to tell you that your ambivalence is understood and respected. He says that should you, at any time, be brought up in front of the courts of Uversa, both he and Prince Janda-chi would willingly speak in your favor."

I confess this took me aback. I'd never considered my intervention would ever rise to *that* level of seriousness. As you know, it was almost inadvertent; the idea had just slipped out of me. Wouldn't this mitigate my error of judgment? Or would my action be interpreted by the courts as one of Caligastia's covert operations on another world?

Now where did *that* thought come from?! That had never occurred to me! Not once. But of course the possibility of my being one of Caligastia's espionage agents would have to have been factored in to the equation. What mischief might I have really been up to?

And then an even worse thought arose in my mind: Might I have actually been doing Caligastia's work without being aware of it? Surely not. That would be too cruel to imagine.

I must have been wearing my emotions on my face as once again Unava stepped forward to steady me.

"Rest assured, dear sister, little will come of it. I have heard no talk of your part in aiding us resist the barbarian invasion, or even passing beyond the few who know. The people here have long believed the idea sprang from Prince Janda-chi, and that is where the situation rests."

I think it was then that I got a sudden glimpse of the past. The images flickered in my mind's eye in an odd way, but I was sure that for one moment I saw Lucifer standing with Janda-chi in the Prince's elegant reception room . . . and I was there with them! I was there, and Lucifer was addressing me . . .

The memory was startling. Or was it a memory? Did I imagine it? The image danced and guttered in my mind in such a strange manner, as though the vision was struggling to stop revealing itself.

And then nothing.

Whatever was happening to me?

Was something deeply buried in me trying to leak through to my conscious mind? And yes, we angels possess what contemporary humans would call an unconscious or subconscious mind, although it functions in a slightly different way from yours.

A watcher—again a point I have probably labored—simply observes. We watch, and we remember. You might think that our memory of the past is photographic, yet the way we store our memories is essentially nonlinear. And—as I have previously explained and for which I've apologized—my recall is associational and not necessarily sequential. Yet this does not mean that my memory is therefore unreliable. Because the links between the memories are a matter of association rather than linear sequence, they can frequently be unpredictable.

While the mortal mind uses sleep and dreaming to process and release what that mind has experienced during wakefulness, it tends to retain whatever is of value for that being's mortal life path and releases what it deems irrelevant. In the case of an observing angel like me, who might expect to remain on duty for many millions of years, it would be impossible to retain conscious knowledge of everything I observe. Yet at the same time, whenever we're recalled to Jerusem, we are also expected to be able to report on everything we might have seen at any point.

Thus my kin are equipped with a multilayered memory system in which whatever we have observed is stored in our unconscious minds in a series of layers that draw their distinction from their associational priorities. In short, we retain everything we observe, but matters of the least significance sink to the lowest layer. If I'd ever have encountered Lucifer with Prince Janda-chi on this world, it would certainly have been significant enough to be stored near the surface of my memory.

As best as I can describe it, that's the main difference between a mortal's and a watcher's capacity to recall. It is also why I felt completely sure I had not seen Prince Lucifer since the time of the revolution. In the same way, I was certain I'd never spent any time with Lucifer *and* Janda-chi on this world (or any other). And yet I couldn't deny the reality of those brief images.

As I write this now, I know that the glimpse must have been of that unexpected encounter I'd had with Lucifer on one of my trips to Zandana. He must have then deliberately closed down any conscious memory I had of meeting him and hearing his reasons for the revolution. But back then, I knew nothing of this with my conscious mind.

I believe this was my first glimpsed recall of that revealing encounter. Or perhaps that was the first sign that the posthypnotic block—the one Lucifer placed on me as I was leaving his presence—was starting to break down.

Unava was solicitous in allowing me to recover from that momentary lapse and gently led me back along a grassy path that wound through the forest, and we moved slowly along it, honoring its bends and twists. We could just as well have traveled in a more direct route, moving though the trunks of the fine old-growth trees, with barely a moment's drop in temperature.

But, no, Unava was taking it slowly, faithfully following the path as it twisted back toward the cliff's edge in the direction of where the lights of the city glittered in the distance. He seemed to be tacitly encouraging me to sense something in the psychic atmosphere of the world. Something new. Something I hadn't remembered from the last time I was here.

Fireflies clustered along the path as it wound back into the forest. There was a strange beauty in this, in the manner those tiny flashes led our way through the trees in the astral half-light.

Here, for those unfamiliar with the astral realms, I should touch on how they appear from a watcher's point of view. As I have previously noted, the astral realms can be thought of as a form of no-man's-land between the third and fourth dimensions. As such, the astral realms of a third-density planet contain key elements of both dimensions.

There is the basic landscape of the first three dimensions—although we experience it from within a finer frequency domain, and, therefore, it isn't what you might think of as solid. And encompassing and inter-penetrating this basic third-dimensional landscape is the fourth dimen-sion, which, you'll remember, is far more subject to the mental and emotional needs of dreamers and those traversing the astral regions.

In the case of watchers—when on another world in which we are presumed to have only a neutral interest—the landscape has no impulse to shift itself to accommodate our emotional or mental needs. When angels of any order venture into a planet's astral realms—seldom a pleasant experience for us—we perceive the forms of the natural world, the morphology of the biosphere, much as it has been molded and held in the hearts and minds of generations of the planet's mortal population.

As I'd noticed earlier, Zandana's lower astral realms were so clear that the path and the trees and the sea beyond were quite distinct—and yet the natural forms possessed the inner glow of the life force. It appeared this held true for Unava as well, as we moved side by side, floating serenely over this winding stream of flickering fireflies. Great trees soared above us, and foreign stars glittered in the dark ribbon of sky that faithfully followed the winding path through the forest.

I believe I spoke first. "I can speak with more confidence now, Unava, when I answer your earlier question. Indeed, I do feel a very considerable difference in the quality of the overall atmosphere of the world. Something definitely has changed on a profound level from when I was last here. It's true."

There was no time for Unava to reply before we turned one last bend and found ourselves emerging from the tree line into a vast open clearing in the forest. In the half-light I could see it was circular, with the circumference limned out by the winking mass of fireflies gathered at the base of the trees. I thought the diameter of this clearing was about one and a half miles, yet what was most uncanny about the sight was that not one single flash of a firefly pierced the darkness anywhere within this enormous circular clearing.

I stopped in astonishment.

The land sloped gently down to encircle a vast flat circular plain of an even deeper and more impenetrable darkness. This created the illusion of almost tipping me into a limitlessly deep black hole. Even though I was floating, I found myself staggering to retain my balance— the illusion was so strong.

Behind me I heard a ripple of delighted laughter. So this was where Unava was leading me!

"Our sacred Lake of Glass is what we call it," Unava told me with quiet pride in his voice when he'd finished having his joke at my expense.

Of course, I'd heard about these so-called Lakes of Glass back in the seminars on Jerusem, but I'd never actually seen one before. We were told that they're found on every mature and developed world—the planet extruding enormous single crystals from her body at the point at which her population, as well as the planet herself, is ready to shift from third to fourth density.

"Our lake is silent now," Unava said, "in the First Darkening of the long night. If we were here sometime later, you would see the Multiverse broadcast circuits in a way that you could never have imagined. The Lake of Glass comes alive with light and color as real-time holograms from a variety of different worlds are beamed instantaneously on spiritual circuits.

"It's like a veritable fairground, Georgia. People from all over

Zandana come to gather on the sacred crystal. When the transmissions come through, the holograms come alive in clusters all over the lake, and our people can wander from one to another, interacting with the projections . . ."

"But how can this be?" I interrupted Unava. "How can they interact? Wouldn't that mean your people were being beamed back to the source?"

"When they are interacting, yes; but only then. Not if you're just walking around from cluster to cluster. It's the interaction that initiates the beam from this end, so that a hologram of the person interacting will appear on the source planet's Lake of Glass."

I must have appeared puzzled, because Unava hurried on answering my unasked question.

"It depends on who originates the communication. There will be times when we on Zandana will initiate the contact, and our Lake of Glass will then become a primary transmitter rather than the receiver of another planet's beamed holograms. I can't explain the technology, so don't ask me how it works. The Lake of Glass appeared about a century ago . . . It seemed to grow out of the ground in the middle of the forest. It thrust the trees aside as it pushed up out of the surrounding matrix. It was like an iceberg. It had this flat top, but as the crystal emerged the body of it became wider and wider, forcing the forest back and creating a great clearing before it receded back into the ground, to end up like this."

Unava gestured widely to include the whole vast circular expanse of darkness. He was proud of what he was showing me.

"Many of our specialists have studied it, as you can imagine, because it was inert until recently. Yet still no one knows how it functions. Our experts suggest only that the structure of the crystal somehow transduces signals within the spiritual circuitry of the Multiverse and reproduces them as interactive holograms. The real puzzle, they say, is how any interaction with a projected hologram from another world triggers an instantaneous return to source. Their best hunch is that the working beam itself is so supremely coherent that data can flow in both directions simultaneously."

He was silent for a while as I absorbed what he was telling me. I knew that the appearance of a Lake of Glass on a planet portended many more important transformations that the world would be undergoing. The more I thought about it, the more extraordinary it seemed to me that Zandana—one of the thirty-seven planets aligned with Lucifer—would be showing signs of moving in to the single most profound transformation from third to fourth density that any world, together with its inhabitants, can experience.

Unava turned back from the Lake of Glass, gesturing for me to follow him back into the forest.

"We must hurry to the city," he said over his shoulder as he moved hurriedly along. "Prince Janda-chi is anxious to meet with you."

"Me? A watcher?"

He must have heard the awkward surprise in my tone. It wasn't comfortable for me to be thought of as Janda-chi's confidante. It was too close to being a spy—at least in Prince Caligastia's view, were he ever to discover it. Unava was clearly unaware of my problem, as he betrayed from his final remark to me as we emerged from the forest to cross the plains on the way to the distant city.

"You are 'just the one,'" Unava said sweetly, seeking once again to reassure me—yet having just the opposite effect. "'Just the very one!' That's what the Prince told me; those very words. It's exactly what he said when he heard you'd arrived!"

I must have looked horrified, but that didn't stop him.

"Prince Janda-chi has recently formed a deep interest in what is occurring on Prince Caligastia's world," he said, and I could hear from his emotional tone that he didn't altogether understand why—and that it troubled him.

He continued, "And since you are the only watcher serving in Prince Caligastia's mission to have traveled to our world for many hundreds of orbits, Janda-chi is anxious to be brought up to date with everything that has been happening on your world."

I should have been privileged by the invitation, but my heart fell. This wasn't an invitation a watcher could refuse. Janda-chi was a

Planetary Prince, and although we might have considered one another as friends under different conditions, I don't think he realized how much I risked by being summoned into his presence.

But if I was going to be perceived as a spy—I thought to myself somewhat desperately—I might as well become one.

What was the worst that could happen?

That I'd be forced by circumstances to become a double agent? That I'd be reporting back to Janda-chi *and* Caligastia, each convinced that I served him and him only?

If I chose to follow this path, I would need to be extremely vigilant and careful with what I said and how I acted. In this way, I thought, I might be able to make a contribution of value to both worlds. But I wouldn't know more until I'd heard what Prince Janda-chi had to say and the questions he might ask of me.

* * *

Mein Host, with all his recent financial successes, had once again risen in Mary Ann's favor. He was being regularly invited up to Mount Chi with a couple of the other senior IPs from the New York Chapter to meet with the Omega and the Four for their interminable all-night discussions.

The next issue of PROCESS magazine was still in the works, and material on the subject at hand was being gathered by the editorial staff. I knew my ward was relieved by this, because to take on designing the new issue when he'd gathered these other responsibilities—which required his constant attention—was to hope for the impossible.

Fortunately, perhaps for Mein Host, the magazine was the last matter on Mary Ann and Robert's mind. The drama long brewing between them—which had occasionally raised its head in the meetings the Omega held with their inner circle—was getting progressively more dramatic. Mild disagreements between the pair could easily erupt into full-blown rows, and the others in the meetings wisely stayed well out of the fray.

Although these rows were clearly uncomfortable to watch, my ward—along with most of the others in the inner circle—didn't take them that seriously. They knew that Mary Ann and Robert had an emotionally dynamic relationship—at least from Mary Ann's point of view—and they must have believed that whatever was troubling the couple to whom they were so devoted would blow over soon.

However, that would be to wholly underestimate Mary Ann's grandiose ambitions, as much as it would be to ignore the infinite cunning with which she set about accomplishing those ambitions.

I've mentioned Sister Verona earlier in my narrative, discussing the fact that she had joined the Process in New Orleans, where she grew up and was educated.

Verona was one of the people my ward had "brought in," or—to use the community's modified form of the colloquial and more revealing—"pulled in." I've heard the question, "So who have you pulled in?" or the more emasculating, "You'll never pull anyone in *that* way!"

While it may well be true that a person's initial attraction to the Process was frequently focused on one or another individual member, it was very challenging for someone to actually join the community full-time.

As all Processeans were openly celibate in the midst of a sexual revolution, this position provoked a wide variety of responses. I've already illustrated one of these reactions when my ward was jumped by that sexually hungry Canadian TV presenter. These were the ones who took a member's vow of celibacy as a challenge to be overcome. Others may not have been quite so bold, but nevertheless harbored the same desires and believed that—in biding their time—they would finally fulfill their unrealistic dream. Most of these hopefuls soon dropped away, discouraged, long before they were allowed to join the IPs in the community.

Processeans knew about this emotional dynamic. It was called "testing." Robert had written extensively about it as a potent and largely unrecognized element of male/female relationships. Whether or not people knew it, they tested one another for the other's authenticity. Most Processeans were unusually attractive young men and women, but if the strength of their beliefs could be overwhelmed by a moment of passion, then what would those beliefs have been worth? They half expected their celibacy to be tested, although not perhaps to quite the extent the Canadian TV lady went to in trying to have her way with Mein Host.

This made Sister Verona somewhat exceptional.

In the community's terms, Mein Host might be said to have "brought her in," and yet it was a credit to Verona's intelligence that, after briefly testing his integrity—as any self-confident young woman seemed bound to do—she accepted the matter of my ward's celibacy. Then, over the months of coming to know each other—and because they shared so many interests—she became increasingly involved with Process thinking and the community's approach to life.

Once an acolyte like Verona had given up her former life and joined the community itself—living in the chapter and devoting herself full-time to the Process Church—the young woman in question would promptly fall under the sway of the matriarchs in the community. This switch-around occurred to a lesser extent with a man who had been pulled in by a female Processean. I was never able to discern whether this dynamic was a deliberate ploy, or if it was perfectly natural under the circumstances. The new member would never have known it before joining the community, but the Process—now increasingly under Mary Ann's control—was a matriarchy.

Mein Host saw little of Verona after she joined the New Orleans Chapter, because by that time he had been transferred to the San Francisco Chapter. They'd always liked one another, but as the group continued to expand during the late 1960s and the early '70s—opening chapters in different countries in Europe and then in the United States and Canada—they seldom found themselves in the same place.

Mein Host has said this was one of the curious aspects of life in the community. He would come to know someone like Verona, for example, they would bond closely during the time she was making her way into the community, and then one or the other would be moved to another chapter. They might not see each other again for months or years, at which point they would find themselves once again in the same place.

You may recall the last time Sister Verona featured in this story. It was when my ward stood among the awkward observers of a pagan sexual ceremony held in the cellars of a Roman palazzo. This event had been organized by Mary Ann and purported to seal Sister Verona's absorption—her sacred marriage—to Father Aaron.

I've also commented on Verona's sharp intelligence, her humor, and her obvious ambition. The latter, my ward has since claimed, was quite evident even in those first months of knowing her in New Orleans. She had always come across as an outwardly self-confident young woman, and, as she rose in the ranks, she might well have become a bully—and may have already been perceived as such by some of those junior to her—but was generally saved by her humor and her mostly happy nature.

In short, Verona possessed some fine, bold characteristics—and some others that were similar to Mary Ann's less pleasant qualities. Verona's intelligence could readily turn acerbic and cruel; her humor was clever enough to bite deep; she didn't suffer fools gladly; and, more critically, she'd started to show herself as a person who, to put it baldly, cozied up to those above her in the hierarchy while treating those below her with some scorn.

As for Verona's ambitions, during that late summer of 1973 they were on the verge of being realized after she'd been invited up to Mount Chi to stay with Mary Ann and Robert and serve as their personal assistant. This sudden promotion created some immediate stresses at Mount Chi as the Four—who were living in one of the wings of the house— thought of Sister Verona as being far below them in the hierarchy. And now this upstart was far closer to the presence of the Omega than they were! Yet the Four had to treat her well because she was so close to the Omega. They would have known that anything they said about Verona would get back to her.

And there was worse!

As was Mary Ann's way, she took Verona under her wing, making her a favorite and keeping the younger woman close to her in their meetings. What this meant from the Four's point of view, however, was that now *all* of them became fair game for Mary Ann's blistering scorn. And there was still a lot of blame going around at that time for the Four's abysmal failure to turn around the New York Chapter's financial situation.

Mary Ann's technique—a dynamic I observed happening time and again—was to juggle the eight or ten people of the Omega's inner circle so there were always a couple of her favorites who shined bright during their time in the sun.

Mary Ann was a woman of extremes, and while she showered her favorite(s) with her love and attention, she liked to do this against a backdrop of bitterly criticizing and belittling the others. She appeared to need this contrast of extremes, as she would have claimed, to keep everyone on their toes, or to maintain the creative tension within the group. Had this ever been articulated at the time, my ward would have accepted it as true.

However, this behavior of Mary Ann's manifested only in the few meetings my ward attended during those months. Before Sister Verona moved in—when it was just the Omega and the Four living in Mount Chi—one of them would generally be the favorite of the moment. This playing-of-favorites dynamic had happened so frequently over the years that I heard my ward and the others joking from time to time about the musical-chairs aspect of it. Everyone had their brief times as the favorite—Mein Host must have had half a dozen of them in his thirteen-year stint in the community—and each had their far longer periods in disgrace. They would have likely claimed it all balanced out in the long run under the twin rubrics that Mary Ann was fond of quoting: whatever didn't kill you made you stronger, and that in order to lead you had to learn how to follow.

These were harsh dicta by which to live and might suggest that Mary Ann was merely a dominatrix—with those of her inner circle being slaves. You could have dismissed them as hypnotized bunnies caught in the blinding light of Mary Ann's intensity.

Yet had you talked to any one of those so-called slaves, each would have told you in their own way that they were completely committed to the Process and devoted to Mary Ann and Robert. They weren't masochists. They clearly didn't consider themselves deluded, or dupes of Mary Ann's wiles. They would have said they were growing in spirit, that they were stronger and more psychically and psychologically adept than ever, and that they were more self-aware and courageous and dedicated than they'd ever thought possible for a bunch of young middle-class English men and women. Indeed, they would have told you they were being prepared for the End of the World, and no one had ever said it would be easy.

It was when Sister Verona, the American, was introduced into this delicate mix of personalities that the Process was changed forever. The inner circle had been comprised of young English men and women who'd been living and working together for more than ten years. They'd placed their lives in the hands of the Beings, together they'd faced the ravages of Hurricane Inez while huddled in that pit at Xtul, and they'd tested themselves almost to the point of destruction to prove themselves worthy. And yet—obvious though it might be to the reader by now—not one of the inner circle had contemplated that introducing an American might result in an irreparable change to the Process.

It wasn't that any of the Four, or the others in the inner circle, individually disliked Sister Verona—although her impulse to sweet-talk her superiors *had* been noted. When she started sitting at Mary Ann's feet, making her opinions known in organizational meetings with the Four, it became painful for me to watch the members of the inner circle struggling with their emotions. They must have known it was another test and that it would have been a very poor show indeed to have complained—yet knowing that made little difference except to make their silence more baleful.

Observing their emotional bodies I could see that they came to be sullenly resentful of the special treatment Verona was getting from the Omega while they, the Four, became the scrim. They were painted black by Mary Ann's sarcastic comments, against which Sister Verona—soon to become Mother Verona—was now shining bright.

What happened next, for all its banal inevitability, came as a complete surprise to Mein Host—as it did to those of the inner circle.

* * *

The time of the First Darkening on Zandana, which Unava had mentioned, turned out to be a period of almost total darkness that fell over the planet when both suns had set—and before the first of Zandana's small moons swung into view, reflecting its cold light on a darkened world. Because of Zandana's figure-of-eight orbit around its two mother stars and its spin around its own central axis, the First Darkening occurred only twice in a Zandanan year.

This darkness had its effect on the lower astral regions, dimming the landscape and bleeding out the colors. Despite this, our way toward the lights of the city of Zandan was still perfectly discernible.

At one point Unava suggested I might enjoy traveling with him inside one of their transit cabins to observe how the natives lived. This was the elaborate system of gleaming rails radiating out and around the city that I'd first seen from the mountains the previous time I was here.

We arrived at the closest terminal, an elegant structure that grew pleasingly out of the hilly landscape and reached up to support the rail on astonishing slim single pylons. When I flash my collaborator an image of the place, he tells me it reminds him somewhat of Eero Saarinen's TWA Flight Center at New York's JFK Airport. I remark that it's interesting that both structures are travel terminals, although of a very different nature—a comment he appears to find rather obvious. No matter—he's the architect—but it should give you a rough picture of the place, with its sweeping roof and high, curved, and canted windows.

Unava and I kept to the corner of the waiting lounge—unperceived, of course—and giving us a good view of the twenty or so natives of Zandana's southern continent waiting along with us. Some were slumped in deep armchairs, reading or watching small flat-screen devices. Others were clustered in groups of two and three, chattering away in curiously birdlike tones, which always gave me the feeling they were really singing to each other. Imagine that! A veritable opera.

Having been subjected to the contemporary diet of extraterrestrial monsters on films and television, you'd probably have every reason to be surprised at how very similar to yourself you'd find a native of this world. If anything, you might think them even more graceful and beautiful than your average mortal from Earth.

On the whole, they tended to be taller and slimmer, both the men and the women. Looking around the lounge I was surprised, in my turn, to observe how almost all of them were faired-haired and blue-eyed. It was a small selection, granted, yet I hadn't recalled on my previous visit seeing nearly so much evidence of what I could only assume was the genetic boost provided by a healthy dose of well-distributed violet blood. Could it really be? My mind was racing . . .

Before I could turn to Unava to ask him whether I was right, there was a slight hissing sound from over our heads; everyone was gathering their bags and moving in an orderly fashion toward a glass-enclosed elevator to take us up to the level of the cabin.

I have to confess that clustering so closely together in the small space—however cleverly transparent—was a disturbing sensation for me. I can't speak for Unava, although he certainly appeared more at ease than I felt.

As you know, on Earth I have always taken great care to keep my distance from mortals, as it was too frequently a wretchedly uncomfortable experience to be within their auric fields. I have no choice but to feel the terrible turbulence of their repressed thoughtforms and the fear and confusion in their minds. Consider what a long time and how much care and consideration has gone into preparing my ward during just this one lifetime, and which allows us to collaborate so closely on this work!

So you might say I was prepared for the worst when I was forced in with the squash of material bodies of those natives of Zandana's southern continent. Though crushed closely together in the elevator, they continued their musical chattering, greeting friends while relaxing their bodies and innocently leaning up against one another, ruefully joking about the crush yet clearly enjoying the sensation. They appeared to know each other; perhaps they traveled on this line regularly. Now that I looked more carefully they did appear dressed for an evening out in the city, and I supposed—given the party atmosphere—it wasn't altogether surprising they were, every last one of them, young and singularly beautiful.

However, that wasn't so much the point.

It was their collective auric field that so bewildered me. To my astonishment, it was warm and welcoming; and not only that, it was almost transparently clear—so clear that I felt it was actually exhilarating.

Unava looked at me sharply then, and I understood I needed to be careful not to alert the occupants of the elevator that we were there. These were sensitive people, his look said, not like what you're used to on Earth. Stay too long in one of their aura's here on Zandana, and he or she will be sure to sense your presence.

So I had this odd sensation of having to shift around, moving through the crush from body to body. After some few moments of entering one, there would be a sudden rush of excitement in that person's emotional and mental bodies and I would need to move on to the next body before any single one of them noticed what was happening.

When the elevator slid to a halt and the doors opened, it was an unusually stimulated little crowd that spilled out and over the catwalk and into the cabin, throwing curious and amused looks at each other.

There was something profoundly different in the general atmosphere of the planet. I could feel it as a palpable reality, even in the lower astral region from where Unava and I were observing. It felt as though the very atmosphere itself was glowing with goodwill.

"You will discover the truth very soon," I heard Unava saying quietly, "once we have reached the residence of Prince Janda-chi."

I must have seemed anxious to him, because the last I recall before we joined the rest of the passengers toward the rear of the sleek cabin was hearing Unava's reassuring words.

"Have no ill concerns, watcher," he said softly. "For what you will hear from the Princes of Zandana will bring you great hope and promise for the future."

After that Unava would say no more, and—as a guest in his world—I knew better than to ask. So we settled in comfortably for the journey up into the foothills, sliding along with the others on a silver rail.

11

Center of the Web

Sexual Ambitions, Follow the Money,
As Lucifer Intended, Sci-Fi Moments,
a Sacred Source, and Joe Haldeman's Miracle

There were probably as many explanations and motives for what happened next in the heart of the Process as there were participants in the drama that was unfolding behind the closed doors of the Omega's wing of Mount Chi.

Mein Host knew little of this except what he'd seen of the gathering friction between Mary Ann and Robert. He tells me that he never for one moment suspected Verona would play such an active part until after everything broke wide open—and then it was all too obvious.

As I wasn't privy to the intimate details of what provoked Robert to "fall in love" with Verona—or so the inner circle was told—I have no doubt Mary Ann had an instrumental hand in it. She may well have set it up as a sexual test of Robert's loyalty to her—a test Robert evidently failed. Did she hope Robert would resist the temptation? Did Robert take it as his opportunity to jump ship? Was Robert hoping for a ménage à trois? I couldn't imagine Mary Ann agreeing to that! She was far too proud. I thought it more likely that she'd simply grown exhausted of trying to mold Robert into her own private messiah and used Verona to get rid of him.

And what of our young sister, now Mother Verona? Was the seduc-
tion of the Teacher merely the summit of her sexual ambitions? Had
she been set up by Mary Ann, or was she the initiator? I've no doubt
she was in love with Robert. I have no doubt that the other women in
the Omega's inner circle would also have imagined themselves to be in
love with him.

Banal though this little drama was in everyday terms—men down
through the ages have forever left their wives for younger women—the
Process terms could never be described as *everyday*. Robert and Mary
Ann were not a run-of-the-mill couple from the suburbs, and Robert
wasn't a corporate shark with his new young secretary. These were people
at the very center of a rapidly growing new religion. For those who knew
them, whether like my ward—who'd seen the divine in Mary Ann but
not in his old friend Robert—or those more strongly focused on Robert,
everyone would have agreed they made a brilliantly effective team.

I may have had my skepticism along the way about the authenticity
of the religious beliefs of the community, yet progressively more people
were filling the chapter's Alphas for their Saturday evening religious
Celebrations. Other chapters were now emulating the psychic fairs and
lecture series that had been developed and perfected in the New York
Chapter. It seemed that their persistence over the years was paying off
at last. The chapters in Boston (though it was actually in Cambridge),
as well as those in Miami, Chicago, and Toronto, were thriving in their
own way.

The Boston Chapter, under the leadership of Richard's younger
brother Jonathan—the one who's hapless parents had made it a matter
of the courts to avoid losing a second son to the Process—was starting
to do unexpectedly well. Donators in that New England city were starting to bring in spectacular amounts of money off the streets—far more
than other chapters with a similar number of donators.

In a matter such as this where money was concerned, Mary Ann
both lauded Jonathan's accomplishment while simultaneously using
his brilliance to whip the less financially successful masters to greater
efforts.

The four Great Gods of the Universe—Jehovah, Lucifer, Satan, and Christ of the Process Church cosmology—may have made minimal rational sense, yet they seemed to be striking a chord of recognition for some of the people emerging from the hallucinogenic sixties. The central tenets of "uniting the opposites" and "loving your enemy" were beginning to take hold of a generation that had been weighed down and divided by the Vietnam War. The community was presenting a belief system that was broad enough—and sufficiently inclusive by virtue of the four god-patterns—to offer a path of personal redemption for different types of people.

It was certainly no overnight success, but the Process Church of the Final Judgment was finally finding its feet.

And once again, everything in the community was falling apart around it.

"Follow the money!" "Follow the money!"

Hadn't that been "Deep Throat's" hoarse, whispered advice to the *Washington Post*'s two persistent reporters while they were trying to unpack the Watergate conspiracy?

To understand what occurred next in the far less public drama unfolding within the core of the Process community and within much the same time frame, it would be more appropriate, perhaps, to counsel "Follow the power!" "Follow the power!"

When the shouting and the tears, the fury, the blame, and the bitter vituperation had lessened somewhat (lessened perhaps, but never forgiven) and the ashes had settled, who then was holding the power?

Well, no surprises there!

What *was* surprising, however, was just how quickly and ruthlessly Mary Ann took over the reins of power—not that she'd ever really relinquished them—and established herself as sole sovereign. This appeared to make little difference to those of the inner circle and the dozen or so other IPs who would have met Mary Ann and Robert on a few occasions, as they clearly already knew who really held the community together.

Robert was a naturally modest man, yet it must have been a disappointment to discover that only a couple of junior IPs chose to follow him and Verona when he tried to set up shop on his own. He spoke at a few public meetings in New Orleans and Boston, but from all accounts he was never able to stir up enough interest in his teachings to make a go of it.

Besides, I doubt if Verona's heart was ever really into it.

It's only my opinion—as I wasn't present for the intimate details of Robert and Verona's life after they broke away from Mary Ann and the community—but from what I'd observed of Verona, her ambitions didn't take her in that direction. She would have had no desire to be a lesser Mary Ann in Robert's life. I suspect it would have been enough for Verona to have taken Mary Ann's husband away from her to establish what she needed to know.

In a way that Robert would have appreciated, he could be said to have had the last word. Soon after he and Verona left the community, they'd met with William Bainbridge, a university academic who had been compiling data for a book about the Process that he would later publish in 1978.

The unfortunately named *Satan's Power: A Deviant Psychotherapy Cult* was a serious study by an academic sociologist, yet because of the mystery of Mary Ann at the heart of the group, he unfortunately completely missed the true inspiration and the driving dynamic behind the Process. This was a fact that Robert and Verona were unlikely to stress in their conversations with the writer.

Naturally, in Bainbridge's considerable research—in talking to many Processeans in various chapters—he would never have heard a word spoken of Mary Ann. More by tacit arrangement than overt instruction, she wasn't mentioned by those who actually knew of her existence. Those without a need to know didn't. After all, it was Robert's messianically lit photograph that hung in the lobby of the chapters, it was his books that were being sold, and it was his religious rants that were featured in the magazines. It was Robert who was the Teacher. Only the elect knew of Mary Ann's existence, and only a handful of Processeans had actually met her in person.

As it turned out, Bainbridge was able to interview Robert and Verona only *because* they had left the community. Mary Ann would have been most unlikely to have ever permitted Robert to be interviewed. From their very early days as Compulsions Analysis—the first iteration of the Process in mid-1960s London—it must have become obvious to her that his verbose analytical style didn't make good press.

Watchers, in my experience, need to develop a healthy grasp of irony in our attempts to understand the dealings of human beings. I don't believe it was a purposeful move on the part of Robert. He wasn't of a vengeful nature, but he must have relished the irony of being able to have the last word.

As mentioned, the book that Bainbridge wrote—while an otherwise diligently researched work—focused entirely on Robert as being the community's leader and made no reference to the vital significance of Mary Ann. Thus from the publication of William Sims Bainbridge's book in 1978 until my ward's 2009 book, *Love, Sex, Fear, Death: The Inside Story of the Process Church of the Final Judgment,* almost nothing was publicly known about Mary Ann's absolutely central role in the community.

When you consider what an anomaly it was to find a celibate matriarchal cult flourishing in the midst of the permissive Swinging Sixties, not only did William Bainbridge miss the point of the matriarchy (through no fault of his own), but the book presented only the community's exoteric mask. The central mystery remained untouched. This has led to an increasingly distorted idea of the Process, which has subsequently been widely exploited on the Internet by people with their own interpretation of the community's teachings.

So perhaps the final irony is that the only purportedly well-researched, serious, academic study of such an unusual community experiment as the Process missed the very essence of what made the community so out of the ordinary.

Satan's Power, for all its sociological analysis, its charts and personality assessments; for all its thoughtful insights and psychological profiles; for all its author's open-minded clarity and generosity of spirit;

for all this mass of objective data—the book made absolutely no reference to the dark goddess at the center of the web.

This was a goddess who was now answering to the name Hecate. If you know your Greek and Roman mythology, this will tell you that something was brewing beneath the surface of the Process Church.

* * *

I was happy to find Zandana's monorail system delightfully slow-moving. Can you understand this in your speed-driven culture? The desire to move slowly? To smell the roses? Isn't that what you say?

For one who can move from place to place faster than you can imagine, as a watcher my delight can frequently blossom when I have no choice but to travel deliciously slowly.

My next pleasant surprise was the fine quality of the interior of the monorail cabin. Previously I'd only seen these vehicles from afar, moving across the landscape with the regularity of a gigantic clock mechanism. If I'd thought at that time about the cabin interiors I would have guessed they were utilitarian—as befitted the simple and straightforward culture of Zandana as I then perceived it.

I really wasn't ready for the quiet opulence I found inside the monorail as the young people were making their way to their seats. The cabin itself was a long, slim tube with windows in unbroken strips down each side—broken only by the vehicle's sliding doors. The cabin was separated by folding screens into seven sections and joined by a central corridor. The seats—like the seats in the transport lounge—looked remarkably comfortable and were arranged in groups within five of the seven sections so as to encourage conversation. The remaining two had a warm, womblike quality. I noticed that a few people were slipping into those compartments, so I assumed they were intended for silent contemplation.

The flooring, I could see, was composed of a soft material that must have been friendly to the feet, given that a number of the young women had slipped off their shoes and were wriggling their toes sensually in its pliable surface.

The cabin was filling up, and the new arrivals greeted the half a dozen individuals already seated in one of the compartments. The atmosphere was strikingly friendly and easygoing, as if the cabin's occupants were one large family who just happened to find themselves traveling together. After I'd seen more of the citizens of Zandan on this visit, I came to understand that this familial feeling was far more general than suggested by the microcosm of the cabin.

The lighting was subdued and seemed to emanate from semitranslucent panels. I could see some people were moving around to allow them more illumination where they were sitting. Now that was odd! Nothing seemed to be plugged into outlets. The panels were simply being moved around from place to place as needed. This was another puzzle to be filed away.

Had I really been away from Zandana *this* long?!

The doors closed with a gentle hiss after the last person was seated, and the cabin slowly accelerated, sliding silently into the darkness, hovering the smallest fraction above its solitary silver rail.

I felt Unava laughing quietly beside me. We were standing together at the back of the cabin. From there I could see up ahead that there was no compartment with a driver. The vehicle would have to have been fully autonomous. And suddenly I was watching from high above, viewing a sleek capsule riding a single rail curling over the hills and forests, silently driving itself farther and farther into the night.

Unava said, smiling, "I see you have observed some signs of our recent transformation."

"Truly, I'm amazed, Unava," I replied after a respectful pause. "I was thinking just how confined my expectations have become. I'm so accustomed to the constant cycles of boom-and-bust on Earth . . . all those times of terrible destruction. It's downright depressing! Everything progresses well for a while. A culture starts to grow and thrive and develop . . . It reaches a certain point and then, boom! The culture collapses, and everything has to start over again."

Unava seemed puzzled at this news, although he must have known how developmentally retarded Prince Caligastia's world had become.

I was then immediately hit by the thought that I might have said too much. I went on quickly in the hope of covering my possible error.

"And yet here you are!" I said forcing some enthusiasm into my tone. "Zandana must have made relatively unbroken progress since I was last here to have reached this point . . ."

"See how the people are at ease with one another," Unava pointed out unnecessarily. "You'll find this the same all over Zandana . . ." And then he seemed to correct himself, for he hastened to say, "Well, all over our great southern continent."

He must have been sensitive to my feeling that this was most likely a clue to the real, overall planetary situation on Zandana. The last time I was here their "great southern continent" was certainly not representative of the state of the other, far less developed island nations. Zandan had been clumsily trying to defend itself from a barbarian invasion on that occasion!

"You *have* been away a long time, haven't you?" Unava asked me reprovingly. "The other nations are now in states of rapid development. Four or five of them are even up to our standards here in the south."

Surely not. I knew that for tens of thousands of years those of the so-called great southern continent had turned their back and spurned the other, far more primitive islands. They believed they had good cause; I understood that. They would say they'd really tried. And yes they had—for tens of thousands of years—before they'd thought to simply leave the primitive natives to their own ways and concentrate on developing their own splendid culture.

"This surprises you, watcher! Ah! Yes! So different from your home world. I see that now."

"But how? How did it happen?" I questioned.

"We now reap the wisdom of that decision to turn away from the arts of war and dominion. You thought it self-serving. 'Culturally selfish' is, I believe, the manner in which you considered our action."

It was true. I had thought that, but I'd no idea where Unava might have picked it up. It didn't do well for a watcher to be found too critical of another world's arrangements.

The reflected light of a moon was now flooding the landscape as the rail started a slow, smooth curving climb up into the foothills of the mountains where the summer villas of the Princes and their administrators enjoyed the cool, off-sea breezes.

"I thought we were going to the city?" I asked.

"You didn't notice everyone leaving the cabin when we last stopped . . . before we switched to the mountain rail?"

When I looked around, it was indeed so. But for a couple sitting quietly in one of the forward sections, the cabin was empty. It was so. And me, a *watcher*!

But Unava was laughing again.

"Conditions on Earth are well-known to us. Rest assured you broke no vow in thinking your truth. Perhaps you can understand now (and this from a Prince's chief of staff!) how severely your expectations of others have become distorted by the miserable state of your world. What you are seeing here on Zandana seems mysterious and impossible to you. It shocks you, perhaps. And yet it is perfectly natural. It is as Lucifer intended."

"But how?" I asked him again. "However have you been able to subdue the barbarian nations so efficiently?"

He pounced on that, of course.

"There you are! Just what I mean. Nobody *subdued* anyone! We don't *hold dominion* over our less advanced brothers and sisters. That's your Prince Caligastia speaking!

"Listen to me, watcher. Had we pressed our advantage rather than retiring to Zandan to mind our own business, we would have been forced to fight and conquer those who sought to bravely defend their own lands. This would merely have imprinted the collective consciousness of the island cultures with the terrible violence of invasion. It would have set up an endless cycle of revenge and retaliation.

"So we didn't do that. And before you say anything, Georgia, about the comparative level of animal predation on the two worlds . . ." (I must have been feeling defensive about the limits of my understanding!) ". . . before you state the obvious, and yes, I know the Earth mortal is a rough and unmade creature, but in believing this excuse you miss the point. We could have invaded a lesser people, but we chose not to. We could have developed advanced weaponry, but we chose not to."

I responded, "Yet you say now, Unava, that somehow the other continental islands are catching up to your state of advancement. Do you not fear their rivalry, their competition? Perhaps they *will* choose to develop weapons. What then? Where will this spirit of peace get you then?"

I realize now how defensive I must have sounded to him, when I was really revealing my own shortcomings . . . my limited understanding. Happily Unava cut me short before I could make a worse fool of myself.

"This is difficult for you. I realize that, Georgia."

I think it was when he said that and I could hear the genuine compassion in his voice that the emotional reality of the gulf between the two worlds more fully struck me. Both planets' early development roughly paralleled one another. They had received their Prince's mission at about the same time. Yet even by the time of Lucifer's revolution, Zandana was showing signs of moving ahead—which I'd attributed to the greater passivity of the natives of this world. But what I was seeing here, now—and what I was hearing between the lines from Unava—felt to me like this was a quantum leap in the collective consciousness.

"Look out the window," he was saying. "We are getting close to our destination. May I suggest you merely observe the beauty of the passing landscape, and we will maintain our silence until we reach Prince Janda-chi's domicile. I am sure he will explain far better than I can the global situation here on Zandana, and in terms you can understand."

And with that, Unava crossed his long arms and turned away from me as surely as his people had once turned their backs on the ignorant barbarians on the other islands.

I didn't miss the metaphor.

* * *

As the New York Chapter grew progressively busier and more successful I found myself getting increasingly concerned about Mein Host's
health. Although my ward possessed the sinewy strength of a tough—
yet slimly—built young man, he was by no means physically robust.

His will—tempered by the brutality he had undergone at
Charterhouse School—was remarkably strong. By now he had become
accustomed to pushing himself beyond his limits . . . if he even *knew*
his limits! Those days he was operating mostly on pure will and the
knowledge that no one else could do what he was doing. It was obvious
to me that he didn't want to let the others down.

I could see for myself that he felt he simply *had* to keep going.

With the success of the psychic fairs and the conferences, pressure
was building for him to create even more of them—as well as to start
a new weekly lecture series. Naturally, it was easier to say "create a conference" than to actually make one happen. Research had to be done.
The various experts needed to be located and, as my ward expressed
it, "schmoozed." It would prove true that these experts liked to be
schmoozed, though some of them they were initially cautious at being
seen to be associated with a church. My ward's intelligence and genuine interest—and his complete lack of any evident desire to preach to
them—most often won the day. Once the centrally important expert
had been reeled in, the remaining participants appeared, in general, to
fall into line. Yet this took a great deal of time, constant attention, and
considerable effort—mainly Mein Host's.

He was given additional secretaries to handle the ever-increasing
load. The phone calls were endless. Letters had to be typed in triplicate,
which—even on the few battered IBM Selectric typewriters they had
managed to "retrieve" in their few months in the city—would be considered a most laborious and tedious affair in the later age of the internet.

In the case of the new lecture series, however, a new twist entered
the game.

Having always enjoyed reading science fiction, it must have been obvious to my ward to hold a series of lectures by well-known science-fiction authors. Still very English, he might not have immediately absorbed that New York—the center of the publishing industry—harbored a hive of writers of every stripe. But it was also, in particular, probably home to more science-fiction authors than any other city in the world.

It is not an original observation to say that authors—men and women, but especially men—who spend most of their professional lives alone in a room facing a blank sheet of paper or its digital representation might be a strange and unpredictable lot when they're let out of their cages. If there is some truth in this, then those who write science fiction might be considered the strangest and most unpredictable of them all.

Writers in general tend to be competitive with other writers, for there are always many more writers than slots to fill. A published writer will anxiously watch for the reviews of their work, and for where he or she had reached in the various bestseller lists, crowing with delight if one of their books overtakes a rival. I have observed this many a time.

Science-fiction authors compete for publishing contracts and sales, of course, but—between one another, as my ward was soon to discover—their mutual competition could become far more intense and challenging. Different from most regular novelists who may be satisfied with describing every minutiae of the human drama—who say things like "there's nothing new under the sun" or "there are only twelve basic plots"—the science-fiction writer, unlike them, competes by using originality of plot and realities never previously conceived of by their best rivals. They are the ones who are busily trying to discover and write what *is* new under the sun.

All very well, you might think. Good for sales. Good for authors. Certainly good for publishers. Good for everybody.

Well, yes, as long as the authors stay in their little bare rooms staring at blank sheets of paper—or their digital simulacra. Yet get a few of these authors together in one place and the fangs—granted the very ingenious fangs—come out. The barbs are exceeding sharp, and points are clearly won by hurling them with the terrifying skill of a whaler's harpoon.

I saw that Mein Host was able to use this peculiarity of science-fiction writers—this intense and almost unwholesome level of competition—to his advantage. When he signed up an Isaac Asimov or an Alfred Bester for a lecture, he found he couldn't keep the other younger writers away— a Spinrad, a Delany, or a Harlan Ellison. He couldn't turn them and their friends away once they'd heard about a lecture through the New York bush telegraph. And for the audience of science-fiction fans at the weekly lectures, that only added to the chaotic fun.

Science-fiction writers were all friends, or friendly enemies. Or at least, everyone knew one another and they watched each other like hawks. Some were boisterous and argumentative, some were tricksters, some were saucy, and some were earnest. Given that Mein Host always took advantage of his position to spend some time with the authors beforehand, some of them used their initial meeting with him to talk about matters they didn't generally discuss with others.

I had observed that by this point in his life Mein Host could frequently have an effect like this on people. You may recall how Brian Epstein used his time with my ward back in the London Chapter's Satan's Cavern in the weeks before he died—during the dog days of 1967—to talk of his unrequited love, his business disappointments, and to confess his homosexuality.

Joe Haldeman, still unknown as a world-class sci-fi scribe, was one such author. The experience he came to share with my ward, while probably not the first time told, was certainly the first time that what he'd described had been taken quite so seriously. There was a good reason for this. My ward was inclined to give credence to out-of-the-ordinary experiences in general, and another remarkable incident had recently been told to him by yet another featured speaker in another field entirely.

Each experience as described would raise absolutely fundamental questions about the nature of mortal death. This provided Mein Host with clues, which he interpreted to mean that death, as I heard him say more than once, "wasn't all that it was cracked up to be."

It was Eva K.'s experience that he'd heard first. She had one of the most serenely beautiful faces of any woman Mein Host had ever met. With fine, chiseled features, high cheekbones, long smooth fine hair, and the clearest of blue eyes, she'd something of the look of actresses like Grace Kelly and Eva Marie Saint—in other words, the classic American blonde. To describe her too closely might be to prejudice her current identity, as my collaborator tells me she has since risen to a position of significance within the international psychological community. Thus I will call her Dr. Eva K.

Doctor Eva K. wasn't yet a doctor of psychology when she first encountered the Process Church in the form of Father Micah during the fall months of 1973. She was studying for her degree at the time— specializing in the psychological aspect of dreams and dream analysis. She was already extremely accomplished at this, as my ward was to discover when he was interviewing Eva for a conference slot. He asked her to interpret a dream he'd recorded some months earlier, and her reading of it was straightforward, well balanced, and apparently meaningful to my ward. It turned out that her intelligence more than matched her beauty.

Eva K. was worldly, self-confident, coolly stunning, and highly intelligent. When she knew my ward better, she admitted to being the secret, longtime, on-and-off mistress of an aging—yet surprisingly well-preserved—married, mustached, American film star. Yet despite this—and although Mein Host wouldn't know it until much later in his life—she was falling in love with my ward. The wise and worldly Eva K. was falling in love with a celibate priest!

Now how worldly and wise was that?!

But perhaps she didn't really know it herself. And it may be that she felt a celibate relationship, a liaison of the spirit, would somehow compensate for her guilty betrayal of another man's wife. Might she have thought that through unrequited love for a celibate priest she could pay her moral dues? I wasn't able to tell. She might even have felt, sooner or later, that she could lure Father Micah out of the Process and keep him for herself.

If this latter proposition was true, she kept her affections remarkably well hidden from my ward for the next few years. It was equally clear that my ward liked Eva K. and appreciated her intelligence and expertise in dream interpretation; but the truth was he had fifteen or twenty Evas in and around the New York Chapter, all of whom he liked and appreciated.

Yet it was clear he felt there was something special about Eva K., and over the succeeding years they became good close friends in the way people can when they consciously choose not to express their friendship within the sexual arena. He never broke his vow of celibacy with Eva, yet she would come to take an important place in his life—as well as inadvertently play a silent role in what allowed his eyes to open three years later.

However, all of this was still to come.

Right now what I wish to focus on is the event that Eva K. described in medical detail, and which occurred early in their acquaintance— some weeks before Joe Haldeman was relating his experience in my ward's sun-filled office.

Eva described how she had been standing in her tiny New York apartment's bathroom, making up her face in front of the mirror over the basin. She told my ward how she'd slipped on the wet floor, falling hard, and catching the underside of her nose on the edge of the basin— driving the bone straight up into her brain. She said she was quite conscious as she fell, and told my ward that she knew she'd killed herself.

She knew she was dead.

Eva K. then blacked out. When she came back to full consciousness a short time later and pulled herself to her feet, she could see in the mirror that she had the slightest bruising around the top of her elegant nose. Apart from that, she said she was just fine.

She had no idea what had happened—only that something very weird had just occurred.

She had no doubt at one moment that she was dead, just as in the next moment she was certain she was alive.

* * *

We were high in the massive rolling foothills—hills that would have been mountains on Earth—when the cabin finally drew to a halt. We waited for the couple in the cabin to dismount. Then Unava guided me out and onto a platform that was cantilevered over a precipitous drop down to the valley below. The cabin slipped silently away, back from whence it had come.

The lights of the city of Zandan far beneath us glowed in the gentle fuzz of a cooling evening mist. Way out in the ocean I could see the lights of what Unava had earlier called flitter-boats skittering across the horizon. I watched, fascinated, while one of these flitter-boats turned back toward the shore. As it drew closer, I saw it was moving with extraordinary rapidity across the surface of the water. It emerged from a patch of mist, and when it did I could suddenly—and with a jolt—see more clearly that the water beneath the vehicle (was it really a ship?) appeared to remain completely undisturbed. There was absolutely no wake, and the surface was as smooth under the speeding craft as it was over the rest of the bay.

Before I could blurt out my surprise, Unava was drawing me away from the view and guiding me along a ramp that swept up to a large structure rising from the bare rocks above us. Far beyond and disappearing into the night, I could see fold upon fold of the massive mountain chain that dominated the vast central area of the southern continent. I knew from a previous visit that the entire region had been designated a natural preserve. The city of Zandan and the lowlands received their precious water from here. It was their sacred source—*the* sacred source—of their religion. Even now in the half-darkness I could see water streaming down in a series of spectacular waterfalls—appearing in the moonlight as alabaster columns of the Temple of the Mountain God—receding off into the darkness and the silver-lined clouds.

I was so absorbed in the magnificence of the view—so ridiculously enchanted by its mysterious untrammeled majesty—that I later felt I must have been trying to delay my entry into this meeting with Prince Janda-chi. This was a meeting I hadn't expected, and for which I felt most awkwardly ill prepared. I can only believe that I must have been a great deal more trepidatious than I knew!

In retrospect—hopefully being somewhat wiser—I now think of that compulsive reaction as one which hung like a celestial curse over us rebel angels. I can say this now: We could never be *absolutely* certain of anything. At one time, before Lucifer's revolution, we celestials knew our functions—you might say we knew our place. We'd been so sure of ourselves. We knew then that whatever we did was good and right and aligned with the loving desires of the Mother Spirit.

Then suddenly nothing was quite as it seemed anymore. Confusion now existed where previously things had been ordered. Were we setting off on a brave new journey? Or were we dropping into a web of Lucifer and Satan's delusion? Were we taking the long return home? Were we part of a great cosmic experiment? Or were we celestial misfits, the interplanetary criminals the MA believed us to be?

These were the doubts and the fears—the grandiose ambitions and the dreams of freedom. These were just some of the demons and thoughtforms carrying the curse of ambivalence and suspicion that beset us all . . .

Great heavens! Am I sounding more like a mortal?

But then again, before I entered the cabin with Unava, I had no concept what I was going to hear from the Prince and his illustrious visitors, or the profound impact this encounter was to have on me.

* * *

Joe Haldeman was thirty at the time—three years younger than my ward. It quickly emerged to their amusement that they shared the same birthday of June 9. They were two young Geminis, both becoming masters of communication, each in his own way. Each one was an incarnated rebel angel, but each, as yet, was completely unaware of his angelic spiritual heritage.

What both men had in common was that each had been showing signs of becoming curious at what lay beneath the accepted surface of consensus reality. For Mein Host, this had been provoked by the reality of the snake that entered through his eye when he was lying on the bedroom floor of Annie Ross's London apartment in an entheogenically altered state.

Although, if I might digress for moment, I have heard my ward say more than once that—in spite of the utter reality of that snake (the snake was me, distorted by his terrible fear)— because he'd experienced it while in an entheogenic trance, there was always the sense that it could have been a hallucination.

But Joe's experience had been no hallucination, and it continued to baffle Joe. The way he explained it that afternoon in the fall of 1973, he was still clearly shaken by the implications of what had happened to him in Vietnam.

Sunlight was pouring through commercial metal frame windows that completed one side of my ward's new and larger office (the lad was coming up fast). The sun's golden beams filtered through the row of a dozen plants hanging from the ceiling behind the window in separate pots—a mass of flowered greenery whose mass of floral strands hung beneath like an upside-down hedge. This gave the room what I had heard my ward once refer to as an example of "some early antigravity experiment gone terribly wrong."

Whether his visitor ever noticed this odd effect was never expressed over the course of their time together. I can vouch from observing Joe Haldeman's emotional body that the profusion of plants—upside-down hedge or not—had relaxed him, encouraging him to open up.

Joe had just completed writing his classic sci-fi novel, *The Forever War*—which would be published the next year—and it established him as both a superb original writer and an acerbic social critic.

Joe had been drafted in 1967 and served as a combat engineer in 'Nam, he explained to my ward while sitting with him in my ward's office. And yes, indeed, he had intended *The Forever War* to be a critical and forthright commentary on the Vietnam War, albeit cloaked as an interstellar conflict between humans and a mysterious Tauran species.

Since the novel hadn't yet been published, Mein Host wasn't yet aware of the book's scathingly brilliant exposure of the hopeless fraudulence of war. This he would discover a few years later when he actually read it. However, it wasn't his book that Joe wanted to talk about. It was something that had happened to him in the war. Something so strange, "so damned mysterious, so, well, so frankly miraculous . . . even if I did believe in that sort of stuff, which I still don't. But I don't know what to make of it."

He explained that as a combat engineer he was most frequently well behind the worst of the action, as he was on this particular day. He felt relatively safe, he said, or as safe as it was ever possible to feel in-country. He was part of a large number of other U.S. Army personnel, mostly grunts with a few engineers and officers, who were working in and around one of the main ammunition dumps when the bomb hit.

Joe believed it was caused by a V.C. rocket, because suddenly the dump exploded without any warning. He said that 184 military personnel were killed outright. Terrible power had been unleashed in another horrifying and tragic expression of the hopeless futility of war.

Yet Joe Haldeman walked out of that explosion barely touched by the fearful blast.

It didn't seem that he was exaggerating, or making the whole story up. He was genuinely amazed and baffled by what had occurred. He was the only man to walk out of the inferno. How *could* this have happened?

He was struggling to believe it was pure luck. How could he have been *that* lucky, when 184 others had been so *unlucky*? It didn't answer anything. It robbed the event of *meaning* to think like that—and surely such an extraordinary situation must have some meaning. If it was meaningless—just a lucky throw of the dice—then did 184 soldiers simply cast an unlucky throw? It was a downright improbability—indeed a statistical anomaly—that would have savaged the body count of American dead for that day had the military authorities been prepared to tell the truth about the Americans who died that day.

Yet it wasn't resentment as much as a perplexed wonderment that Joe alone had survived which appeared to trouble him so. Surely his survival *must* have some greater meaning. His fellows' deaths weren't completely meaningless, were they?

This wasn't survivor's guilt. Nor did it appear that Joe was wrestling with any sense of unreasonable self-importance. He didn't seem to feel that he had been saved for any particular purpose. He said it wasn't that he felt especially bad that he'd survived when so many others had died. Neither did he feel that the awful animal rush of guilty joy at being alive at the expense of the others. Of if he did, he claimed it hadn't lasted long.

This event hadn't turned Joe into a prophet. But being an extremely intelligent and curious man, it had forced him to look more deeply into the nature of reality. The explosion had shown him something he was still struggling to understand—a truth just beyond his conscious awareness. This was a truth that was so vitally important that he couldn't afford to let it slip through his grasp, and yet it was so elusive that it always managed to escape him.

Joe Haldeman, as my ward told Juliette later, had his "snake moment."

Yet it was an exchange Joe and Mein Host had toward the end of their unexpectedly long discussion that made my ward so thoughtful afterward. Whether the implications of what he believed he had stumbled on had struck Joe in the same way, he never discovered.

But then again, I wonder if the concept of "sidestepping death"—as my ward came to call the phenomenon when he thought he understood it better—was something designed more for him to study, and of which to take special note.

Mein Host couldn't have been consciously aware of what awaited him in a scant few months: an event that would finally open his eyes to the true nature of death, as well as answer the question at the center of Joe Haldeman's enigma.

My ward would soon discover for himself—with an unshakable certainty—the answer to one the deepest mysteries of life. Oh, nothing so grandiose as the meaning of life, but the more modest and pragmatic realization that *every human life has meaning.*

The life of every single human being is *inherently* meaningful. Yet most humans will only discover the profound truth of this when they pass from third-density life.

12

Furious Transformations

Prince Janda-chi's Residence, Evolutionary Polarization, Norman Spinrad's Joke, the Foundation Faith, and Enter a Succubus

I had no idea what to expect as Unava guided me past the ornamental waterfall and into the entrance hall of Prince Janda-chi's summer residence. I barely remembered the place from the last time I was here. It was so long ago it was now almost unrecognizable.

There was no front door, for example; no obvious barrier to entering the place. The dwelling was, or appeared to be, completely undefended. This must be one of the most special places on the southern continent—on the whole planet, if you think about it. After all, he was one of the Planetary Princes of the entire world, and yet the house seemed to be open and welcoming to everyone.

I was asked to wait in a small ancillary chamber. It was windowless, and a hidden door slid closed behind me after Unava had disappeared, presumably to speak with the Prince. He was probably updating him on my reactions and questions during our trip here, I thought. I felt an almost imperceptible movement in the room, as if it gave a slight shiver. This was followed by a slight tingling starting at my head and moving steadily down my body. It took a few moments, but by the time the sensation reached my waist I realized I was being scanned by some hidden device.

That took me aback, I can tell you. Most natives of Zandana—or most other material visitors—likely wouldn't have been aware of the scan, but it let me know the dwelling really did have its hi-tech protections. The Prince must have cloaked the scanning rays so as not to appear more advanced than the indigenous natives and their own technological progress. This in and of itself told me he was still maintaining the course he had set under Lucifer's guidance.

In the case of Zandana, both of the Planetary Princes had originally located their city of Zandan—their equivalent of Dalamatia—and settled on the same continent. After many generations of peaceful attempts to advance the cultures of the other island nations—as Unava had told me earlier—they had chosen to focus their entire efforts on their own cultural development down in the south.

I realized I had never even been to the other island continents, and I'd visited Zandana at least half a dozen times. There was simply nothing of much interest on the islands. Here in the south "is where the action takes place" was the way I thought about it.

Before I could start to feel inadequate—a watcher is simply meant to impartially observe—another hidden door slid open in the chamber to reveal an enormous meeting room. Unava (mysteriously) was there to greet me again and ushered me into the room. He was friendly enough, yet I couldn't help but feel nervous as I followed him cautiously into the cavernous space.

I sensed the presence of Prince Janda-chi approaching well before I saw him. Unava must have retreated silently behind me, because for a few moments I felt I was completely alone in that vast and gently glowing space.

At that moment it was almost completely bare. High canted walls melded into a roof way above me. The walls appeared to be carved out of bedrock, and yet they were geometrically facetted into a multitude of triangles and trapezia, which scattered rays from small floating light panels that were similar to those I'd first seen in the transport lounge.

I turned to see where Unava had gone. The hidden door had disappeared seamlessly into the wall behind me. The wall was the only vertical feature in the room, and as I looked more closely I could see it was composed of a mass of thin shelves reaching up to the ceiling. On top of the shelves sat row upon row of small transparent boxes, each one containing what seemed to be a tiny multicolored glass sphere. There were thousands upon thousands—perhaps millions—of these little colored balls. They were like transparent marbles that might have sparkled and flashed had more light been directed on the wall from the floating panels.

Something must have detained the Prince.

I could hear the faint cry of a child far above me, then—one after another—the cries of small children joined with the first until a chorus of sleepy, angry cries was echoing indistinctly through the passages and corridors. It sounded like a Greek chorus commenting on my arrival.

If this was what was delaying the Prince then it might take him a little longer to get down here than he thought.

Hearing those kids gave me a good feeling though. I thought of Caligastia, who I reckoned really didn't like human children. I found it unusually touching that a Planetary Prince would actually have children in his dwelling. In his dwelling! Prince Caligastia would have been appalled.

I was no wiser about the purpose of those masses of little colored spheres: Were they performing a function, or were they simply an unusual decorative feature?

Turning away from the puzzling wall, I moved toward the massive curved window at the far end of the room. I could see from there how the architect had cleverly cantilevered the structure out over yet another precipitous drop; this time it was facing the mountainous natural reserve!

The natural reserve?! Is *that* what I was seeing? How could that be?

The land fell away into a deep valley before it climbed up through the mists and dropped away again, folding into the far mountains, soft-silvered by the moon, and then shading imperceptibly into the distant darkness.

But how could this be? Wasn't it what I'd glimpsed earlier from the ramp?

I suddenly felt ridiculously disorientated. Everything was the wrong way around. It made no sense to be seeing the mountainous reserve. Not through this window, anyway. I'm usually good with directions. Watchers have to be.

Entering with Unava, I'd had no feeling of being turned around—yet here I was looking in completely the opposite direction. There were those alabaster columns of water I'd seen earlier. The Temple of the Mountain God, I'd called it, rather proud of my imagery, yet also finding myself questioning where just such an image might have come from.

I must have been distracted by that thought, because I didn't feel the Prince's approach until I saw his reflection in the window. In a moment of confusion, it seemed to me that the Prince was outside the window, slowly floating over the valley. His image was slightly distorted by the curve and blemishes in the glass—giving the impression that he was weaving and dancing his way toward me.

Was he, I wondered, enhancing his movements slightly to exaggerate the effect?

I could just make out that he was smiling before I turned to greet him, so I assumed he knew what he was doing—he may even have instructed his architect to create that effect. And it worked! I couldn't take my eyes off his dancing figure.

It struck me then that we might both have been confused. I'd not yet adjusted down to the Prince's frequency domain, so I must have appeared more like a ghostly form to him. I trusted he wouldn't take it as an insult—it was considered bad form in such encounters between beings from different domains not to have matched frequencies prior to meeting face-to-face. (Need I add that all but a very few sentient beings have faces?)

I quickly downstepped into a mutual frequency domain. I synched my senses to that domain as I was turning to greet the Prince, so that—by the time we both actually met—we had physically materialized enough to embrace.

This surprised me. It was the first time he'd been so openly warm to me. My previous dealings had been chiefly with Prince Zanda, who tended to be a more detached presence. I'd always enjoyed Janda-chi, Prince Zanda's executive assistant, but I can't say I knew him that well. Yet here he was, all smiles, apparently happy to see me and pressing me to his broad and comely bosom.

The attentive reader will recall this is the first time I have spoken about actually physically embracing another being.

Of course, my friendly Transport Seraph Eleena embraces me, as she embraces every being who travels within her heat shield. But that is rather different. Eleena and other Transport Seraphs may not much enjoy transporting rebel angels, yet they have no choice but to do so if required. I regarded myself as most fortunate to have made such an ally of Eleena, although I knew if it came down to the wire she would be aligned with the MA. I would be deceiving myself if I thought she wouldn't betray our friendship without a second thought.

If it has seemed unusual that there should have been such an obvious lack of physical affection in my narrative, I would explain that this was the result of the increasing polarization of the energies present primarily on Earth. The further the world in question deviated from what the MA considered the tried-and-true patterns of planetary development, the greater the polarization of the energies present on that planet. This, in turn, increases the propensity for extremes of thought and action among the protagonists.

This held true to a much lesser extent on Zandana and doubtless appeared in one form or another on the rest of the thirty-five worlds that had broken away from the MA at the time of the revolution. By isolating the entire System, the MA had cast off those worlds from the overall cultural developmental pattern that it had established and perfected over the eons. This had been practiced on billions of worlds seeded with organic life, then nurtured through their evolutionary processes. Those worlds had been settled in light and life.

In our cosmology lectures back on Jerusem, we had been taught about the existence of seven massive Superuniverses that in total comprised the Multiverse. This Local Universe of Nebadon was located in the seventh Superuniverse and was numbered 611,121 out of the total of seven hundred thousand Local Universes. This underscored for us how much of the Multiverse was already populated with intelligent life. In cosmic terms, I recall being told that the Local Universe of Nebadon had come very late in the day.

There were even some hints given by one or two of the more open-minded lecturers that suggested preparations were already under way for what might occur when the entire Multiverse would be settled in light and life.

The result of being isolated from the MA's natural patterns of development has allowed the individual, isolated planets to progress—or regress—largely according to the actions of their Planetary Princes. Although this was never mentioned in the MA's lectures, it was becoming more obvious to me that the policy of isolating worlds was a lot more purposeful than first met the eye.

It came to me that a system-wide rebellion would provide the MA with the chance to introduce change into the stable and well-organized Multiverse—and do it without negatively affecting planets outside that System. A rebellion was, if you like, an experiential way of assessing a variety of different factors, from the preparedness of Planetary Princes to operate free of the MA's oversight to creating arenas in which mortal beings could develop the muscle of faith.

This became clear to me as I was standing in Prince Janda-chi's enormous rock-hewn room, the mountains and valleys stretching out before me into the darkness. I saw in those moments of unusual clarity how planets like Zandana and Earth were being used to foster greater individuality and self-reliance.

Whether this meant that such rebellions and revolutions and the subsequent isolation of the planetary Systems involved were intentionally provoked—or were permitted in the grand scheme of things— remained a mystery to me. Perhaps they were simply the product of unanticipated individual actions—as the MA's local agents appeared to believe.

What I did realize, however, was the profound difference in the clarity of the World Mind that I was experiencing on Zandana. Given a few moments of being on my own, I found I possessed a degree of lucidity of thought I had not experienced on Earth.

It was as I was enjoying this sensation of mental clarity that I saw a slight movement reflected in the massive window that curved up above me.

Then I felt the presence of Prince Janda-chi again.

And I still had no idea of why he'd called me here.

* * *

As fall turns to winter, New York City can become beset by biting cold winds blowing down from Canada; winds that howl through the avenues bringing freezing rain and turning street-bought umbrellas inside out.

Sometimes the winds bring violent arctic snowstorms. They are pretty at first, granted, and the snow paradoxically warms the city's air. But then the snow turns into dirty gray heaps stacked on sidewalks, and it morphs into deceptively deep puddles of slush that fool the unaware and melt into ice-cold water in one's shoes. More often, however, it would be a terrible, freezing gale that would turn a donator's extremities blue and numb, however bundled up that donator might happen to be.

The weather made no difference to donating. Donators were sent out in rain, wind, or snow, and they were expected to take care of themselves. The bitter cold days naturally thinned out the crowds of people on the streets of Manhattan and thus could radically reduce the number of potential buyers of PROCESS magazine.

When Mein Host was out donating or selling magazines in such difficult conditions, he found this could work both ways. If someone could actually be stopped in a snowstorm or a gale, then he could be almost sure of a sale—or a larger than expected donation—purely from sympathy or admiration. But it could also lead to long and frustrating days wherein money was scarce, which put an even greater emphasis on bringing increasing numbers of people into the Chapter.

The weekly science-fiction lecture series was filling the new theater, the Alpha, with enthusiastic audiences, and the well-known writers who were giving the lectures appeared to be enjoying themselves. As well, they provided the fodder for some good stories that were exchanged later at the evening meeting. More than one pretty young Processean, for example, reported being pinched on her bottom by the avuncular but saucy Isaac Asimov.

After the lectures were over, the coffeehouse became a hothouse of animated discussion. It was in the course of just one of these discussions when my ward had an encounter that—had he known better—would have made a fine story for the evening meeting. But he didn't know any better—and that was the practical joke he fell into. He was the butt of a joke that he only realized many years later.

It occurred after Alfred Bester's lecture. Bester was an enigmatic figure in the sci-fi world who had written unusual and brilliant books. He had drawn a large and rapturous crowd, which included a few other eminent, but younger science-fiction authors.

Mein Host, who had organized the event as usual, was moving between the tables in the coffeehouse, greeting and talking to people, when he approached a table at which two or three writers and friends sat chatting.

It was Norman Spinrad who beckoned my ward over to their table, introducing him to those sitting there one by one. The last person, a fair-haired, bearded, middle-aged man, was the author Chip Delany.

It happened that Samuel Delany—"Chip" to his friends—had written a work that my ward greatly admired: the trilogy titled The Fall of the Towers. As well, he had written what my ward believed to be among the finest of science-fiction novellas—some of which earned Samuel Delany a Hugo Award or a Nebula Award for Best Short Story of the year. Delany, who lived in the city, was on my ward's list to be invited to lecture, but he'd never managed to make contact with the man. Now here was Samuel Delany sitting at the table in the coffeehouse and smiling patiently up at him.

Being asked to slide into the seat next to "Chip," with Norman Spinrad settling in opposite them and the others craning forward to hear above the babble of conversation in the Cavern, my ward was invited to ask Samuel Delany some of the questions his books had raised.

Norman Spinrad appeared to be encouraging my ward with his questions while Delany answered as best as he was able. Few writers really appreciate being closely questioned on books written many years earlier, yet Delany seemed to be deriving unusual pleasure as he stumbled through his curiously improbable answers. My ward said afterward that—going by the man's answers—he reckoned he understood Delany's books better than the writer himself did.

Sitting there on opposite sides of the table, Spinrad and Delany seemed to have some secret passing wordlessly between them that they were keeping suppressed beneath a veneer of friendly banter—which included Delany's strange replies. The man's bright-blue eyes sparkled with humor while he gave his convoluted answers to my ward's questions about *Babel-17* and *The Einstein Intersection,* two of his favorite novellas.

The others around the table seemed to be behaving strangely too. They were craning forward to hear the words dripping from the lips of the Great Man, yet they seemed to be giggling at odd moments.

Mein Host appeared not to notice this because he was so focused on talking with Delany, yet I could feel his growing disappointment over the course of this sci-fi bantering. As he said afterward at the evening meeting, Sam Delany was a nice enough man but nothing like he'd imagined him. He told the others that he simply couldn't get any real sense out of him. And yet there were those wonderful, visionary books.

It was only many years later when my ward chanced to see an author photograph of Samuel Delany on the jacket of one of his more recent books that he finally got the joke.

Chip Delany, of course, was never the smiling, blue-eyed, bearded man, introduced by Norman Spinrad, who seemed so loftily amused by my ward's enthusiasm for his books. Samuel Delany was an African American—one of a very few African American science-fiction writers—and in my ward's opinion, among the finest in the field.

So in the end there did turn out to be some truth to my ward's observation that the Samuel Delany he met was nothing like he'd imagined he would be from reading the man's books.

Matters at the Omega were in the process of furious transformation. With Robert and Verona out of the picture—and Mary Ann finally in complete charge—her first action was to change the name of the community to the Foundation Faith of the Millennium and to excise Lucifer and Satan from their complex theology. Moving forward, the emphasis was to be placed entirely on Jehovah—with whom Mary Ann now believed herself most closely identified.

In terms of their "god-patterns," Mary Ann claimed to be a J/S: a combination of the dogmatic and autocratic patterns of a Jehovah and the passionate and creative/destructive patterns of a Satan.

The fourth of their so-called Great Gods of the Universe, Jesus Christ, presented more of a problem. Mary Ann, at her most hopeful, had always promoted Robert as a Christ figure. Indeed, many of the junior Processeans—who weren't aware of Mary Ann or of her place in the community—had thought of Robert in these exalted terms.

With Robert gone, Mary Ann would have known that she needed to tread carefully. She would have let go of Lucifer and Satan without a second thought—and no doubt to the relief of some Processeans, as Satan and Lucifer had always been a hard sell—but Jesus Christ was a far more controversial figure to drop from the new cosmology. He needed to remain, but from now on Christ would have to remain in the background, playing a secondary role to Jehovah.

The hymns and chants were changed, and some with an undue emphasis on Lucifer or Satan were quietly dropped. The responses in the assemblies were rewritten to reflect this new direction. Any sign of the Process Church was removed, any mention of the Process was somehow diverted, and the coffeehouse—which had been called Satan's Cavern back in London, then the Cavern in America—now was simply "J's Place."

My ward has joked that perhaps the most onerous—and certainly the most painful—of these transformations was the "appallingly kitsch, ridiculously heavy" gold-colored Star of David that they now had to wear around their necks.

The six points of the star touched a circle drawn around it. The circle's diameter was about two and a quarter inches. The metal itself had a thickness of slightly more than an eighth of an inch. It was heavy, and it was dangerous. Two large Fs, one inverted against the other, painted navy blue and indented into the gold-painted pewter star, had replaced the elegant silver serpent-and-cross design previously worn.

My ward has said he assumed the design of the pendant must have been dreamed up by Mary Ann as a way of placing her stamp on her new organization—the Foundation Faith. I have heard him say he thought the pendant was both ridiculously ostentatious (as he later came to think of Mary Ann) and a continual punishment to wear. Any sudden movement slammed the star into the wearer's body, ensuring that at least one or more of the six well-placed points drove hard into the chest.

In the drawing office, four or five Processeans were typically bowed over their drawing boards, engrossed in their work. Their activity entailed much leaning forward, then suddenly straightening up. The momentary squeals of pain and irritation became a background chorus to the radio in the corner that was constantly playing popular music of the 1960s and early '70s.

PROCESS magazine had been renamed, not surprisingly, FOUNDATION magazine, and the staff was busily at work—leaning over their drawing boards, then straightening up—producing the first issue of FOUNDATION magazine.

Mary Ann had instructed Mein Host to make sure the design of the new magazine appeared very different from its former incarnation. I had watched him throwing everything he knew and more into developing a unique graphic style for the half a dozen issues of PROCESS, and now he was being told to develop an entirely new and different style. As if it was as easy as waving a wand!

I could see he took on this new task willingly, however. He tells me it didn't occur to him at the time that his design work had been treated so casually by Mary Ann, yet I could tell his heart was no longer in it.

Gone were the elaborate four-color, handmade, color separations; no more hand-drawn psychedelic fonts were allowed. The graphic exuberance needed to be toned down for it had to look like a more normal magazine.

This turning back to a more conventional graphic style in magazine design soon became representative of the community's more general attempts to appear respectable.

As a spurned wife might be expected to speak poorly of the husband who had abandoned her, so Mary Ann used her split from Robert to dismiss the Process—along with her husband, whom she claimed responsible for the failures of the past.

Yet for all Mary Ann's imperious actions and her cavalier dismissal of Robert's role in the community, Mein Host, along with the others in her inner circle, remained troublingly loyal to the Oracle. If by this stage my ward still considered Mary Ann as the incarnate Goddess, his belief in her must have been starting to wear somewhat thin.

However, by this time he was being promoted again, this time to take overall charge of the New York Chapter, which was currently the headquarters of the Foundation Faith of the Millennium.

* * *

"Unava has been showing you around?" Prince Janda-chi asked after the formal greetings were over. "I trust your visit has been satisfactory."

Taking my arm in a friendly fashion, he guided me over to a cushioned seating area sunk into the floor in a small chamber off the main room.

"Unava tells me you were surprised to see our progress," he said after seating himself in the pit opposite me.

I suppose it was then that the full reality of where I was hit me. I hadn't come to Zandana with any thought of being conducted into the Prince's presence; in fact, rather the opposite. I'd hoped that so long after the thwarted barbarian invasion the Prince would have forgotten my idea. I'd blurted it out more as a joke before I could stop myself. Making love not war would never have worked on Earth.

In fact, I was surprised when Unava had found me so soon after I'd arrived. I was hoping for some rest and relaxation, a chance to get away from the stresses and turbulence of life back home.

"Very gratified, my Prince," I said courteously, still unsure why I was here. "What you have accomplished since my previous visit surpasses any expectation."

The Prince nodded his lovely head in appreciation, while telling me that what I was experiencing had been brought about by the promise of the imminent arrival of a magisterial mission made some fifteen hundred Zandana-years ago. It seemed they had spent the time preparing, straightening up their act as it were—yet there was still no sign of the mission.

There was a long silence while I imagined the Prince was collecting his thoughts. I saw this was every bit as unusual a situation for him as it was for me. I appreciated it couldn't have been easy for him to spend time in my presence. In spite of the smiles and the warmth of his initial greeting, I was still an unhappy reminder of the disastrous impact of the rebellion on his Lanonandek brother, Prince Caligastia.

Janda-chi's face turned stern while he seemed lost in thought, and I suddenly recalled something touched on the last time I was here . . . or was it the previous visit? Wasn't it suggested that I might become an intermediary between the Planetary Princes on Zandana and Earth?

I'd given it little thought—except to believe that it didn't sound like an optimal function for a watcher. Watchers are not negotiators; we are not even ambassadors. We're not really go-betweens, and I certainly didn't believe we were spies! We weren't trained for that sort of activity—or prepared for it—so I didn't take the idea seriously at the time. Frankly, I hadn't given it a second thought. Yet here was a Prince of Zandana with a solemn look on his face, showing every sign that *he* had *not* forgotten.

While I waited for him to speak, I was able to look around the vast chamber from my perch in the side chamber's conversation pit. It was only then that I saw how I'd been tricked into believing I was facing in the wrong direction. The sealed windowless chamber in which I'd been scanned must have been an elevator. I remembered experiencing a slight shiver in the chamber without knowing what it was, and without feeling any upward movement.

"It rises in a spiral," Prince Janda-chi said, now smiling again, obviously proud that his feature worked so well. With a watcher too! There was a wide-eyed childlike quality to his laughter, and I thought once again how different he was from Prince Caligastia. Beings of the same order too.

Smiles over, he said with no preamble that he'd been made aware through his interplanetary midway network that Prince Caligastia was proceeding with his plans to interfere with the Earth's planetary grid.

"I have no doubt that you, as a watcher, understand the implications of this better than most. If this should be allowed to occur it will sabotage the very meaning and purpose of the mortal ascension process. You must understand this. If he succeeds in short-circuiting mortal ascension, it will be the end of him—and his planet too."

This was altogether extremely odd.

One of Lucifer's main complaints—if I remember rightly (I believe it was even in his manifesto)—concerned what he believed to be an excessive amount of attention given to mortals and their ascendant Multiverse careers. Yet here was Prince Janda-chi lecturing to me about the importance of mortals and their natural ascendance process.

"It will push the MA over the edge," he said, looking me firmly in the eye. "Betraying atomic secrets is one matter. That was criminal enough . . . but interfering with the grid? No, that would be more terrible than you can imagine."

I wasn't quite sure how to react.

Did Prince Janda-chi really expect me to communicate the seriousness of Caligastia's action to him? Or was he subtly plying me for further information? Was he perhaps implicating me in his game? He *was* a rebel Prince, after all. And a Planetary Prince needed to be a far more complicated being than a mere watcher.

But no. His emotional body showed no sign of deceit.

"Much has changed these past few millennia," he said, his voice suddenly soft and saddened. I thought it best to remain silent as I still wasn't sure what was expected of me or even where my true loyalties lay.

I must have been transparent, because his next question cut to the heart of my ambivalence.

"Am I correct in saying that it is to Prince Lucifer you pay allegiance?"

Where was this going? I had to be cautious here. Astar had mentioned the last time we'd encountered one another that she'd heard some conflicts were blowing up among the leadership of the revolution. It hadn't overly concerned me at the time, but now it suddenly felt terrifyingly serious. It wasn't difficult to work out that if the rebel angels fractured into different groups, we would lose all credibility as a unified force of freedom fighters—which is how we thought of ourselves.

"And yet you serve on a world falling under Prince Satan's aegis?" It was no question. He would have known this. As, of course, he would be aware that his own world was among the nineteen overseen by Prince Lucifer.

"Perhaps if I'd had a choice . . . ," I murmured, playing for time.

"And your sympathies for your Prince Caligastia?"

I dreaded the question. I am not able to lie. I can dissemble, but I cannot tell a deliberate lie. Besides, a watcher's lies are just too obvious.

"Prince Caligastia troubles me," I said as tactfully as possible. "I have ceased to understand his motives . . ."

"Do you not realize what he is doing, this Prince of yours?" Jandachi's beautiful face contorted in anger, and he was almost shouting across at me. "Caligastia's actions have disgraced us. We will be tainted by his sins . . . all of us! How can he not understand that! He is making any resolution in our favor absolutely impossible! *He* is absolutely impossible!"

He was shouting at me by this time; perhaps he was watching the frightful possibilities of a failed revolution pass before his eyes.

When I try to recall such an event, I find it can irritate me how, in such moments, my mind can easily wander, and I can only recall snatches of what the Prince was so furious about.

Now that I think about it, this does make an interesting contrast to those times I'm narrating incidents from my ward's life. In such cases, when I have scant recollection of our dialogue, I'm able to appeal to his recording angel for help. But I have no recording angel of my own to whom I may turn when I write of other beings.

So this is essentially what I've recalled of that curious speech.

"We can only succeed in our revolution," Prince Janda-chi said when he'd cooled down somewhat, "if we present the MA with a respectful and unified front. This, watcher, you must understand. Satan and Caligastia between them are risking any hope we have of demonstrating the worthiness of our claims. They are ruining our plans."

The Prince threw up his arms, gesturing toward the massive window in the large room and the mountains beyond.

"You have observed how well we nurture our land. Unava tells me you think of Zandana as your other home world."

I nodded my agreement, but I was still emotionally shaken by the Prince's outburst. A Lanonandek Son of Prince Janda-chi's order was equipped with a far stronger and more flexible emotional body than any angel of my order. His sudden shift from anger at Caligastia's antics on Earth to his apparent interest in my affinity for Zandana must have left me behind emotionally, because at this point my recollection became less clear.

(I've since considered it possible that Prince Janda-chi tried to throw a not so successful blanket of amnesia over what he'd told me when we were sitting together in the pit. Again, it's something Lanonandeks can do!)

Putting together my dimly remembered snatches of what turned out to be a long and sometimes angry, sometimes sad monologue, I do recall him frequently betraying his terrible frustration at what had become of some of the revolutionary planets. If I caught the gist of it, he'd said two of those thirty-seven worlds had already destroyed themselves, and another one was well on its way. He said that there had been the normal mass planetary evacuations, but he confessed it had been a shocking disappointment for the rebel leadership to lose entire planetary biospheres.

Apparently this had never occurred when planetary Systems were governed under the MA's direct supervision.

And it was certainly the last thing Lucifer wanted to have happen.

I recall thinking at that point that Prince Janda-chi appeared singularly well informed about the inner workings of the revolution. He made an unexpected contrast—this I do recall—between those worlds overseen by Lucifer, and those falling under Satan's aegis.

Yet it was for Prince Caligastia that he retained his most bitter ire—even blaming him for the long-delayed appearance of the Magisterial Son and his mission on Zandana. He claimed that Caligastia was holding them back.

He said he didn't believe Caligastia was insane—he never had. From what he knew about life on Earth, he felt he had detected a subtle edge of intentionality lurking beneath every significant action taken by Prince Caligastia. Talking about this had further infuriated Janda-chi and set him off on another rant, this time rather improbably accusing Caligastia of being one of the MA's agent provocateurs, embedded in Lucifer's revolution and acting in a manner to completely discredit it. (Now, *that* was a new one to me!)

He said he might have understood it better had his brother, Prince Caligastia, been merely inept or confused. Yet to think that Caligastia had been deliberately driving his planet into ruin to bring the entire revolution into disrepute—that was truly utterly reprehensible and dishonorable beyond belief.

* * *

Observing my ward's emotional body throughout the fall months of 1973, I could see that something was changing. The colors of his aura were becoming muted and dull. He had been working harder than ever, now having to add designing the new magazine to the creating and administering of the conferences and lectures series. He counted himself lucky to get four hours of sleep a night.

He now had six or eight full-time secretaries, one of whom had inserted herself in the role of executive assistant. I'll call her Sister Marion.

The first thing to know: Sister Marion was definitely not an incarnate rebel angel. She was a very normal, passionate, average-looking human being in her late twenties; not very bright, but painfully loyal and with an un-self-conscious boldness that I observed could deeply embarrass my ward if he was anywhere around to witness it.

Sister Marion had fastened herself onto my ward with a tenacity fueled by a commitment that horrified him when she told him what it was. She had promised Jehovah she would take care of Mein Host and serve him until death! She had dedicated her life of service to my ward, for heaven's sake!

You might wonder how this situation had come about. My ward wanted to know, and she had been finally persuaded to reveal what had happened. It had occurred, she said, back when she came around daily to work at 242 East 49th Street during the time that my ward and half a dozen other priests were living there together. This had been during the low period, after they had acquired the First Avenue Chapter, and the reality of what an impossible financial challenge it presented was sinking in.

It was true, the morale amongst the senior and mid-level Processeans had dropped to the lowest level I had ever seen. People were exhausted from overwork, and depressed to see so little manifesting from all their efforts.

Marion had said what touched her so deeply was that Mein Host had remained optimistic and enthusiastic throughout this period—spending time encouraging those who needed a bucking-up and, as she said, "being invariably cheerful and kind whenever the others were in a murk."

It was his "generosity of spirit" that had apparently sealed the deal for her. And off she'd gone to pray to Jehovah—Marion was a J/C, Jehovah/Christ, the most self-righteous of the god-patterns—to make her selfless, if not ridiculous, pledge to care for her Father Micah through thick and thin.

And my ward didn't even like the woman!

No doubt there are some men who would be thrilled to have a woman so deeply committed to their welfare, and my ward himself would tell you that Marion was certainly helpful to him in many ways during his time in the community.

I have observed that one of the unacknowledged blights of a celibate community is the development of frequently unbalanced emotional attachments. As there is no chance for sexual fulfillment—a time when the suitability of two people can become clearer—sexual delusions can metastasize and persist far beyond their natural shelf life.

I make no apology for my ward for making use of Marion. He knew her nature. He didn't like it, but it was useful to him. He was aware she was one of those people who bully their juniors and suck up to their superiors. But she was organized and efficient, and she brought him fried eggs and tomatoes in his office for lunch. She kept away the people who wanted a piece of him, and, unbeknownst to him, she became known as "the dragon lady" guarding the gate of his office.

She clearly admired Mein Host, and might have thought—but would never have admitted, even to herself—that she was in love with him. My ward evidently chose to ignore her unexpressed affection, if he'd even noticed it in the first place.

He clearly disliked being associated with her in any way other than the most official. The difficulty here was that Sister Marion had a jones for singing in public. After one such event, he made sure to avoid her performances in the Cavern, which she did with all the confidence of someone who'd never been told the unfortunate truth. She was a little girl who relished showing off—growing up in a household of indulgent parents, a bunch of condescending aunts and uncles, and an adoring younger sister. Why, no one was likely to tell her she sang out of tune, or that her dancing was more like prancing, or that she was trying too hard, or that her precocity was an embarrassment—because, dammit, she was so darn cute!

Sadly, what is cute in a seven-year-old is seldom as appealing in a woman approaching thirty. Marion seemed to be unaware of this discrepancy, because—when she performed in the Cavern—she exuded sexuality with the innocence of a seven-year-old emulating a sultry torch singer. I once heard my ward telling Mother Juliette, who generally shared his opinion, that the worst part of Marion's performance was that she had no idea just how banal and awful it really was.

Marion must have been a fan of the Welsh pop singer Shirley Bassey, because her favorite song was the sexually suggestive hit song by Ms. Bassey, "Big Spender," which Sister Marion delivered with every exaggerated bump and grind that the lyrics demanded.

Bumpity-bump: "The moment you walked in the joint . . ."

Bump-bump: "I could see you were a man of distinction, a real big spender . . . ," she sang, her hips swiveling, one hand clutching the microphone, fixing her gaze on one *man of distinction* after another, pointing with a forefinger and moving between the tables, swaying and winking.

"I don't pop my cork for every man I see . . . ," bump, wink, sway—erotic energy pouring out of her as if she was flaunting her sexual unavailability in the faces of the customers.

"Hey, big spender! Spend a little time with me."

Groin grinding, more winking and undulating, Sister Marion's face now red with effort, weaving and wriggling her plump body between tables full of bewildered patrons.

"I could show you a good time.

Let me show you a good time."

And a final triumphant flourish, arms thrust in the air, face flushed and excited, expecting—no, demanding—the applause she must have received as a precocious child.

Could Sister Marion really have been so unaware of the sexual dissonance she was exhibiting? Did she never realize the effect she was having on other people? Was she unable to register what a tawdry impression she made with her crude exhibitionism?

For a fuller picture, it should be added that Sister Marion was no sylph. She was a healthy well-rounded young woman who looked like she'd never lost her puppy fat. Her Process (or Foundation) uniform always seemed a size too small for her, giving her the impression that at any moment she was about to burst out of her clothes. This curiously inflated look was emphasized by the shape and color of her face as well as by her bossy manner.

Sister Marion's was an undeveloped face, unformed, with the chubby cheeks of a baby, bright brown eyes, a small nose, and full sensual lips. Her hair tended to be frizzy and uncontrollable, and for a time she wore it in the style of an Afro or, as she sometimes called it in a moment of rare self-mockery, "a Jewfro."

On the whole, Marion was a woman who took herself rather too seriously. Her manner might have been generously called "outgoing" by someone unaware that she seemed to be living on the verge of hysteria. She was pushy and opinionated, and she liked to poke her nose into everyone's business. She had a quality common to all petty dictators: she had to know every detail of what was going on around her, just in case it might reflect badly on her.

I know Mein Host would agree in retrospect that he treated Sister Marion in a disgracefully offhand manner. He was never cruel or unkind, but it would have been obvious to anyone not blinded by devotion that he was trying to push Marion away, to get her to keep her distance and not crowd him. But that was impossible.

In that same conversation with Juliette that I mentioned earlier he'd said that he "couldn't fight Jehovah, for God's sake!" and they'd both had to laugh at that.

"Seriously, Juliette, you see the jam I'm in? I can't really tell her I think she's deluded, can I? I can't just invalidate her vow to Jehovah—however stupid I think it is. I'm trapped. I just can't dislodge her—and you know how I feel about her."

"Very flattering it must be," Juliette joked, not really understanding what so annoyed him about Marion. "She's useful. Look at what she does for you. I know you don't like her, but put up with it for a while . . . for her sake. She's utterly devoted to you . . ."

He retorted, "You're not getting it, Juliette. It's not as if I was given a choice! Nobody asked me whether I wanted her to take over my life. She just glommed onto me; told me Jehovah had told her to do it. What the hell am I going to say to that?!"

Mother Juliette wasn't having any of it.

"Don't be so spoiled, Micah!" she said sharply. "Put up with it . . . sooner or later she'll get the point and glom onto someone else. Mark my words."

Juliette was right, of course.

Although I'm sure she couldn't have imagined it would take another seven years for my ward to finally manage to dislodge this unwanted succubus—which is how he was referring to her by that time—to get her finally out of his life.

Mein Host had initially tried to discourage Marion from her vow to Jehovah—with mixed feelings, he would be the first to admit—but he soon found he had little choice but to surrender to her conviction of absolute rightness, while having to admit (to himself) that she was actually making his life flow a lot more smoothly. If he had to compromise, he was going to make her "work her ass off" for the vow.

I know Mein Host feels that this reveals him at his most opportunistic and hard-hearted. And yet, I don't believe he ever really stopped trying to get her to "move along."

However, there is no need to dwell any longer on Sister Marion, soon to become Mother Marion for her dedicated service. She moves into the background as my ward's executive assistant for the next four years. In the winter of 1977 she would come briefly back into the forefront of his life for a final round that would tax them both to their limits.

Until then, she would continue to irritate and embarrass him, the whole time feeding him and caring diligently for him. She would efficiently filter out the trivial and turn away those she called "star-fuckers." She would be envied and hated by young women who joined the community—brought in ("pulled in?") by my ward—and who therefore believed they deserved some personal time with him. She guarded Mein Host with a terrible ferocity.

Because of the protection Marion was giving him, he now was available to work on even more projects. A successful two-day conference that he put together on alternative medicine led to an even more controversial gathering of experts speaking about alternative cancer treatments. It brought in a full house.

Mein Host now had overall responsibility for a chapter of some twenty IPs, a growing crowd of OPs (Outside Processeans—referred to as "disciples"), along with design work on the new magazine. This was on top of creating the conferences and events that brought in the money.

He was in an almost terminal state of exhaustion. I could see that his immune system—accustomed by this time in his life to a wide variety of stresses and strains—was starting to show weakness.

If there is some truth to the astrological idea that those born under the sign of Gemini are particularly vulnerable to a weakness of the lungs, then my ward was beginning to add some credence to that belief. Although he had quit smoking cigarettes some years earlier, a lung inflammation that had been incipient for the previous few months was now active, and, as a result, he started to break out in fits of racking coughs, his sputum getting greener and uglier with every cough.

But the lad was English!

The birthplace of the stiff upper lip.

He was the product of a harsh, self-denying education.

Would such a man take notice of a trivial complaint?

13

Nigredo

Princely Manipulation, Amnesia Tricks,
Panentheist Insights, Grants for Satanists,
Atlantis Revisited, the Spy, and the NDE

I'd previously described Prince Janda-chi's face as lovely. And lovely it was—until it started contorting in anger.

I couldn't understand quite why he was venting his bile on me: it wasn't as if I could do anything about what was happening on Earth. I was merely a watcher. So I just watched and listened.

At some point I noticed a sudden and distinct shift in the Prince's mood during his prolonged monologue—when he was accusing Caligastia of being a venomous traitor to the true revolution. The savagery drained out of his tone. It was as if he had said enough, or perhaps too much.

His face quickly relaxed to lovely again.

Then to my surprise, he rose to his feet—smiling yes, but without another word he turned and strode off across the great hall to disappear through another hidden door that slid open and closed silently behind him.

In that moment, between the door sliding open and then closing, I was sure I could hear the distant joyful shouts of children floating across the hall to where I still sat in the pit.

I felt happy for the Prince. I remember that because what followed was far more troubling. A certain sense of unease had fallen over me while I was still sitting in the pit, but I couldn't grasp what was causing it. My thoughts were interrupted by Unava, who silently appeared to escort me out of Prince Janda-chi's residence and back to where I could pick up the monorail again.

Unava, still in astral form, didn't communicate as we moved back down the long ramp, and although I didn't feel he was being overtly unfriendly, I did get the distinct impression he would be glad to see me gone and back on Earth, minding my own business.

When the cabin arrived, Unava showed no sign of getting on it with me, which I took as encouragement to spend some more time going slowly and thinking through what had occurred in the Prince's residence.

Dawn was breaking over the distant horizon, the ocean turning blood red as the planet sunk gradually into the new day. The cabin was empty, and, after briefly accelerating to its optimum speed, it appeared to be making no local stops.

To my left, the rolling foothills were still in darkness as they rose up into the massive central mountains. I was unable to see the forms of the mountains. Their very tips, lit red by the sun, seemed to hang suspended in the darkened sky like a huddled clan of crimson arrowheads.

The feeling of unease returned as we descended into the lowlands, and it soon crystallized into a rather disturbing thought. Perhaps the talking and ranting Prince Janda-chi had been indulging in was really a smoke screen. Could his entire performance have been designed to distract my attention? And all the while the Prince was downloading everything I knew that lay beneath my conscious awareness. (Lanonandeks can do that too.)

And I hadn't even noticed it!

Oh yes! Prince Zanda was good, alright.

Now, of course, I can say with more certainty that Prince Janda-chi was trying to pick up what I'd been told during my interview with Lucifer.

That was the jewel of information I possessed, and, as you'll know, I wasn't even aware of it!

That must have been what Prince Janda-chi was trolling my mind for—and I still don't know if he reached deep enough to read it accurately!

It would have been Lucifer's talk of his experiment in what he'd called "cosmic alchemy" that Prince Janda-chi was really after. It would have settled many of the Prince's doubts to know Lucifer's plans for Earth. The concept that the planet was being developed as the base stage—the Nigredo—in a mighty work of planetary alchemy would have mollified his angry reactions about what was occurring on Earth, while giving deeper meaning to Prince Caligastia's actions.

However, as I sat in the empty cabin traveling steadily along its single rail, I consciously knew nothing of this. So I was left with the worrying thought that Prince Janda-chi wanted me to pass along his critical opinions directly to Caligastia.

Although that too seemed highly improbable.

Why would any Planetary Prince use such a clumsy method of criticizing or influencing another Prince? I then had an even more disturbing thought: Could Prince Janda-chi have been setting me up for an unpleasant confrontation with Caligastia? Or might he have been using me as his proxy for some private scheme of his own?

You can see how confused and troubled my mind was as I was trying to make sense of what I seemed to have strayed into.

It is only in writing this narrative that I've come to think that Lucifer must have so effectively erased all conscious knowledge of his Great Work from my brain that Janda-chi would have caught very little, if anything, of it. Perhaps that's why he went on and on blaming Caligastia for every offense he could think of—he was actually, fruitlessly, trying to grab the jewel.

Whether Prince Janda-chi managed to break through the amnesia barrier makes little difference to my story, though it does serve to further illustrate something of the psychic manipulation of amnesia that can occur between Multiverse personnel. It has been helpful to me, however, when I'm trying to identify those times this secret that I was unwittingly carrying came closer to the surface.

I hadn't yet understood, let alone accepted, that I was being used as an unconscious conduit for information passing between the senior leadership of the revolution. It was only when I was deep into this narrative that what had previously been hidden from me was coming to the surface.

I've had to have faith that there must have been a good reason for this long period of amnesia, or for being told of Lucifer's plans in the first place. And me, a mere watcher!

However, as I sped slowly along alone in that monorail cabin on Zandana, I had no conscious awareness of what I was carrying and what had made me of such interest to such as Prince Janda-chi.

Now, as I write these words, I am still unaware of this "good reason." Yet I am confident if I pursue this narrative wherever it may lead, I will discover why I was accorded this privileged insight. I may also discover why this revelation was then so effectively erased in my consciousness that I doubt even Janda-chi's artful extractive psychic skills had succeeded in bringing anything of value to light.

More recently, I've felt a deeper understanding stirring somewhere beyond the edge of my conscious awareness—so close and yet so far away. I just couldn't grasp hold of it. It made me think this particular issue is perhaps more relevant to my ward than to me.

Now I can see that to have known of Lucifer's cosmic alchemy so long ago—and to have spread that knowledge around—would have deprived the revolution of its dramatic spontaneity. This could never have been permitted. Every being needed to be fully committed to their role.

I suspect it's only today, writing in a time that many people believe will bring either global catastrophe or planetary transcendence, that knowing Lucifer's motives becomes of value. Understanding there was always a submerged current of intentionality—running unperceived beneath the drama of what has come to be known as the

Lucifer Rebellion—provides a deeper contextual framework and gives meaning to what is currently occurring on the planet.

As I draw close to a natural interlude in my story I owe it to myself to briefly summarize what I feel I've learned over the course of this narrative.

The most personally significant of these insights I must attribute to my close working relationship with my mortal collaborator over the course of writing these volumes. I know now, thanks to his compassionate nature, that all beings—all the players in the Lucifer Rebellion on both sides of the conflict, both good and bad, caring and cruel, loving and despised—are aspects of the Great Spirit, the Creator of all. My collaborator (the panentheist) likes to remind me that we are all aspects of this Creator Spirit. As such, we both transcend the Multiverse and yet are immanent in every form—material and immaterial—and in every subelectronic particle—those known and those yet a mystery. This Creator Spirit who we are part of and who is part of us is, by nature, both impersonal and personal, and who, in the form of the Supreme Deity, is imbuing and informing both mortals and celestials alike.

It is in the depth of this revelation that I can glimpse, if only for a moment, that every being is playing its part—knowingly or unknowingly—in the Creator's Great Work of refining the dross of living experience into the true gold of spiritual attainment.

So I am left with this thought: If there was a deeper alchemical purpose to Lucifer's plans for Earth, then can his actions be more meaningfully understood as a localized reflection of the Creator Spirit's desire for the spiritual refinement of all beings?

"Be ye perfect, even as I am perfect."

Isn't *that* the admonition that gives purpose, direction, and meaning to every living being—each according to its capacity for perfecting itself?

* * *

If, from time to time, I've painted some of the activities of the Process community in a poor light, I should also point out some of the good they managed to do. Though it must also be said that everything the community accomplished in the outside world—the "world of men" as they condescendingly called it—was invariably conducted with a mix of intentions.

Back in Toronto, for example, my ward and Andrew—the production manager of the magazine—had filled out an application for a grant from the Canadian government for the community's so-called social work. "So-called" because up until then, they had done no social work worthy of the term.

As I watched the two of them concocting their answers, joking about what to write, it was obvious they really weren't taking this seriously. In fact, they had forgotten about the application when news came through a couple of months later that they were being granted more than forty thousand Canadian dollars for their social outreach programs. These were social programs that Andrew and my ward had dreamed up when originally filling out the paperwork for the government.

It was this grant, more than any deep humanitarian urge, that required the community to create a soup kitchen for Toronto indigents, as well as a free clothing store. It must have soon become obvious to the Omega that doing this—actually serving needy people—turned out to be excellent public relations. Other chapters were therefore instructed to emulate the Toronto Chapter—although, because they were in America, they would have to do this without the largesse of the Canadian government.

The perceptive reader will have already deduced that starting and running a soup kitchen and free clothing store need not actually cost anything. Especially when both soup kitchen and store fitted tidily into the unused basement of the house they were using as the Cavern. The food was retrieved for free from supermarkets keen to clear their shelves of perfectly edible items a few days after their due date had expired, and the clothes were culled from the overstuffed cupboards of Toronto's generous—and sometimes guilty—citizens. On several occasions I overheard an expression new to me used to describe the grant: they had called it "money for jam."

When the grant to the Toronto Chapter ran its course, the contract was not renewed. After a sneering article appeared in the *Toronto Globe and Mail* attacking the liberal Trudeau agenda with the outrageous headline "Grants for Satanists!" the whole messy affair became an embarrassment for Pierre Trudeau's government in Ottawa. After boldly and fruitlessly trying to defend their decision to award the grant they quietly dropped the Process Church from their books.

However, the exercise did bring some real benefits.

The various chapters, once they had started their soup kitchens and attended to similar tasks, found it was to their advantage to be seen doing good works, and thus they continued distributing food and clothes for the poor and needy. Besides, the free stores provided volunteer work for the disciples; most of the gathering of food and clothing and tending of the store was left up to those who were trying to "work their way" into the community.

I'd overheard this arrangement described as a win-win situation more than once by the IPs. It provided useful work for the volunteers, it was good publicity, they were able to collect forty-four thousand dollars, they were bringing a lot of new people into the chapter, and it wasn't costing them a dime!

However, it *was* costing them something.

It was a rather more subtle form of currency that, over time, would take its toll.

It was evident to me from the start that few, if any, of the IPs had any genuine interest in soup kitchens or giving away clothes. I saw no sign of any real enthusiasm, for example, from my ward. Their humanitarian work seemed to be purely an expedient innovation. It might have merely added another level of hypocrisy to the community's activities were it not for the subtle moderating influence the work was gradually having on the IPs within the community.

As I've already noted, the Process had long claimed to have rejected humanity, for they felt they'd been collectively rejected *by* humanity. The title of one of Robert's books, *Humanity Is the Devil,* says all that needs to be said on this topic.

Yet when the chapters started including free stores and kitchens, the coffeehouses began to attract a different kind of customer. They started becoming gathering places for the homeless, the poor, and the needy. The Toronto Chapter coffeehouse, for example, briefly became a local hangout for homeless transvestites. Young Americans, exiled to Canada by their rejection of the draft for the war in Vietnam, frequently gravitated there. With the mental hospitals releasing patients stupefied with medication, more of the mentally troubled also found their way to the Process coffeehouse. And of course there were always the addicts.

This in turn forced each Processean to constantly have to deal directly with human beings who were often at the end of their tethers. Claiming that humanity was the devil might make a provocative title for a book, but it was merely an idea—a naive abstraction.

However, being confronted with a constant flow of people who needed genuine help—each with his or her own story as to how they had arrived at their sorry state of affairs—had the overall beneficial effect of gradually softening the Processeans' hard-hearted and cynical attitudes toward humanity.

There was something illustrative of the paradoxical nature of the Process in this, an unusual uniting of opposites. An expedient and self-serving action—the writing of the grant proposal and the use of the money—became transformed by circumstances and necessity into acts of authentic kindness and caring. Processeans found themselves unexpectedly doing socially useful work, feeling good about it, and growing from the experience.

* * *

The city of Zandan and the surrounding landscape were at their most glorious at daybreak, when the second of Zandan's two suns—the older and smaller one—started flooding the world with its curiously copper-colored light. I'd watched the light turning from red to copper as it crept down the mountains. When the hills and the faraway mountains were finally fully lit by the rays of the sun, I noticed a curious optical effect: the landscape had flattened out as though I was looking at a painted diorama.

I actually had to rub my eyes to try to make the effect go away; but no, it stayed in place until the planet had dropped sufficiently in its orbital path to allow the sun to throw deeper, sharper shadows. And this happened before my eyes. There was magic in this. I was glued to the window, fascinated by what I was watching.

I find I have no convenient metaphor for this odd visual effect. My collaborator is suggesting that perhaps it could be somewhat like watching a photograph sitting in a developing pan, an image that gradually appears on a blank white sheet of photographic paper until the entire form is clearly visible. Not bad. It did have something of that quality—as if I was watching a vast painting slowly coming alive as it gradually gained the substance of a third dimension.

You can see how distracted I was by this unexpected beauty—and I'd intended to use this trip to consider what had happened back with Prince Janda-chi.

I still didn't know how long I would be in the monorail cabin, or indeed where I was going to end up. I thought for a time it was going to take me into Zandan, but no, we brushed the limits of the city without stopping. It was then I realized that it looked like I was going to be deposited back at the Seraphic Transport Center.

Someone evidently didn't want me on Zandana any longer!

Disembarking from the cabin, I found that Eleena, my friendly Transport Seraph, was there already, sitting on her own in the transport lounge and apparently waiting for me.

It still puzzled me as to how she did that! It wasn't an inevitability that she'd be there already and ready to carry me, but it has occurred enough to suggest that she must be wired in some way of which I was unaware.

Eleena looked more worried than I'd previously seen her. But it wasn't until I was enclosed in her embrace and we were on our way to Earth that I heard her voice in my mind.

"It seems you are not aware of it," she said, "but you are being recalled to Earth. There have been many changes since you have been away."

That concerned me, I can tell you.

Whatever might I have done wrong? I immediately jumped to the conclusion that it must have been Prince Caligastia who had sent for me, and so soon after the time I'd spent with Prince Janda-chi. I dreaded facing him. I still wasn't sure whether Janda-chi wanted me to tell Caligastia what he'd said about him.

Eleena must have picked up on my sudden frisson of fear, because, held in her embrace, I felt a delicious warmth starting to suffuse my body and relax my mind.

"Have no fear, sister," I heard Eleena's sweet voice again. "Sleep, my sister, sleep, and when you awaken your mind will be clear."

I slept and dreamed there'd never been a rebellion among the angels. I saw life continuing on Earth much as it always had, with Lucifer and Satan still fulfilling their duties as System Sovereigns, Prince Caligastia being his old jolly self who had reigned in his midwayers, and the Prince's staff still walking the planet . . .

I awoke as Eleena was decelerating and the landscape in my dream had started to turn dark and threatening. She was right. I was certainly more clearheaded than I'd been earlier, and I no longer felt fearful at the prospect of facing Prince Caligastia.

When I disembarked I found that Eleena had deposited me in the Transport Center located in the Middle East and not where I'd embarked from the Seraphic Transport Center on the North American continent. Surely Eleena must have known I'd been avoiding the Middle East STC because of its proximity to Prince Caligastia's domain.

Of course, that started me worrying all over again, and I confess to having what I can only call another of my fits of cowardice.

Why had Eleena done that?

Did she know something that I didn't?

The Middle East STC was set in the fifth dimension among the forested hills close to the settlement that later became known as Salem, and later still, Jerusalem. It was right in the middle of Prince Caligastia's area of primary influence. Did this mean that I *was* going to have to confront the Prince?

Yet as I emerged from the Transport Center after bidding an anxious adieu to Eleena (who wasn't giving away anything), I found no agent of the Prince there to conduct me into his presence. Also, as I was still feeling no draw from him, I began to relax again.

It always takes me some time to grow accustomed to the ugly and difficult conditions of the Earth's astral regions. After the astonishing clarity of Zandana's astral regions, the Earth's lower astral regions often felt like wading through a syrup of anger, guilt, and terror.

I meditated sitting on a rock overlooking the eastern end of the Mediterranean Sea—a body of water that seemed to have increased in size since I was last here—until I felt once more in a state of balanced equilibrium.

It was then I felt the draw.

It wasn't toward Prince Caligastia, to my intense relief, but to Atlantis, that rocky volcanic island that had so preoccupied me during the natural catastrophes befalling the planet in the thirteenth millennium. I recalled the bravery of those cetacean rescue missions from Sirius, and everything that I'd learned when I accompanied one of the dolphins south to where they were attempting to relocate the remnant of the Atlantean civilization.

Those had been terrible and wonderful times. The island had taken a dreadful battering, destroying almost all signs of the culture that had developed there. Yet within a couple of millennia of the catastrophes the island had repopulated itself, and a new culture had started to develop. There'd been some more geophysical disasters that had struck the island in the tenth and seventh millennia, but they were less devastating.

The last time I'd been on the island I could see that Atlantis was rapidly becoming the most advanced civilization in the world. The earlier Nile Valley civilizations had been collapsing as the climatic changes rendered the region largely arid—and the Sea People were starting once again to dominate the entire region around the Mediterranean.

This much I already knew.

The waves lapped against the rocks on the beach far beneath me. I idly watched two fishermen in a small vessel—more of an elaborate canoe—casting out small nets, one from either side of the boat. It looked to me as if they were scooping the fish out the water. I could hear their shouts of glee and laughter echoing over the sea.

Was it this image of fish-scooping, I wondered, which had called Prince Caligastia to mind? An odd association, I admit. But there it was. One moment it was the fishermen's triumphant shouts, the next I was back with Caligastia, who was crowing over his plans to overlay the planetary grid.

Had the Prince already completed his complex of buildings, the ones he was planning to use to anchor and reimprint the grid? It must have taken some ingenious maneuvering by the Prince to convince his midwayers to cooperate in getting these structures built.

I knew that the quickest way I was going discover if the Prince had yet activated his Reincarnation Express would be to follow the draw I was feeling and make my way to the island of Atlantis.

* * *

Soon after the first check arrived from the Canadian government an odd and rather unkempt man started coming to the Toronto Chapter coffeehouse.

He was older—in his early fifties—than most of the young homeless people drawn to the Process Church. He was thickly built with somewhat of a beer belly, and although he was only of medium height, he had the swagger of a smaller man. His gestures were flamboyant and would have been thought effete in a less thuggish man. His dark hair was greasy and thinning. It was invariably unbrushed and fell over his eyes, only to be pushed back in an habitual gesture. His skin was greasy too, and it would sometimes display an angry red boil on the back of his neck. As they saw more of the man over the weeks, I'd heard my ward commenting that the poor guy always seemed to have a cold sore on his lips.

But it was the man's eyes that gave him away.

Bill Clement's pupils were as black as a raven's wing.

His eyes too glittered with a bird's hyperalertness. They were eyes that darted constantly hither and thither, assessing details and gathering the information; obsidian marbles squinting darkly through a constant cloud of cigarette smoke. But more than that, they were eyes that told you they'd seen the most terrible things in their time.

As Mein Host came to better know Bill Clement over the following weeks and months, it quickly emerged that Bill was a spy. He was an agent in the intelligence arm of the Royal Canadian Mounted Police (RCMP), and he'd been sent by his agency to report on the Process Church after rumors of the "Grants for Satanists!" percolated up to it. In fact, it was much to the credit of Bill Clement's positive reports that the grant money—which had been divided into quarterly checks—continued to flow despite the negative publicity being generated by the political opposition.

I doubt the RCMP thought that in sending Bill Clement to spy on the group it was sending one of its top agents. It couldn't have been one of their most pressing assignments.

Bill may have been past his prime as an agent, but he made excellent company, as my ward and his friend Peter—now Father Malachi—found out on getting to know him. Bill was a great raconteur—sharp, funny, irreverent, sardonic, and brutally frank—when he felt like pouncing.

He liked to stand up for full effect when telling one of his stories, and then it was possible to see another, more feminine, aspect of the man. When, for example, he would be trying to derisively imitate one of the transvestite regulars, it was obvious he was enjoying his performance rather too much. He would hold his cigarette with the very tip of the fingers of his right hand, gesturing with his left with a languidly limp wrist, his voice high and piping and those obsidian eyes rolling under fluttering eyelids.

Bill's persona was that of a hard and cynical man who'd seen the worst in people and who'd watched the horrors. He had even participated in doing the worst that humans can do to one another. And like many other men who have developed what they hope are impenetrable carapaces, Bill had a soft and tender interior, which had become almost entirely stifled by his macho persona.

Mein Host in particular was drawn to Bill Clement, having been the first to suspect him of being sent by an intelligence agency. I noticed—in talking about it to Malachi—that he ascribed his intuition to a familiarity derived in some way from his mother's work with the British spy agency MI6.

It is only now as I write these words that he is finding out that his draw to the RCMP agent was, in fact, because Bill was a fellow incarnate rebel angel. However, in the agent's case, he would die some years later without ever having learned that.

Bill came and went over the months, so Malachi and my ward got to know him well. Having been exposed so quickly as an agent had convinced Bill that the Processeans really did possess psychic abilities. This must have allowed him the security to open up and speak the truth about his life and his service as an agent. The stories and details were horrifying, and they fascinated his listeners. Happily they are irrelevant to my story, as the conclusion Bill reached was one of disrespect and disillusionment and a bitter hatred for the agency he represented.

Somewhat like Gordon Creighton—another covert intelligence agent who'd befriended my ward in London back in the sixties to find out what the lad knew about UFOs and extraterrestrials—Bill Clement soon found himself doing most of the talking. It was as though this cynical, suspicious, and profoundly disappointed man had finally found people to whom he could talk honestly without fear of exposure.

He would have quickly concluded there was no public worship of Satan here, that whatever they might be doing behind closed doors was harming no one—and actually seemed to be making them kind and approachable people. The two Processeans, in their turn, knew that as long as they kept their spy charmed—and nothing charms a man so much as talking about himself to a rapt audience—they would keep the grant money coming in.

One of the more intriguing pieces of manipulation he talked about to my ward was a perfidious technique used by Canadian intelligence to deal with troublesome opposition groups. Rather than opposing them and trying to stamp them out—he contrasted this with the approach taken by Hoover's FBI—the government simply threw money at them.

He told them this was believed to be more effective than merely infiltrating the group. The money was sure to make the group's leadership dependent on it—or it would bring up the group's latent conflicts. And then, slowly and surely, that group would either break up or grow soft and cease to be a threat.

Yes, it was clever—and typically Canadian Bill would say—but he hated seeing all that youthful enthusiasm and healthy rebellion (he *would* say that, wouldn't he!) being snuffed out by greed and materialism.

Over the months, Bill came to genuinely love the Processeans and their community, and would contrast the commitment and purity he saw in their lives with the cynicism and corruption of the government he had continued to serve after returning from fighting in the Korean War.

What Bill was really saying, although he could never put it into words, was that he was waking up.

He saw he had made a series of bad choices, but he'd made them in good faith. He'd then watched his health and mental stability steadily deteriorate. The woman he loved had abandoned him, his work for the agency had long disgusted him, and the drugs he was taking were turning on him. He claimed they were for his heart, but my ward's early experience with amphetamines left him in no doubt that Bill's meds were uppers. The man felt he was slowly falling to pieces. Bill Clement was not a well man.

So perhaps there is another paradox here.

The RCMP sends a spy to report back on the nefarious activities of the community, and the said spy finds himself far more in sympathy with the community than with the masters who sent him. This was a spy who'd arrived in poor health—angry and sour—who despised himself and hated his work, who was disenchanted and world-weary, and who, when he was finally recalled, would return to Ottawa a very different man.

Whether or not Bill was ever able maintain his new state of openness and clarity when he returned to the fold my ward would never discover. He lost contact with Bill after the grant money dried up, and the agent disappeared back into his secret world. Soon afterward my ward was transferred to from Toronto to New York City.

Yet for those few months my ward was able to watch the transformation of a most unlikely man, while also deriving deeper insights into the state of corruption at the heart of even the most apparently laid-back and humanitarian of the world's governments—that of Canada.

Bill Clement, in his turn, would serve as a good example of the state of mind in which so many incarnate rebel angels of that generation found themselves.

I give these brief glimpses into some of the characteristics of the incarnate rebel angels that my ward encountered over the course of his life so that he may retrospectively learn more about what I've recently heard him calling a new symbiotic mutation: Homo angelicus. I do it also for those who happen to read these words, for most surely you too are an incarnated angel.

A normal human being—a "first-timer"—would be unlikely to find my narrative of any personal interest.

* * *

As long as I've been observing Earth—with its horrors and misfortunes, its tragedies and triumphs, its crimes and corruption—I have occasionally caught a hint that beneath the events lurks a deep underlying sense I can only describe as divine humor.

It was when I reached Atlantis—after quickly checking out that Prince Caligastia's forces had indeed completed his structures and had likely already activated the device—that I was able to observe one of these strokes of divine humor.

Let me lay out the setup.

Prince Caligastia conceives of a nefarious scheme to recycle mortal souls by closing their access to normal mortal ascension, thus essentially enslaving them to his will through an endless cycle of incarnations.

His scheme goes into action and—for reasons beyond the scope of this narrative—it isn't entirely satisfactory. Many souls get through—too many for Caligastia; it insults his pride. He has to tighten the screws. Still too many souls get through and make it up the ascension ladder.

Caligastia has to change his strategy. Perhaps if he simply focuses his device on a particular region of the planet and modifies the grid to affect that one area. Where better than an island, and a relatively advanced one at that? Where better than the island nation of Atlantis?

Thus it was on this particular visit to Atlantis—as I moved invisibly through the marketplace and saw the superb quality of the worked copper and the ingenious bronze implements laid out, the likes of which I'd never seen before—that I started catching on. I looked more carefully at the human beings who jostled past each other down narrow passageways, who gathered in groups in the open squares, clustering around the central fountains or in the shade of trees, drinking and palavering.

I didn't believe it at first. How could this be?

I tuned in to the emotional bodies of one person after another, and—of the first ten I examined—seven of them were incarnate angels. Only three were normal mortals—first-timers. Three out of the ten! That meant there were seven angel incarnates out of every ten mortals I examined. If those numbers held true when I'd looked at more people then I would be witnessing a most unusual event.

I had never witnessed this before—not in these numbers.

Recently, a few small clusters of incarnate rebel angels had been appearing here and there, because it was considered an unnecessarily harsh and cruel punishment for even the toughest of angels to incarnate alone, without others of her kind with whom to relate during her early mortal lifetimes.

I think I might have mildly panicked, because I bustled around examining the emotional bodies of anyone standing or sitting long enough for me to get a stable image. By the time I had viewed the emotional bodies of more than two hundred mortals—both male and female—I realized my original analysis held true over the larger count.

This indeed was startling. Could it be that more than two-thirds of the citizens of Atlantis were reincarnated rebel angels?

So that had been the MA's response to Caligastia's reincarnational scheme for breeding slaves! Rather than short-circuiting the normal mortal ascension process and enslaving those souls in his cyclical trap—Caligastia really should have understood that the mortal soul is inviolable—Caligastia was being fed rebel angels for his Atlantean experiment.

I am able to detect angelic incarnates by looking at their emotional bodies. Compared to a normal mortal, the emotional bodies of the species Homo angelicus are weak and tender affairs—especially during one of their early mortal lifetimes. I have since learned it generally takes between ten and twenty mortal lifetimes—not necessarily on this one planet, but on other third-density worlds as well—for an incarnate angel to learn to bring her emotional body up to full and appropriate strength.

Much of this training over hundreds of mortal lifetimes is being brought to completion with a final mortal lifetime on this planet and other of the surviving worlds in which the rebellion played itself out. Because now—in the dawn of the twenty-first century on this world—a great transformation will soon be upon us all.

Every watcher knows this to be true.

But like mortals, we know not when—or how—it will occur.

We only know that with such large numbers of mature rebel angel incarnates currently serving on the planet—more than one hundred twenty million I am told as I write these words, and still more coming in every day—this is a sure sign of the coming transformation.

The conditions I find among the mortals in the world today—although very different in scale and complexity—are also surprisingly similar to those I found in Atlantis on that visit.

Yet the single most important difference is that nine millennia ago this world was locked into Prince Caligastia's revolution. Now, in the first years of the twenty-first century—with the Lucifer Rebellion reconciled and Prince Caligastia recalled to Jerusem and no longer a diabolical presence on the planet—rebel angel incarnates will have a chance to express the brilliance of this mutation.

It is fitting in this time of profound transformation on Earth that those originally involved in the rebellion amongst the angels should now find themselves matured into a new species that will fulfill its final responsibilities by nurturing and aiding its fellow human beings through the imminent changes of the world.

*　*　*

It was raining hard in Manhattan throughout the afternoon and well into the evening of the night that Mein Host died.

I could see he'd been heading in that direction for some months. As I've fretted about before, he was working himself to death—and there was nothing I could do about it. His companion angels had done little to intervene, so I had no choice but to observe.

Mein Host's destiny came to a head one day mid-November of 1973 when he fainted and fell down hard on his office floor. I have already commented on his racking cough and the weakness of his lungs—as I have also previously mentioned his childhood lower back injury. As a spindly thirteen-year-old, he had been physically picked up by a large senior boy and hurled on his back during a snowball fight at Charterhouse. This resulted in a vulnerability that seemed to reoccur every four or five years—generally the result of extreme stress. It froze him at a forty-five-degree angle and made it an agony for him to move around.

My ward had just taken charge of the New York Chapter a month or two earlier, and in the intensely competitive and critical atmosphere existing between the senior Processeans he was obviously trying to put on a good front. He mustn't be seen to be weak.

After he'd fainted and fallen, he was found by Sister Marion, who fussed over him until he agreed to go home and rest.

It was only a fourteen-block walk from the First Avenue Chapter back to 242 East 49th Street. He'd done it every day, twice a day. It was unheard of to take a taxi in those penny-pinching times. So, barely able to walk—pulling himself along sets of railings whenever he had the chance, propping himself up against signs and traffic lights, the rain pouring down and soaking him through by the second block—he dragged himself back to the house.

I will let my ward describe his experience given that I merely observed it from the outside. This is what he wrote in his 1984 book, *The Deta Factor: Dolphins, Extraterrestrials & Angels,* and although he has written about it since, this description hits all the correct chords. This was after he had arrived back at the 49th Street house and—because he was a water person—had drawn what he called "one final bath."

"I knew I was finished," he wrote, "but I had little idea what lay in store for me.

"Within moments of stretching out in the bath, I found myself—to my utter amazement—hovering somewhere out in space, my body clearly visible in the bath far down below me. The next thing I knew I seemed to be in a valley as real and as solid as any landscape I have seen in my travels.

"A monorail car was sweeping down toward me on a single, shining curve of metal. Then, mysteriously, I was inside the monorail cabin, together with nine or ten other people. I can see them today in my mind's eye: opposite me sat a black man playing a trumpet with great beauty.

"Somehow at that moment I knew we were all dying at the same time. A voice came to me over what I took to be a speaker system—although it may well have been directly into my mind. It was very clear and lucid and quite the most loving voice I have ever heard.

"'You are dying,' the voice confirmed for me, 'but we wish you to make a choice. You can indeed pass on to what awaits you on the other side. . . .' At this point I was given to see my body very casually sinking under the water of my bath somewhere below me in a simple and painless death.

"'. . . or you can choose to return to your life. We wish you to know, however, that you have completed what you came to do.'

"The voice was utterly without attitude—wholly kind and considerate—and with no bias whatsoever as to which option I might choose.

"I thought for a moment with a crystal clarity I have never since experienced, and knew in my heart I desired to return to the world. On announcing my decision, there was an expression of delight so profound that the monorail cabin dissolved around me, leaving me once again suspended in space—this time before a seemingly endless wall of angelic beings. Such music and singing welled around me as I have never conceived of—or perceived before or since. I disintegrated into the overwhelming beauty of the sounds.

"The next sensation was of becoming aware I was standing on the edge of a vast, very flat plain. Beside and slightly behind me stood two tall beings dressed in white—or simply creatures of light. I couldn't see clearly, for my attention focused on what lay in the center of the plain. It was an immense structure I can liken only to an extraordinarily elaborate and beautiful offshore oil rig. It shone with gold and silver and had at each corner the faces of people and animals. Somehow it was in constant movement, yet in itself, it did not move. Intuitively I knew at that moment I was seeing the same structure that Ezekiel describes with such elegance, although I find it difficult to retain the image in my imagination.

"I was led into this enormous place and taken to a brightly lit room where I was gently laid out on a flat surface similar to an operating table. Beings clustered around me, murmuring soft encouragement. Some apparatus appeared, and I have a dim recollection of being hooked up to it. There was a moment of intense pain, except it was not truly pain. It wasn't quite shock either but some combination of both sensations. I felt as if in some way my blood had been completely changed—as if the tired old vital fluids had been switched in one infinitely rapid moment.

"I recall that after the 'operation' I was taken 'somewhere.' I am still, to this day, rather embarrassed to admit that I believe it was heaven. I have no conscious recollection of this last journey—my only clue being a strange sense of familiarity with a description of 'heaven' that I came across some years later in Robert Monroe's book *Journeys Out of the Body*.

"The next thing I was aware of was descending gently again to my body, which was still propped in the bath, the water now cool. When I got out to dry myself off I found myself completely healed, my back straightened and the thick phlegm in my lungs gone. From being terminally ill I found myself fully restored and stronger than ever."

In 1973 a near-death experience (NDE) was still largely unknown to those who hadn't had one, and was generally dismissed by science as a hallucination until Raymond Moody's 1975 book, *Life After Life,* opened up the area for serious review.

I know a few more pieces have slipped into place as my ward has subsequently contemplated the experience that so profoundly changed his life, but the essentials, he assures me, are exactly as written above.

He has since recalled a female voice coming from behind him as he lay on the operating table. She told him that the pain would be extremely intense, "but it will only last for a very short time." He also now believes the instrument penetrated him either through the belly button or close to it. I can now confirm it was through his belly button.

He also claims to no longer be embarrassed at a mention of his visit to "heaven." As well, he remembers that he was told—when he was in heaven—that he wouldn't recall being there upon returning. Apart from happening to read Robert Monroe's somewhat similar experience and resonating with it, the amnesia has held firm.

He has had no further memory of heaven.

Mein Host has frequently said that his NDE was the most profound spiritual event of his entire life. And it would be hard to imagine a more profound experience for any mortal to undergo.

Now, forty years later, with a number of books having been written by those individuals who've had a near-death experience, with innumerable internet sites devoted to NDEs, with serious scientific papers focusing on various aspects of the NDE, with popular cable TV shows featuring those who've returned to life after being clinically dead, with some surveys suggesting that as many as eight million Americans have experienced an NDE—with all this attention the near-death experience remains as enigmatic and as unexplained within the current laws of physics and biology as ever.

As my ward likes to say, "You had to be there!"

Turning Points

More about Near-Death Experiences, a Telling Lacuna, and Incarnated Rebel Angels on Atlantis

Georgia was quite correct when she commented a few pages back that she felt she was coming to a natural pause in her narrative. It is certainly true from my own point of view.

My near-death experience on that rainy November afternoon in 1973 was a turning point in my life. I had never undergone such a profound experience before, and I have never been through anything like it since.

At the very least, it hit the reset button in my life.

Anyone who has had a full-blown NDE knows they never come back the same person. This held true for me although it took me about seven years to absorb the encounters I'd had in my NDE and assimilate what I'd learned over the course of it.

I was grateful that I'd had some experience of altered states of consciousness, or I would have been a lot more freaked out by what seemed to be happening to me. I give full credit to entheogens—to power plants—for that small advantage when consensus reality disappeared, to be replaced by some different state and place altogether.

The most immediate and profound learning for me was the absolute authenticity of the transcendent reality in which I found myself.

Previously I'd acknowledged and believed in the existence of other levels of reality and had occasional glimpses, but there is a fundamental difference between belief and experiential knowledge.

To know that life continues after death—because I've been there—completely changed my approach to life. How could it not? But knowing that life carries on after we die raises far more questions than it answers. It also renders much of contemporary science and traditional religion either irrelevant or plain silly—all while simultaneously provoking a need for true scientific inquiry and requiring a reassessment of the meaning and function of religion.

Writing these words today when so much more is known about NDEs, the concept that I had "completed what I'd come to do"—as the voice told me—makes a great deal more sense. Back then, when I'd lived a mere thirty-three years, it is weird and puzzling to be told with such transcendent certainty that I'd completed my tour of duty. Plus I'd no idea exactly what it was that I had come to do in the first place! But I never doubted what I'd been told.

Then to be given the choice to move along or return to my life! I still find it hard to take in that extraordinary offer.

Even now, when I've read about hundreds of NDEs and viewed many experiencers talking about what happened to them—in almost every case the people are sent back—or at least shown why they should return to their physical bodies. I have only come across a couple of experiencers who were actively given the choice to return or not. To be fair, these are only the ones like me who chose to return. From what I witnessed in my NDE, there would likely be a great many more people who would choose *not* to return to their physical bodies, but instead would want to continue on in the heavenly realms.

Possibly the most radical concept to be revealed by the NDE that flies in the face of most contemporary belief systems is that life really does have a deep purpose and meaning—deeper than we can understand. Not only that—which like any generalization is easy to say—but more importantly, that every one of us, each individual human being, lives a life that possesses its own unique purpose. There are specific tasks to be taken on during an incarnation, and when they are accomplished it is time to move on.

Naturally, this concept, like almost anything associated with the NDE, raises all sorts of paradoxes—from free choice versus predestination, to reincarnation and the issue of suicide, and how we can determine what our purpose is and which specific tasks give our lives meaning.

While my inner life was transformed by my NDE, I was still stuck in the community and in Mary Ann's web. I was doing relatively well apart from my steadily deteriorating health prior to the NDE, as Georgia related, so I had no thought of radically changing my life. I still felt that the community was doing good work, and I was learning a lot by being in charge of the New York headquarters.

I must have told a few people close to me in the group, probably Juliette, about my NDE, but I met with such blank faces that it brought home to me how improbable it must sound—even to people in a spiritual community. After that I kept my experience to myself until I published an account of it in my first book in 1984, from which Georgia took the description included here.

In spite of my desire to continue with the Process community, within a couple of months or so of the NDE, I found myself having to face an unpleasant reality.

Directly after getting out of my bath and drying off, my mind still full of the experience, I sat down and wrote a four-page account of the most transcendent event of my life in a letter to Mary Ann, the one person I believed would affirm and understand what I'd just been through. Remember, no one really knew about NDEs, or talked about them openly until Raymond Moody's book came out two years later and the work of Elisabeth Kübler-Ross, on death and dying, became better known in the late 1970s.

I didn't for one moment think I was going crazy. The NDE was far too lucid and meaningful to have been a delusion or a hallucination. But I still had no idea what it was, or whether other people had ever gone through the same weird experience. I wanted—no, I needed—for Mary Ann, my Goddess in the body, to somehow make it alright.

After a month passed, then two and three, I heard nothing back from her. There was no acknowledgment of my letter, no reference to the NDE when I'd seen her subsequently, no message passed down from her—no nothing.

Luckily I had my hands full running the New York Chapter, so I didn't brood on it. The near-death experience was self-confirming. It was only much later—long after I'd left the community—that I realized how strange and awful this complete lack of response really was. And how telling too!

If I had really grasped the significance of this at the time I think I might well have up sticks and left. But of course I didn't—at least not for another four years.

As I pondered this retrospectively, I realized Mary Ann was simply unable to countenance any spiritual experience not initiated by her, or that didn't include her in some way. She had truly become the victim of her own propaganda by that time, and I'm sad to say I was still unable to see through it.

What I now know had changed in my life was that I was introduced to an entirely new direction to take, but this was still securely locked away in my superconscious mind. I was consciously unaware of what would become the driving interest of my second life—that of nonhuman intelligences—yet looking back I can see how every major decision I made over the next four years brought me closer to achieving that end.

It wasn't going to be easy to leave. People I'd been close to for fifteen years would feel let down and betrayed. I'd be castigated as a traitor, I'd be taken to court (with the case thrown out), and I'd become subject to psychic attacks and vicious bad-mouthing.

However, I would emerge from this conflict—still some years distant in Georgia's narrative—stronger and more optimistic than ever, and with a sense of purpose driven by the insights gathered from my NDE.

Although I had encountered angels face-to-face in the course of my

NDE, it would be another seven years before I actually had a chance to communicate with them—and thus kick off another phase in my life.

Georgia, it seems to me, has left off her narrative in this volume at a significant point in her long life, just as she has ended here with the near-death experience in *my* thread.

True to how Georgia and I work together, I have little idea of what lies ahead in her story. I deliberately don't want to look or to know at this point. It would spoil the fun for me.

I just know that Georgia has continued to surprise me at every turn over six volumes so far, at the same time answering some of my most long-held questions.

As she moves her narrative from the troubled seventh and sixth millennia, through prehistory, recorded history, and then into the modern era, her discovery of those rebel angel incarnates present on Atlantis is sure to become an insight she will want to take note of and which she'll want to follow up on.

I can only say that I can't wait to hear what Georgia has to tell me of her journey through human history—there is much I still don't know.

Thank you, Georgia.

APPENDIX

The Angelic Cosmology

Different versions of the so-called War in Heaven appear so frequently in indigenous legends and mythologies from around the world—as well as in the sacred books and traditions of major religions—that the war is more than likely based on a real event. I believe the most authoritative account can be found in *The Urantia Book,* where it is referred to as "the Lucifer Rebellion."

Thirty years after first reading *The Urantia Book,* I still regard it as the most reliable source of information about both extraterrestrial and celestial activities. It is broken down into four parts devoted to the following subjects: the Nature of God and the Central and Superuniverses, the Local Universe, the History of Urantia (their name for this planet), and the Life and Teachings of Jesus Christ. (For a definition of terms common to both *The Urantia Book* and this book, please refer to the glossary.)

According to the Urantia model, there are seven Superuniverses, which together compose the material Multiverse. These seven Superuniverses form the substance of the finite Multiverse and circle the Central Universe, which can be visualized as the hole in the center of the toroidal form of the Multiverse.

Each Superuniverse contains one hundred thousand Local Universes, each of which has its own Creator Son (ours is Christ Michael, or Jesus Christ) and its own Divine Mother—these are the

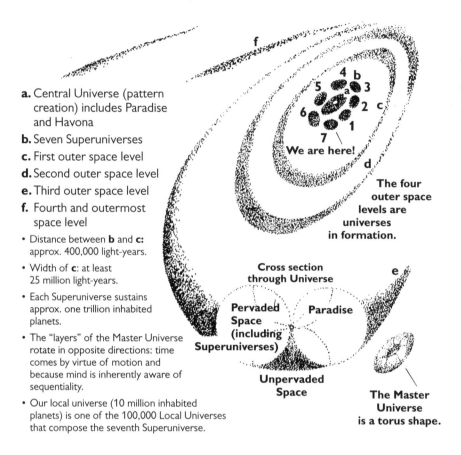

a. Central Universe (pattern creation) includes Paradise and Havona

b. Seven Superuniverses

c. First outer space level

d. Second outer space level

e. Third outer space level

f. Fourth and outermost space level

- Distance between **b** and **c:** approx. 400,000 light-years.
- Width of **c:** at least 25 million light-years.
- Each Superuniverse sustains approx. one trillion inhabited planets.
- The "layers" of the Master Universe rotate in opposite directions: time comes by virtue of motion and because mind is inherently aware of sequentiality.
- Our local universe (10 million inhabited planets) is one of the 100,000 Local Universes that compose the seventh Superuniverse.

Master Universe Structure (adapted from *The Urantia Book*, p. 129)

Creator Beings of their domain. This pair of High Beings modulates the energy downstepped from the Central Universe to create and form the beings and the planetary biospheres with their Local Universe. Each Local Universe sustains ten million inhabited planets broken out into ten thousand Local Systems.

Each Local System, in turn, contains one thousand inhabited—or to be inhabited—planets, and each has its own System Sovereign (ours was Lucifer) appointed to govern the System. Each planet, in turn, has a Planetary Prince (ours was Prince Caligastia), who oversees their particular worlds.

According to *The Urantia Book,* Lucifer and Satan (Lucifer's main assistant) came to believe that an elaborate conspiracy had been con-cocted by the Creator Sons of the Local Universes to promote the existence of a fictitious Unseen Divinity, which the Creator Sons then used as a control device to manipulate the orders of celestials and angels within their creations. Having announced the existence of this conspir-acy, Lucifer demanded more autonomy for all beings, and for System Sovereigns and Planetary Princes to follow their own approaches for accelerating the spiritual development of their mortal charges.

The revolutionaries quickly gained followers, and the rebellion spread rapidly to affect thirty-seven planets in our System, with Urantia, our planet Earth, being one of them. Choice was given to the many angels involved with supervising System activities as to whether to join the rebel faction.

Lucifer's charge—that too much attention was being given to ascending mortals—appeared to ring true to a large number of angels, as well as the thirty-seven pairs of administrative angels: the Planetary Princes and their assistants who were responsible for the orderly pro-gression of mortal (human) beings on their worlds. The revolution was effectively suppressed by the administration authorities and recast as a heinous rebellion, its immediate consequence being the removal of Lucifer and Satan from their posts in the System.

At the time of the Lucifer Rebellion, the vast majority of the fifty thousand midwayer angels on Earth—40,119 to be exact—aligned themselves with Lucifer and Satan. They were destined to remain on our planet until the time of Christ, when, according to *The Urantia Book,* it was one of Christ's occulted functions to remove them. It is a brief reference and no further details are given in the book as to where the rebel midwayers were taken. However, with the removal of these rebel midwayers, a mere 9,981 loyalist midwayers remained here to ful-fill the tasks of five times their number.

As a result of this, in contrast to a normal planet (one not quar-antined), on which angelic companions and the presence of helpful midwayers and extraterrestrials must be commonplace knowledge, we earthlings have slumbered in our corner of a populated Multiverse, unaware of who we are and how we got this way. Having been quarantined and isolated from normal extraterrestrial activity for the long 203,000 years since the rebellion, we first lost touch with, and then forgot entirely, our rightful place in the populated Multiverse. Given this, we were bound to evolve as a troubled species. Our world is one of the few planets that, due to the Lucifer Rebellion, has been thrown off its normal pattern of development.

This disquieting situation, this planetary quarantine, has persisted for more than two hundred thousand years, only to have finally been adjudicated, in my understanding, in the early 1980s.

Given that the planetary quarantine has finally been lifted, the rest of the Multiverse is now able to make legitimate contact with us. More recently what we are witnessing is both the return of the rebel midwayers (the beings of the violet flame), who are now coming back to assist us in the coming transformation of our world; and, perhaps of more personal interest to my readers, the many angels who aligned with Lucifer at the time of the rebellion are incarnating as mortals. It appears these rebel angels and watchers are being offered human incarnation as a path to personal redemption, as the world is emerging from an interminably long dark age to shake off the shadows and fulfill its remarkable destiny.

Glossary

Many valuable insights from many different sources have contributed to the themes and fundamental questions that this series of books, the Confessions series, seeks to explore, but the most reliable and comprehensive exposition of God, the Universe, and Everything that I have come across remains *The Urantia Book*. A number of the concepts and words below are drawn from it and marked (UB), but the definitions are the author's.

Albedo: the second stage of the alchemical process resulting from the slow burning out of the impurities present in the first stage.

Angel: a general term for any order of being who administers within a Local Universe.

Atman, Indwelling Spirit, Thought Adjuster (UB): an essence of the Creator that indwells all mortal beings, human and extraterrestrial.

Bioplasm (UB): a constituent of an individual's genome required to reconstitute a biological duplicate of the bioplasm's donor, or for calibrating a cloned physical vehicle to its intended environment.

Caligastia (UB): a Secondary Lanonandek Son who served as Planetary Prince of this world and who aligned himself with Lucifer.

Cano (UB): young Nodite aristocrat who mated with Eve, the female visitor.

Central Universe (UB): the abode of the original Creator God/s—the Father, the Mother/Son, and the Holy Spirit (UB). If the Multiverse is a torus, then the Central Universe is the hole in the middle existing on a far finer frequency and from which energy is downstepped to form the building blocks of the Multiverse.

Citrinitas: advanced state of spiritual enlightenment whereby the alchemist can make an ultimate unification with the Supreme.

Creator Sons (UB): co-creators—each having a female complement, the Mother Spirit (UB)—of each of the seven hundred thousand Local Universes (UB). The co-creators of the Local Universes modulate the downstepped energies from the Central Universe to design the life-forms for those beings existing within all the frequency domains of their Local Universe.

Daligastia (UB): a Secondary Lanonandek Son who served as Caligastia's right-hand aide.

Demons: negative thoughtforms.

Devas: the coordinating spirits of the natural world. All living organisms are cared for by devas (or nature spirits). In the human being the deva is that which coordinates and synchronizes the immense amount of physical and biochemical information that keeps our bodies alive.

Extraterrestrial: mortal beings such as ourselves who hail from more developed worlds with access to our frequency domain.

Fandor (UB): a large semi-telepathic passenger bird, said to have become extinct about thirty-eight thousand years ago.

Frequency Domain: the spectrum of frequencies that support the life-forms whose senses are tuned to that specific spectrum.

God: in *my* personal experience, God is both the Creator and the totality of Creation, manifest and unmanifest, immanent and transcendent.

Guardian (Companion) Angels (UB): function in pairs to ensure their mortal wards grow in spirit over the course of their lifetimes.

Janda-chi: the second of the two Planetary Princes on the planet Zandana.

Jesus Christ: the Michaelson (UB) of our Local Universe (UB) who incarnated as Jesus Christ in the physical body of Joshua ben Joseph; he is also known as Michael of Nebadon (UB).

Lanaforge (UB): a primary Lanonandek Son who succeeded Lucifer as System Sovereign.

Lanonandek Order of Sonship (UB): the third order of Local Universe Descending Sons of God who serve as System Sovereigns (Primary Lanonandeks) and Planetary Princes (Secondary Lanonandeks).

Local System (UB): our Local System, named Satania (UB), is believed to currently possess between 600 and 650 inhabited planets. Earth is numbered 606 in this sequence (UB).

Local System HQ Planet, Jerusem (UB): the political and social center of the Satania System.

Local Universe (UB): a grouping of planets that comprises 10 million inhabited worlds.

Lucifer (UB): deposed System Sovereign and primary protagonist in the rebellion among the angels.

Lucifer Rebellion (UB): a rebellion among the angels occurring 203,000 years ago on Jerusem that affected thirty-seven inhabited worlds, of which Earth was one.

Master Universe (UB): the Multiverse that contains the seven Superuniverses (UB).

Melchizedek Sons/Brothers (UB): a high order of Local Universe Sons devoted primarily to education and who function as planetary administrators in emergencies.

Midwayers or **Midway Creatures (UB):** intelligent beings, imperceptible to humans, who exist in a contiguous frequency domain and serve as the permanent planetary citizens.

Mortals (UB): intelligent beings who emerge as a result of biological evolutionary processes on a planet. Souls are born to their immortal lives as mortals, whose physical bodies live and die before they are given the choice to continue their Multiverse career.

Mortal Ascension Scheme (UB): the process by which all mortal beings who live and die on the material worlds of the Local Systems pass up through the seven subsequent levels to Jerusem, where they embark on their universe career.

Mother Spirit (UB): with the Michaelson, the female co-creator of a Local Universe.

Multiverse: the author's term for the entire range of frequency domains, on every level of the Master Universe (UB).

Multiverse Administration (MA): the author's general term for the celestial administration, with special reference to the Local Universe bureaucracy.

Nebadon (UB): the name of this Local Universe of 10 million inhabited planets.

Nodites (UB): descendants of the illicit interbreeding between selected mortals and, on realizing they were doomed to physical death, those of the Prince's staff who followed Caligastia's uprising.

Nodu, Nod (UB): Nodu is Georgia's informal, but respectful, name for the member of the Prince's staff who opposed Caligastia and who, in time, led his people to the Islands of Mu.

Satan (UB): Lucifer's right-hand aide who co-instigated the angelic rebellion 203,000 years ago.

Serapatatia (UB): Nodite Prince who persuaded Eve to accelerate the visitors' mission by mating with Cano and creating a singular Nodite bloodline with a healthy dash of violet blood.

Seraph(im) (UB): a high order of angels whose functions include that of companion (guardian) angels or, like Georgia, observing angels.

Seraphic Transport System (UB): Transport Seraphs, living beings that carry nonmaterial beings—watchers as well as ascending mortals—to the other worlds on a variety of frequency domains within the Multiverse.

Solonia (UB): the seraphic "voice in the garden" (UB) who admonished the visitors and had them leave their garden home and start their long journey to settle in the Land of the Two Rivers.

Superuniverse (UB): a universe that contains one hundred thousand Local Universes.

System of Planets (UB): a grouping of planets consisting of a thousand inhabited, or to be inhabited, planets.

System of Satania: the System of planets within which Earth is but one of the more than six hundred fifty inhabited worlds of the one thousand planets within its administrative domain, and the locale of the Lucifer revolution.

System Sovereign (UB): the administrative angel, together with an assistant of the same rank, who is an overall authority of a Local System. Lucifer and Satan were the pair in charge of this System of planets.

Thoughtforms: quasi-life-forms existing in the astral regions, drawing their limited power from strong emotional thoughts projected out from human mentation, both conscious and unconscious. Thoughtforms can be negative or positive. Localized negative ones are referred to as fear-impacted thoughtforms.

Transport Seraphim: order of seraphim specifically created as sentient vehicles to make interplanetary transit available in the fourth and fifth dimensions.

Ultraterrestrial or **Intraterrestrial Beings:** the beings who inhabit our neighboring frequency domain and who *The Urantia Book* calls the midwayers or midway creatures.

Unava: chief of staff to Prince Zanda, the senior of the two Planetary Princes of the neighboring planet Zandana.

Universe Career (UB): a mortal's destiny, unless chosen otherwise, to rise through the many hundreds of levels of the Multiverse to finally encounter the Creator.

Violet Blood (UB): the potential of an infusion of a slightly higher frequency genetic endowment, which results in more acute senses and a deeper spiritual awareness and responsiveness.

Zanda: senior Planetary Prince of Zandana, a planet named in his honor and to which Georgia has made frequent visits.

Zandan: the principal city of the planet Zandana.

Zandana: a neighboring planet developing within approximately the same time frame as Earth and whose Planetary Princes also followed Lucifer into revolution.

Index

About the Author

Timothy Wyllie (1940–2017) chose to be born in London at the height of the Battle of Britain. Surviving an English public school education unbroken, he studied architecture, qualifying in 1964 and practicing in London and the Bahamas. During this time he also worked with two others to create a mystery school, which came to be known as the Process Church, and subsequently traveled with the community throughout Europe and America. He became art director of PROCESS magazine, designing a series of magazines in the 1960s and '70s that have recently become recognized as among the prime progenitors of psychedelic magazine design. In 1975, Wyllie became the director of the New York headquarters and organized a series of conferences and seminars on unorthodox issues such as out-of-body travel, extraterrestrial encounters, alternative cancer therapies, and Tibetan Buddhism. After some fractious and fundamental disagreements with his colleagues in the community, he left to start a new life in 1977. The record of Wyllie's fifteen years in the mystery school of the Process Church and the true account of this eccentric spiritual community appears in his book *Love, Sex, Fear, Death: The Inside Story of the Process Church of the Final Judgment,* which was published by Feral House in 2009. It is slowly becoming a cult classic.

A profound near-death experience in 1973 confirmed for Wyllie the reality of other levels of existence and instigated what became a lifetime exploration of nonhuman intelligences. Having created his intention, the Multiverse opened up a trail of synchronicities that led to his swimming with a coastal pod of wild dolphins, two extraterrestrial encounters—during one of which he was able to question the ET mouthpiece as to some of the ways of the inhabited Multiverse—and finally to an extended dialogue with a group of angels speaking through a light-trance medium in Toronto, Canada.

Wyllie's first phase of spiritual exploration was published as *The Deta Factor: Dolphins, Extraterrestrials & Angels* by Coleman Press in 1984 and republished by Bear & Company as *Dolphins, ETs & Angels* in 1993.

His second book, *Dolphins, Telepathy & Underwater Birthing,* published by Bear & Company in 1993, was republished by Wisdom Editions in 2001 under the title *Adventures Among Spiritual Intelligences: Angels, Aliens, Dolphins & Shamans.* In this book Wyllie continues his travels exploring Balinese shamanic healing, Australian Aboriginal cosmology, human underwater birthing, dolphin death and sexuality, entheogenic spirituality, the gathering alien presence on the planet, and his travels with a Walk-In, along with much else.

Wyllie's work with the angels through the 1980s resulted in the book *Ask Your Angels: A Practical Guide to Working with Your Messengers of Heaven to Empower and Enrich Your Life,* written with Alma Daniel and Andrew Ramer and published by Ballantine Books in 1992. After spending time at the top of the New York Times Best

Sellers in religion, *Ask Your Angels* went on to become an international success in eleven translations.

The Return of the Rebel Angels continues the series he began with *Dolphins, ETs & Angels* and *Adventures Among Spiritual Intelligences,* presenting further in-depth intuitive explorations of nonhuman intelligences. It draws together the many meaningful strands of Wyllie's thirty-year voyage of discovery into unknown and long-taboo territories in a coherent and remarkably optimistic picture for the immediate future of the human species, with the inconspicuous help of a benign and richly inhabited living Multiverse.

The Helianx Proposition: The Return of the Rainbow Serpent—A Cosmic Creation Fable, also thirty years in the making, is Wyllie's illustrated mythic exploration of an ancient extraterrestrial personality and its occult influence on life in this world. Published by Daynal Institute Press in 2010, it includes two DVDs and two CDs of associated material. The CDs contain nineteen tracks of the author's visionary observations, augmented by Emmy-winning musician the late Jim Wilson, master of digital sonic manipulation.

Confessions of a Rebel Angel, Wyllie's first collaboration with Georgia, emerged in 2012, published by Inner Traditions • Bear & Company, who followed up with *Revolt of the Rebel Angels* in 2013, *Rebel Angels in Exile* in 2014, *Wisdom of the Watchers* in 2015, and *Awakening of the Watchers* in 2016.

BOOKS BY TIMOTHY WYLLIE

The Deta Factor: Dolphins, Extraterrestrials & Angels, 1984 (currently in print as *Dolphins, ETs & Angels,* 1993).

Ask Your Angels: A Practical Guide to Working with the Messengers of Heaven to Empower and Enrich Your Life, 1992 (cowritten with Alma Daniel and Andrew Ramer).

Dolphins, Telepathy & Underwater Birthing, 1993 (currently in print as *Adventures Among Spiritual Intelligences: Angels, Aliens, Dolphins & Shamans,* 2001).

Contacting Your Angels Through Movement, Meditation & Music, 1995 (with Elli Bambridge).

Love, Sex, Fear, Death: The Inside Story of the Process Church of the Final Judgment, 2009 (editor, with Adam Parfrey).

The Helianx Proposition: The Return of the Rainbow Serpent—A Cosmic Creation Fable, 2010.

The Return of the Rebel Angels, 2011.

Confessions of a Rebel Angel, 2012.

Revolt of the Rebel Angels, 2013.

Rebel Angels in Exile, 2014.

Wisdom of the Watchers, 2015.

Awakening of the Watchers, 2016.

BOOKS OF RELATED INTEREST

Awakening of the Watchers
The Secret Mission of the Rebel Angels in the Forbidden Quadrant
by Timothy Wyllie

Wisdom of the Watchers
Teachings of the Rebel Angels on Earth's Forgotten Past
by Timothy Wyllie

Rebel Angels in Exile
Pleiadians, Watchers, and the Spiritual Quickening of Humanity
by Timothy Wyllie

The Return of the Rebel Angels
The Urantia Mysteries and the Coming of the Light
by Timothy Wyllie

Confessions of a Rebel Angel
The Wisdom of the Watchers and the Destiny of Planet Earth
by Timothy Wyllie

Revolt of the Rebel Angels
The Future of the Multiverse
by Timothy Wyllie

Dolphins, ETs & Angels
Adventures Among Spiritual Intelligences
by Timothy Wyllie

Bringers of the Dawn
Teachings from the Pleiadians
by Barbara Marciniak

INNER TRADITIONS • BEAR & COMPANY
P.O. Box 388
Rochester, VT 05767
1-800-246-8648
www.InnerTraditions.com

Or contact your local bookseller